To Begin at the Beginning

To Begin at the Beginning

An Introduction to Christian Faith

• •

THIRD EDITION

Martin B. Copenhaver

WILLIAM B. EERDMANS PUBLISHING COMPANY

GRAND RAPIDS, MICHIGAN

Wm. B. Eerdmans Publishing Co.
2140 Oak Industrial Drive N.E., Grand Rapids, MI 49505
www.eerdmans.com

First published 1994 by Pilgrim Press
Cleveland, OH
This edition published 2017

ISBN   978-0-8028-7416-0

Library of Congress Cataloging-in-Publication Data

A catalog record for this book is available from the Library of Congress

Biblical quotations are from the New Revised Standard Version of the Bible, copyright
© 1989 by the Division of Christian Education of the National Council of Churches of
Christ in the U.S.A. and are used by permission.

To

Charles and Marian

Alanna and Todd

May the God of our fathers and mothers also be the God of our children.

Contents

CONTENTS

Preface

This book is for those who want to consider—or reconsider—the Christian faith and need a place to begin. The Christian faith is not a series of propositions or a body of knowledge to be assimilated; thus it is not learned the same way as, say, calculus or Shakespeare's plays might be learned in an academic course. It can be misleading even to speak of learning "the basics" of the Christian faith, because it is not a subject matter to be mastered as much as it is a story to be told and a life to be lived. First we hear the story, and then we are invited to take our part in the story.

Bringing out this third edition is my attempt to tell the old, old story again. Søren Kierkegaard made a distinction between a genius and an apostle. He observed that a genius is someone who brings forth something new into human understanding. By contrast, an apostle tells an old story. It is the strange and awe-inspiring story of God's interaction with the world. This story may not be new, but it renews us, whether we are hearing it for the first time or we have heard it all before. So we do not tire of it any more than we can tire of the words "I love you," which, of course, is just the message that this story brings. So I am not concerned, here or elsewhere, with saying something new. I am no genius. Rather, my aim is to get the old story right—in a manner befitting an apostle. We can be grateful that we are blessed with the best story around, a story that is both worthy of our trust and endlessly interesting.

Introductions

Before we set out on this journey together, perhaps we should introduce ourselves.

About You

Let's start with you. That is, let me describe the kind of person for whom this book is intended. I assume that you are someone who is looking for a basic introduction to Christian faith and practice. As a child, you may have gone through all the levels of church school and even collected a few perfect-attendance awards along the way, but at this point in your life you want to start from the beginning and get a background in the basics. You now want to explore what you may have learned once. The material may be the same, but *you* are different now. When we are children, much of our Christian education is an attempt to answer questions that have yet to be asked. Now that you are an adult, the questions are your own. They have immediacy, perhaps even something like urgency.

Or you may be in the exhilarating flush of a relatively new relationship with the Christian God and now, like someone experiencing a new love, you want to know as much as possible about the beloved. At such a stage in a relationship, there is so much you want to learn that it is hard to know where to begin.

Or perhaps you do not identify yourself as a Christian, but you are interested in learning more about Christian beliefs and practices.

Whatever the case, you want a place to bring your most fundamental questions about the Christian faith. Perhaps you have already read other books or taken part in other Christian education offerings, but they always seemed to start somewhere in the middle. Such ventures were worthwhile, but they would have been even more so if you had been able to build on a more complete foundation.

You may feel a bit self-conscious, even apologetic, about your need for some basic background in the Christian faith. This may be the case especially for those who already have been active in Christian community, but it is also true of others. You may feel that, somewhere along the line, you should have "picked up" this background knowledge. Therefore, you may be tempted to preface even your most heartfelt questions with an apology: "This may be a stupid question, but..." Or "I should probably know this already, but ..." Teachers know that the most penetrating questions often are prefaced in this way, yet for those who are eager to learn, it can also be freeing to know that such apologies are unnecessary because no prior background is assumed.

Maybe you are among those who are prompted to explore religious questions anew because of the questions of children. Children want to know how, if you cannot see or hear God, you can be sure God is there. Why do people have to die? Where is Jesus now? Does God answer all prayers? Did all of the things recorded in the Bible actually happen? And then there is that largest of questions in the smallest of words: Why?

Often, in attempting to answer these questions, we not only discover that the answers are not immediately available, but that the questions are our own. That is, many adults come to a church to have their children's questions answered, even when those children turn out to be the ones in their own hearts and minds. They want to learn more about the God who has laid claim to their lives. They want to know what it means to be a disciple of Christ. In the local parish, I have learned to take seriously the questions of all the children of God. This book is one attempt to do just that.

About Me

I am the president of Andover Newton Theological School, where we educate those who wish to become pastors and other religious leaders. I spend my days in the company of scholars and students whose lives are focused on teaching and learning about Christian faith and practices. For the thirty-four years prior to assuming this role, however, I was the pastor of a local church. I suppose I could call myself a theologian because I have devoted a good deal of my life to the study of God. But most of what I have learned about God has not been through books. Rather, the best that I have learned about God has been via faith communities. To be sure, life in the church includes the careful study of the church's book, the Bible, and the learned reflections of subsequent generations. Nevertheless, much of what I have learned has been through worshiping and serving with a community of people who are attempting to live out this story in their life together. When we're standing at an open grave, or talking with someone who is trying to hold together the jagged pieces of life, or serving a warm meal to a homeless family, the gospel defies abstraction and takes on the dimensions of life.

As a pastor, I learned that searching questions can be posed in any setting and circumstance. They may be presented pointedly in a study group or with seeming casualness in a curbstone conversation. They may not come in the form of words at all, but in the inarticulate sighs of someone who is wrestling with the twin demons of grief and fear. Such questions may even appear when least expected, popping up amidst the agenda items at a church meeting, like a sapling that appears between the cracks of a sidewalk, reaching for life. Questions about the God we know in Jesus Christ can appear anywhere that God is, even in the most unlikely place of all—our lives.

About This Book

This book is entitled To Begin at the Beginning because it is intended to be a starting place for those who want to consider—or reconsider—

the essential tenets of the Christian faith. I should point out some of the limits of such an undertaking, because you will discover them yourself soon enough. The biblical story itself is so panoramic that any attempt to do it justice in a small book is like trying to draw a mural on a teacup. Theologians who attempt to summarize the mysteries of God and the meaning of Jesus Christ often fill a bookshelf with learned tomes before they declare their "introduction" finished. Those who try to write about God often seem more intent on touching every base than does a seasoned baseball player. After all, the stakes are so much higher.

Someone who taught me much about preaching once said, "Every good sermon is a little bit heretical." By that he did not mean that the preacher makes false statements, but rather that he or she cannot say everything on a single Sunday. A good sermon is a little bit heretical because it must, by necessity, leave some important things unsaid. To tell one part of the story accurately, one must set it in the context of the rest of the story, which is simply impossible on any one day.

So you should know from the beginning that this book is a little bit heretical. There is much that it does not cover. What you have here are a few broad brushstrokes on a canvas, which I hope will give you some sense of the scale, shape, and color of what I hope to portray. The details will need to be added later, but at least you will have a canvas on which to paint those details as they become clearer to you through further study.

This book is best read with others. Christianity is, first and last, a religion of community. It is together that we are most able to discern and follow God's ways. That means, among other things, that we are invited to share our insights, however fragmentary, and express our doubts, no matter how dark or deep. Above all, it means that there is no such thing as a stupid question, for such questions are nothing less than opportunities for further growth.

I hope that this book will in some way be an invitation to discipleship. Its aim is not merely to create further knowledge but also to prompt further commitment. In order to grasp the Christian faith or to be grasped by it, we must live it, not merely study it, because the Christian faith is only understood from the inside. It is only by living the Christian faith that we can hope to see the truth and attractiveness of it. So this book should be seen not as a travelogue that can inform and delight you while you sit in a comfortable armchair. It is more like a guidebook that will help you only when you read it in the middle of a journey.

PART ONE

The God We Worship and Serve

CHAPTER 1

The God of Creation and Covenant

To begin at the beginning...

But where does this story begin? One might assume that any telling of the Christian story would begin with the creation of the world. After all, the first words of the Bible are devoted to accounts of creation, and many of the historic creeds of the Christian church begin with affirmations about God as Creator. What better place to begin?

In one important way, however, the story begins elsewhere. If the story of God's dealings with the world were a story that had been followed from the very beginning, then naturally it would start with creation. But this is not the case. The people who wrote the creation stories were obviously not eyewitnesses. In fact, the creation accounts were not even the first parts of Scripture to be written. No one was assigned to cover the story of creation until after the people of Israel had witnessed the astonishing ways in which God had dealt with them.

The Hebrews' initial convictions about God were not the result of philosophical musings about the origin of the universe. Rather, their faith arose out of their encounters with God midstream in the flow of history. This is a story that begins in the middle of human history, in the midst of life. It begins when God called the people of Israel out of slavery in Egypt and entered into an everlasting covenant with them. Only then did the people begin to ask what this mighty and mysterious God was up to before the Exodus. So we begin this story, not with the spirit of God brooding over the waters before creation, but with a particular people encountering a God who was revealed to them in specific ways at a certain point in their history.

The Exodus

The Exodus is the focal event of Israel's faith. It is also, in one sense, a creation story, because it is the story of God creating a people and giving them life. The enslaved people cried out for help, and God responded: "I have observed the misery of my people . . . I have heard their cry . . . I know their sufferings. . . . So I have come down to deliver them" (Exod. 3:7–8).

Notice how the statement builds, making more wondrous claims with each step. The first two affirmations suggest only that God sees and hears what is going on. The third indicates that God is not a mere neutral observer: God assures the people that God identifies with their suffering. But the fourth affirmation is decisive. Here God assures the people that their God is intervening on their behalf. No longer merely an observer, even a sympathetic one, God has actually become an actor in the drama, willing to enter the stage of history to intercede on behalf of the helpless.

It may not be all that important to believe that the Exodus occurred in the way filmmaker Cecil B. DeMille depicted it, with the waters of the Red Sea held on either side as if by invisible dams, thus allowing the Hebrews to flee "with unmoistened foot," as the old hymn puts it. Whatever the circumstances surrounding that escape, it was an astonishing turn of events that the people of Israel could not explain without seeing God's saving hand in it. The eye of faith could see God's fingerprints all over the Exodus, and the people sang a great hymn of celebration at the end of the Exodus, which includes these questions: "Who is like you, O Lord, among the Gods? Who is like you, majestic in holiness, awesome in splendor, doing wonders?" (Exod. 15:11). These are rhetorical questions, of course, and the answer is obvious: no one. Only the majestic God of the Exodus could make a way out of no way.

It was not out of detached theological reflection that the people of Israel came to believe in a God who could intervene in history. Rather, they believed in such a God because they had already seen God intervene on their behalf in the Exodus. It would forever be impossible for them to go back to the beginning without recalling their experience of a God who encountered them in the midst of life. In such a context, indulging in detached reflections about God would seem the most egregious irreverence, if not downright impossible. The Exodus was such a decisive event that nothing in the Hebrew experience could be understood in the same way again. When one otherwise ordinary day can flash with such a powerful revelation of God, the rest of Israel's days can only be approached differently, sustained by memory, drawn by hope. When the Lord of the universe is so powerfully evident in a particular place, no place is barren enough or trying enough to force the conclusion that God is totally absent.

God's special intervention in the Exodus came to be seen by the people of Israel as the definitive sign of God's special relationship with them. We sometimes resist the claims of those who view themselves as singled out for special privilege, associating such claims with arrogance. It is particularly important to note in this context, then, that when the people of Israel came to understand themselves as having a special relationship with their God, they did not perceive that they deserved such a distinction.

God did not respond to the Hebrews' pleas for help because the Hebrews were good people; the Exodus was not a matter of giving righteous people their due reward. The Hebrews were not picked out of the crowd of nations because they were particularly winsome or worthy. In fact, it was for no good or discernible reason that God helped this undistinguished and unlikely people—except that God loved them (Deut. 7:8). God's love for Israel, which was evident in the Exodus, is an example of *grace,* a word and concept that signifies something that is given even though it is completely undeserved. And at the same time that the people of Israel saw themselves as having been chosen for a special relationship with God in particular ways, they also understood that that special privilege also brought special responsibilities.

The Covenant with Israel

The Hebrews had little time to rejoice in their new freedom before it became clear that this new and special relationship with God did not free them from hardship. Part of God's promise was that after their escape the Hebrews would inherit a new homeland, a land flowing with milk and honey, a land where their descendants could live from then on. But for years after their escape, the Hebrews simply wandered in the wilderness like children separated from their parents. Their days were so filled with trial and uncertainty that some of them even pined for the good old days when they were slaves.

It was during these wanderings, at a place called Mount Sinai, that the fuller implications of what had happened between the people and God were revealed. In the Exodus the people experienced God's gift of freedom and special favor; they also received God's promise of prosperity and progeny. But now it was time for them to learn about their end of the deal.

The Exodus was, indeed, an instance of grace. But in response to that free and unmerited gift, the people of Israel were expected to behave in particular ways. The prophets later summarized this understanding when they envisioned God saying, "You shall be my people, and I will be your God" (Jer. 30:22; Ezek. 36:28). Here the promise and the expectation are inseparable: both are inextricable parts of this new bond between God and God's people. After the Exodus the people of Israel knew that when God promised to be their God, it meant that there would not always be a distance between them. This God meant to be active on their behalf in powerful ways. But if God could not be counted on to keep a distance from Israel, to be God's people also meant that they would need to continually respond to the intrusive presence of this God in their lives. For God to be in the middle of human life was a welcome realization at first. But it also meant that this God would meddle in human life, which is not always so welcome.

In particular, the Hebrews knew that they were expected to respond by observing the law that, according to the scriptural account, was given to them by God through Moses on Mount Sinai. The Ten

Commandments are the summary of that law, but it takes the better part of four biblical books (Exodus, Leviticus, Deuteronomy, and Numbers) to spell out the details. It was by observing the law that the people of Israel could do their part to live out the new relationship with God established in the Exodus.

It was a particular form of contractual arrangement known as a *covenant*. The Hebrew word *berit*, which is used most often to express the idea of covenant, is literally translated "shackle" or "chain." The term was originally used in reference to any form of binding agreement, but it eventually came to describe this unique relationship between the people of Israel and their God. At first we might wonder how we could call this gift an instance of grace because it seems to carry such a hefty price tag. When we survey all that is expected of Israel in this relationship, the covenant can begin to sound more like the familiar quid pro quo of a contractual agreement than a free and abundant gift bestowed on the Jews without regard to their merit. Yet, even though the covenant does carry expectations for Israel, the sides are by no means equal. It is God who extends a strong and constant hand to Israel, not the other way around. All Israel is expected to do is respond by grasping the hand that is freely offered.

Indeed, unconditional love—like what God offered the people of Israel—does not mean the absence of expectations. We see this same dynamic in human relationships. A mother may say to her son, "I love you. You did not earn this love, and there is nothing you can do to diminish it. I will always love you, no matter what." And yet this mother, vowing unconditional love, will not cease to have expectations of her child. She will still expect her son to treat her respectfully, to do his homework, to help around the house. This does not mean that the mother's vows of love are insincere. Her love is not bought with obedience, nor will it be withdrawn in response to disobedience. Her love is a given. Nevertheless, expectations still flow from such unconditional love; often the greater the love, the greater the expectations. Perhaps this principle is more clearly understood in reverse: a complete lack of expectations is a sign not of love but of something more like indifference. So we can affirm that God's covenant with Israel was characterized by both unconditional love and great expectations.

7

One reason we have a hard time comprehending such a relationship is that it is so unlike most of our human experience. We are accustomed to love having a price tag—perhaps tucked away, largely hidden, for the most part unnoticed—but unmistakably there nonetheless. It is a familiar pattern that, in grammatical terms, starts with the imperative and moves to the indicative: "You do this and I will love you." When we speak of God's relationship with us, such as in the covenant, the order is reversed: "I love you. Do this." First comes the indicative, a statement of fact; only then comes the imperative, the command. God's covenant with Israel begins with a statement of God's faithfulness, and only then does it move on to commands. To confuse the order is to misunderstand the startling nature of the relationship God established with Israel.

It's true, some authors of Hebrew Scripture expressed the conviction that God may get so impatient with Israel's rebellion that God will revoke the covenant promises (like parents who occasionally entertain thoughts of disowning their willful children). Like all deep and lasting relationships, the relationship between Israel and God was severely tested. More than once, Israel seemed to quit the relationship entirely, and the authors recognized that there were times when God was probably tempted to do the same. At certain points in Israel's history, the covenant ties became so strained and frayed that prophets and kings told the people that such a bond needed to be renewed or reestablished entirely. Yet even when Israel responded to God with every kind of hot rebellion or cold indifference, the covenant promises remained.

The Law

When a network television newscaster spoke at the graduation ceremony of a major university, he began his remarks by intoning a list of the world's ills, a familiar litany filled with statistics about the rise of violence, drug use, poverty, hate crimes, and homelessness. It was a bleak picture. But this television icon did not leave his audience on the edge of despair. When he had crushed nearly everyone under an avalanche of depressing observations, he concluded his speech something like this: "But there is a way out for our world. There is a course of action upon which all of us can agree. If all of us were to act on these simple principles, the world would be a far different place. First: 'You shall have no other gods before me.' Second: 'You shall not make for yourselves a graven image.' Third: 'You shall not take the name of God in vain.'" And on he went, straight through the Ten Commandments. When he had finished the list, he sat down.

This was certainly a remarkable occasion: a network television newscaster speaking out in favor of the Ten Commandments. (Can you imagine what such an endorsement might be worth?) Nevertheless, it should be clear from our considerations here that this famous newscaster was quite wrong. The Ten Commandments are not for everyone. The Ten Commandments are not abstract principles that govern all of life, as universally understood as, say, the laws of nature. If they were universal principles, we could cite them without reference to God. We could have come up with them ourselves. If their authority came from their inherent reasonableness, they could be the findings of a focus group or a think tank.

The power of the commandments, however, stems not from their inherent wisdom and reasonableness. Rather, their power comes from their source—that is, God—and from the context in which they are given, as implicit in the covenant that bonds Israel with God that is also part of our story as Christians. The Ten Commandments and the fuller explications of the law are not so much general principles about how we should treat one another as they are ways in which we respond to the ongoing presence of the God who has chosen to be bound to us. They have a special claim on us because they were given by the God who delivered the people of Israel out of exile in Egypt and established an unbreakable covenant with them.

That is why the commandments are introduced with this reminder: "I am the Lord your God, who brought you out of the land of Egypt, out of the house of slavery" (Exod. 20:2). These are not universal principles; rather, they are particular words given to a people who have been drawn into covenantal relationship with the God who now addresses them. As God once gave them the gift of freedom from slavery, this same God gives them another gift: telling them how they might escape becoming slaves to false gods or to themselves, and how they can know more fully the freedom of life lived in relationship with this amazing God.

Consider this homely comparison. A small child is loved by her parents and picks up much about the ways of the family even before she has the capacity to fully understand them. She learns that when she cries her parents will hold her and comfort her. She learns that, when she spills her milk, her parents will help her clean up the mess and give her a fresh glass. She soon knows that, no matter what she does, her parents will not abandon her. Then, when she is older and able to understand more, her parents spell out some of the rules that govern their behavior toward other humans and give definition to what it means to be part of this particular family. They say things like, "In this family we do not hit," "In this family we do not lie," and "In this family we do not curse." These rules (or "commandments") are thus set in the context of an ongoing relationship; they are given to a child who has already experienced a particular way of life within that family. The rules are nothing new, but are more like a summary of what has guided the family all along.

How different it would be if these rules were wrested out of context and simply posted on a bulletin board in school, introduced by the words, "From now on these are the rules all students will be expected to follow." In such a setting, the rules would be so weak, so seemingly arbitrary and groundless, that if they were to be maintained they would have to be backed up by severe punishments for those who did not obey. Under such conditions we would expect the vice principal's office to be very busy. Something like that happens when the Ten Commandments are separated from their context in the covenantal relationship.

The newscaster who quoted the Ten Commandments is not the only one who has been led to the conclusion that they are common-sense, universal principles that are valuable regardless of their source. But if they merely represented common sense, we could have come up with them ourselves. And if that were the case, then we would have to recognize that the same humanity that came up with them also came up with Hiroshima, Auschwitz, and Soweto. At one time or another, to some people, those ideas have also seemed like good ones, manifestations of common sense. "You shall not kill" may seem obvious, but at other times, when left to our own devices, other responses have also seemed obvious.

Such are the conclusions that we are allowed to draw when the Ten Commandments, like other stipulations in the law, are cut off from their source of life. The commandments are not simply common sense. They have grown out of an uncommon relationship with a peculiar and particular God. They are not binding on everyone. They are given to those who see themselves as bound to God in a sacred covenant.

Previous Covenants

When the Israelites looked back to the dimmer reaches of their history, they did so from the vantage point of the Exodus. Old Testament scholar Lawrence Boadt says: "Genesis can be understood somewhat like a special background briefing that government officials often give to newspaper reporters before a big event. Israel understood that God had begun something big in the exodus, but they also knew that God did not just act on a whim. He had been involved in the world and in their story from the beginning."[1]

The background of the story, supplied in Genesis, traces the roots of the covenant back to a time before recorded history. Before the Exodus, even before there was an Israel, there was a promise given to Abraham that would establish him as the progenitor of the Hebrews. Abraham was living in the ancient land of Ur when God told him to leave his father's house and travel to a country that God would show to him. God also assured Abraham that he and his descendants would possess the land of Canaan and that they would be blessed, not only with prosperity but with progeny as abundant as the stars of heaven or the sands of the seashore. Abraham, needing no more motive than obedience, packed up his family and left for this unknown land. This simple (and simply momentous) arrangement was a covenant, the precursor of the covenant God would offer to Israel after the Exodus. After God offered this promise to Abraham, many years would pass before the implications of what had happened would be understood, and many more before the promise would be realized. But from that moment on, neither God nor the people to whom God was now bound would ever be the same.

The story of Genesis traces the covenant back even further. Before Abraham, when God's special relationship with Israel was no more than a twinkle in God's eye, God established a covenant with Noah. God vowed that, after the Flood, never again would God wash away the evils of creation in a gesture of destruction. Never again would God give up on humankind and attempt to start over from scratch. To seal the deal, God placed a rainbow in the sky to remind the people, and to remind God, of this everlasting covenant. It was a covenant offered to all humankind through Noah; but the Hebrews held it particularly close. The rainbow was a reminder that, before God made a special covenant with Israel in the Exodus, even before God made a promise to Abraham, God was at work binding God's own self to Noah, the one from whom all nations and peoples would issue. Recounting this story helped Israel remember that, even though God made a special covenant with them, this covenant had a larger purpose. Through Israel, all people were to be drawn to the one true God.

Back to Creation

Only after experiencing and recounting this remarkable history of God's covenant with God's people was Israel's imagination drawn to the creation of the world. The biblical creation stories themselves were not the result of one person's speculation. By the time the stories were written down, they had already passed through many minds and varied traditions. Not only that, there are two distinct stories of creation in Genesis, each marked with a different set of fingerprints. The first story of creation is found in Genesis 1:1–2:3, the second in Genesis 2:4–24. Even a cursory reading of the two reveals their differences: the first one (Gen. 1:1–2:3) contains the famous affirmation that God created the heavens and the earth in six days. In the second story, God made the heavens and the earth in a single day of extravagant creativity. The first creation story begins with God creating light and darkness out of nothing, then earth and sky, then waters and dry land, then stars, then the moon and the sun, then fish and birds, then land animals, then humankind, before God finally rests on the seventh day. (It is interesting to note that this progression is strikingly similar to the order found in theories of evolution.) The second creation story (Gen. 2:4–24) is far less sophisticated and probably represents traditions that are earlier than those appearing in the first story. It says nothing about God creating the earth but rather assumes that it already existed. In the second story, humankind, rather than being the culmination of the creative order, is created first. This narrative begins with God's forming Adam out of dust, and then it moves on to the creation of plants and other animals, much as one might put a turtle in a terrarium and then place other living things around it to provide it a pleasant environment. The second narrative tells of Adam and Eve, characters who are totally absent from the first story.

What is important to us is the fact that there are two distinct stories of creation found back to back in Hebrew Scripture. If these stories were intended to be read as history, as is sometimes argued, this would certainly not be the case. If we were compiling a history of our country, for example, we would not include a second chapter that contradicted the first in key respects. Instead, we would attempt to reconcile the differences, something that the compilers of Genesis did not do. We would include two distinct views only if our goal were something other than to present history. When we read any written document, it is important to ask what form of literature we are reading, because our approach will be different depending on what we are reading. If we read a novel in the same way we read history, we will be misled in our reading. If we read poetry the same way we read a science book, we will draw some peculiar conclusions.

The reason the compilers of Genesis were not troubled by the contradictions of the two creation stories is that they did not mean them to be read as history. The authors were interested in other matters entirely. A historian approaches a past event with one set of questions: *What* happened? *When* did it happen? *Why* did it happen? A scientist considers an object of study, asks what happened and when, and then moves on to the central question of *how* it happened. Those who wrote, compiled, and responded to the creation stories were certainly concerned with what happened and why; however, they were most interested in *who* was active in creation and what that says about who we are.

On this central question, the two creation stories agree: God is the "who" behind creation. The world and everything in and beyond it are not the result of a random series of events. Rather, they are the creation of a loving God who was active from before the beginning and is at work still. Like any great work of art, the world is a reflection of its Creator. The windflowers that dance in a gentle breeze remind us of the tenderness of God; the staggering power of a hurricane speaks of God's power. In humankind, the most intricate and complex of all creatures (and those loved most dearly), the reflection of this God is seen most clearly. And despite the cruelties of nature and the occasionally more vivid cruelties of humankind, God declares this creation good.

The implications that flow from these simple affirmations are many and powerful. We are not the masters of our fate, the captains of our souls—as much as we might like to believe so. Instead, we are mere creatures, radically dependent on the Creator God at every turn. God did not create us as a painter creates a painting, hangs it on a wall, and then goes on to other endeavors. God creates more like a cellist "creates" a sonata. If the Creator were ever to stop creating, the creation would also end. To say that God created us is to affirm that we are not gods ourselves. If we are to discover how to order our lives, we must look beyond ourselves. We may have the power to end life, but only God has the *authority* to do so. We may think of ourselves as masters of creation, but we are mere stewards who are accountable to the true master.

If everything that exists came to be by mere chance, we must be content to have our lives tossed about by similarly purposeless winds. But if everything we are and everything we see is part of a good creation, then we must work for good in the world in partnership with the one who created it and declared it to be good. The order and purpose of the universe may sometimes be hidden or even temporarily thwarted, but we cannot give up on creation, even on that part of creation we think of as ourselves, because the Creator of it all has not yet given up.

Leaning Toward the Future

In the creation and the covenant, Israel received two gracious gifts from God. As the years unfolded, however, it became increasingly clear that something had gone woefully amiss. G. K. Chesterton observes that it is "strange that people can doubt the doctrine of 'original sin,' the only doctrine that can be verified through observation." The people continued in their warring madness. They neglected the needs of the most vulnerable in their midst. They lusted after other gods, including perhaps the most seductive of all, the god of self-reliance, and they ignored the presence and commands of the one true God. When they did worship this God, it was sometimes no more than a hollow ritual. Israel's leaders, charged with leading them in the ways of truth and drawing the people into closer relationships with God, often made matters worse by leading the rebellion.

God's covenant remained intact through it all, but the people seemed persistently unwilling or unable to hold up their end of the relationship. God occasionally sent messengers to the people of Israel to chastise them for their rebellion and to point them back in the right direction. These people were called prophets. They warned about what would happen if the people continued their disobedience, which is why the term "prophet" came to be associated with prognostication. The prophets were simply speakers of truth. Their intention was to inspire people toward obedience in the present, and one way they did this was to offer compelling pictures of the future that would result if the people continued on a particular course.

The great Jewish scholar Abraham Heschel shares a legend about a magical kingdom faced with a dilemma because its grain crop was poisoned. Anyone who ate the grain would go insane, but if they didn't eat, they would starve to death. It was a terrible predicament. Eventually the king called his subjects together and told them, "I have made a very difficult decision. I have decided that we must survive; therefore, we will eat the grain. But we will designate selected people to feed on the small uncontaminated food supply. We must always have someone around to remind us that we are crazy." This is the role that the prophets played for Israel. The prophets were sustained by God's truth so that there would be someone to remind the people that they had abandoned the truth.

The prophets continually warned the people that their faithlessness was approaching the boundaries of the infinite because it tested the infinite patience of God. The words of the prophets resounded with urgency because they knew what was at stake. It was not simply that Israel's transgressions were growing tiresome, but that the people's rebellious posture threatened the whole deal. The very covenant on which their life was based was in danger. Nestled in the midst of the prophets' warnings, however, were declarations of hope. The Old Testament scholar John Bright has said: "The prophets could never believe that the national ruin was the end. True, they could see no cause for hope; but they never lost hope because they never lost God."

And thus, the prophets held, if the old covenant was not merely a bit frayed at the edges, but rather threatened at its very core, God would offer a new and different kind of covenant. Hosea spoke of a new and faithful marriage that would be established between God and God's people (2:2–16). Jeremiah (31:33) and Ezekiel (36:26–28) envisioned God's offering a new covenant in which the law would now be written on the hearts of the people. Isaiah anticipated a more faithful servant of a different kind who would come to lead the people in new ways (Isa. 42:18–21; 52:13–15).

Something had clearly gone wrong with the world—created as good, intended for good, and yet mired in the ways of disobedience and decay. This was beyond tinkering or mere adjustment. The people needed a new creation so that they could start anew. God would have to start at the very beginning with a new Adam. And a new covenant was required, one founded on a new basis and not as dependent on the rebellious human will for fulfillment.

It was this new beginning, this new covenant, that the prophets proclaimed and awaited. They leaned toward it just as a plant on a windowsill leans toward the sun that is just out of sight. They anticipated this new covenant with urgency. They even rightly anticipated some of the broader outlines of this new covenant. What they could not fully anticipate was the surprising and peculiar way in which this surprising and peculiar God would bring it all about.

CHAPTER 2

The Jesus of the Incarnation

According to the Gospel of Luke, soon after Jesus's public ministry began, he returned to his hometown of Nazareth. When he attended worship in the synagogue there, he was asked to read the Scripture and offer a sermon. This was common practice, as there were no "ministers" in the synagogue. An invitation to read and preach could be extended by the ruling elders to any member of the congregation. Since Jesus had been away for a time and was now home again, he seemed a fitting choice for the honor. The reading from the Law for a particular day was established by custom, but the preacher was allowed to choose his own reading from the prophets. Jesus stood up to read from a scroll these words of the prophet Isaiah: "The Spirit of the Lord is upon me, because the Lord has anointed me; he has sent me to bring good news to the oppressed, to ... release the prisoners; to proclaim the year of the Lord's favor ..." (Isa. 61:1–2).

So far, nothing unusual. It was a familiar passage that declared the triumphant coming of the Messiah, God's anointed one, who Israel anticipated would usher in a new age in which God would reign. The Jews were used to hearing these and similarly hopeful words from the prophets. Ever since the covenant had been established between Israel and God, the people had received such words of promise and awaited their fulfillment. Exile and suffering tested the faith of the people; the rebellion and apostasy of the people, in turn, certainly tried God's faithfulness to them. Nevertheless, through it all, the promises remained: God would do something new through God's anointed one. God would establish God's reign in tangible ways in the here and now of life, ushering in a new era through the one God would send.

When Jesus finished the reading, he rolled up the scroll and sat down, assuming the customary posture for a preacher in the synagogue. Jesus looked around at the people. His father and his brother were there. His next-door neighbor was probably there, as well as his father's business associates. They all knew Jesus. Jesus met their eyes, and the first words out of his mouth were: "Today this scripture has been fulfilled in your hearing" (Luke 4:21). In other words: "You and your mothers and fathers, and their mothers and fathers before them, have been waiting for the Messiah and the new age he is to usher in. Today your waiting is over. I am the one." Luke then records the people's reaction to this startling declaration. All of them spoke well of Jesus. They were certainly amazed, but they were also receptive to the "gracious words that came from his mouth" (Luke 4:22). But then a second—and very different—reaction followed. The people asked skeptically, "Isn't this Joseph's son?"

The two reactions seem to contradict each other. One seems to indicate belief, the other disbelief. The discontinuity between the two reactions has led some commentators to conclude that their origins were in two separate accounts of the story that were later brought together. That may be the case; but in another way, Luke's account records a mixed response that we can easily recognize. On the one hand, the people seemed to recognize that there was something different about the one addressing them in the synagogue. Jesus spoke with authority, and the people sensed that God was in Jesus in a way they had never before witnessed or experienced; they responded with receptivity, if not yet full belief.

On the other hand, the people were unsettled by the realization that it was Jesus saying these things and Jesus to whom they were responding in this way. Jesus, of all people! Jesus, Joseph's son! It can't be, they told themselves. We can imagine them saying: "I remember when his baby teeth fell out! I remember him when he used to play behind our house! I knew this kid before he learned the books of the

Bible." The people might certainly have been able to believe that the Messiah would come and establish God's reign in a way they could not anticipate—but Joseph's son?

The people who heard Jesus preach in the synagogue simply could not hold together the image of Jesus as the Messiah and their intimate knowledge of him as a human being. It assaulted their understanding of the way the world is put together and the way God works. The idea that the almighty God could be found in something as familiar as this human life was difficult to accept, if not downright bizarre.

The Folly of the Incarnation

This story reminds us that we are not the first people to find it difficult to affirm the divinity of Jesus. And the problems we have in accepting such an affirmation did not first arise in the scientific age. The people who lived in Jesus's day had no easier time than we do believing that God could be incarnate—that is, "enfleshed"—in a human being. In some ways, not much has changed in two thousand years. To be sure, those who listened to Jesus speak in the synagogue that day did not hear him, or anyone else, claim that Jesus was "the Son of God." They were too early to be familiar with Paul's retrospective credo that "God was in Christ, reconciling the world to God's own self." The refined theology of the creeds, which affirmed that Jesus is fully God and fully human, was still centuries away. These were all subsequent ways to explain the mystery that stood before them in the synagogue. For now, it was more than enough to realize that it was the common and lowly Jesus who was making such uncommon and mighty statements about himself. From the moment Jesus began to preach, the people could not fully accept or understand the ways in which the human and the divine seemed uniquely present and inseparable in Jesus.

Paul, writing a generation after Jesus, addressed the entrenched skepticism of his age: "Jews demand signs," he wrote. That is, the Jews wanted some kind of proof for the claim that Jesus was the Messiah.

And "Greeks desire wisdom": that is, sophisticated people that they were, they would not subscribe to any religion that did not stand up to the best of human logic. All of this teaching about Jesus being both God and human is a stumbling block to them, sheer folly. Paul did not try to marshal reasons why belief in Jesus made sense. Instead, he readily granted that, via the way the world measures things, Jesus was weak, and belief in him was foolish. For Paul, recognizing the very unlikelihood and bizarreness of God in human flesh is an initial step toward greeting his coming as welcome and wonderful. If we cannot hold in our minds the twin affirmations that Jesus is God and human, then, paradoxically, we are on the right track. What distinguishes believers is that they come to see that this very "folly" is what everything else depends on, for in such foolishness is the very power and wisdom of God.

The tension of that remarkable affirmation, however, never slackens. Holding the human and divine together seems like trying to hold opposite poles of a magnet together. We don't believe we can do it. Even the name "Jesus Christ" seems to pull apart. *Jesus*, after all, is a common name, like Mary, Scott, or Lisa; but *Christ* is an honorific title, the Greek form of the Hebrew word "messiah," meaning "anointed one," the one through whom God works to bring people into a right relationship with God. When we refer to "Jesus Christ," we are affirming a powerful and difficult paradox: the common person Jesus is also the one who is the unique manifestation of God.

Ways beyond the Paradox

The humanity and divinity of Jesus Christ are so difficult to hold together that throughout history humankind has found various ways to relieve the tension of this assault on our hearts and minds. Most people have been able to do this by either denying the humanity or denying the divinity of Jesus. People who deny the divine in Jesus are the most numerous and the easiest to spot, and they affirm a wide spectrum of views about him: they might see him as a charlatan out to deceive the gullible or as the greatest product of the human race, with unequalled insight into the ways of God. As different as these views might seem, what unites them—and other views in between— is the conviction that Jesus is human through and through.

People who deny the human in Jesus are usually harder to spot because, through their fervent insistence that Jesus is divine, they seem very "religious." The vehement emphasis on Jesus's divinity distracts us, while the humanity of Jesus slips away virtually un-noticed. This is what happened in the early centuries of Christian history: some people accepted that Jesus was God but found it diffi-cult to believe that he was human in any real sense of the word. This happens today as well—subtly at first, usually through an unwilling-ness to attribute to Jesus doubt, impatience, anger, or other human characteristics. Soon Jesus becomes a god in human disguise, God's costume for an earthly masquerade, as if, at the stroke of midnight, God will shed the mask to reveal who was behind the mask all along. This view is often accompanied by great zeal and piety; but it, too, is a way to escape the "folly" of the statement that Jesus was fully human *and* fully divine.

We have had almost two thousand years to take the "folly" out of Jesus's coming, and we have become quite good at it. We have had time to let our mind's eye see, not the Jesus who was sent, but the Jesus we would have sent. After all, we would not want God to come in the person of a lowly carpenter, smelling of a manger, looking like a vagabond, and speaking in a dialect. If our God were to come as a person, we would want God to do so without getting mucked up in anything very human. And this is the Jesus, purged of things human, who often parades in front of our mind's eye.

In a church I once served, a print of a drawing by Rembrandt hung above my desk. In the drawing, Jesus is preaching to a small assembly. A child lies on his belly and draws in the dirt with his finger. A few others gaze off into space, lost in reflection. Most have their eyes riveted on the preacher. If we, with the crowd, focus on Jesus, we notice nothing about his appearance that sets him apart. He is just Joseph's son. There is nothing prepossessing in his stature or coun-tenance. His hands are large workman's hands that have served long hours in the building trade. His face could not be called beautiful, reminding us of how Isaiah describes the Messiah: "He had no form or majesty that we should look at him, nothing in his appearance that we should desire him" (Isa. 53:2). If his figure were put in the crowd of listeners, we might not even notice him.

But if our eyes again shift to the listeners, we appreciate that they see more than this. They know that this is no mere backwoods faith huckster. On the contrary, this is the one on whom everything depends. A halo does not show, nor do calloused hands hide, that they are in the presence of God. This face is not so ugly that only a mother could love it, but it is plain enough that only the faithful could see God in it. And they do see it. A child once stared at this drawing above my desk and asked, "Who's that?"

"That's Jesus," I replied.

"Oh," the child responded, more than a little surprised, "I didn't recognize him."

And little wonder. He looks so ordinary that it should not surprise us that Rembrandt found models for his portraits of Jesus by wandering through the Jewish ghetto of Amsterdam. In many pictures of Jesus that hang in Sunday school rooms or elsewhere in a church venue, Jesus is made to stand apart in his humanity, as if his humanity were somehow different from ours. We are led to believe that if we saw him at a lunch counter or stuck in a traffic jam, we would know him. The human eye would be able to perceive that this one is different from all others. And if Jesus were set apart like that, we might assume that only a fool would not see the living God in him. We would do well to wonder why so many fools lived at the time Jesus walked the earth, people who had the advantage of seeing him with their own eyes and yet did not assent to him. The reason, of course, is that the human eye is not enough. Jesus Christ is a vision that only the eye of faith can see.

It is a temptation (and not a small one) to distance Jesus from things human. The temptation insinuates itself into our perceptions in small ways at first. It starts by making Jesus distant from the little things, the staples of human life. It becomes difficult to imagine, for example, that Jesus ever had to sneeze. It's hard to believe that Jesus ever had to pause and fumble around trying to find the right words.

And it's difficult to picture Jesus passing the evening with friends, perhaps listening to Peter regale them all with stories about when he was a fisherman, stories that everyone had heard before but that prompt Jesus to laugh again all the same. If we have trouble visualizing Jesus participating in these snippets of human reality, we are well on the way to denying that he shared with us the more central aspects of human experience.

Jesus as God Sharing Our Lives

It may seem sheer folly to affirm that Jesus is fully divine and fully human, but it is only when we are able to let this folly stand that we are able to receive its full benefits. It means that nothing we experience is distant from God.

We often feel alone in the trials, toils, and snares of human life. Misery loves company, or so goes the old adage; but profound misery is more isolating than anything else this side of death. Abject misery does not seek company, because it knows no company. A cry of misery can have no accompaniment. Into the most important areas of life we go single file. We are born single file, and we die single file. We enter life's darkest days single file, and face our greatest disappointments single file—and necessarily so. Where we go in those moments, no one else can follow. Those moments hold a kind of loneliness that cannot be quenched; there is no companion anywhere who can share them.

Then we hear about the cries of suffering that are attributed to Jesus. On the cross, Jesus said, "I thirst," and perhaps more poignantly, "My God, my God, why have you forsaken me?" These sound like words of need, despair, even doubt—which is, of course, just what they are. It is difficult to let those words stand, raw and unexplained, yet there are gracious benefits for doing so. A Jesus who experienced the full range of human circumstances and human emotions must surely have experienced bodily agony and the sense of being forsaken. After all, in Jesus, God came to live among us—not as God in a human costume that could be shed whenever things got rough, but human to the bone, human enough to experience need, deep despair, and even the perceived absence of God. If Jesus never experienced these, it would mean that he never experienced the kind of human life that we live, a life filled with such things. Through Jesus we can appreciate the philosopher Alfred North Whitehead's definition of God as "the fellow sufferer who understands."

John Westerhoff tells of a mother whose child was late in leaving his nursery school room. The child explained to his mother that, as class ended, one of the other children had broken a pottery dish she had made. The mother asked, "So you had to stay and help her pick it up?" "No," the child replied, "I had to stay to help her cry." In Jesus, God came to us (in part, at least) to help us cry. Jesus is uniquely able to bear such burdens because, as a human, he has traveled the same uneven roads we have, and as God he has the endless empathy of the divine, which is not easily worn out, as human empathy is.

The Apostles' Creed contains this affirmation about Jesus: "Jesus Christ was crucified, dead and buried. He descended into hell." The last part of that statement always used to trouble me, until one day someone told me that, for her, it was the most treasured part of the creed. When I asked why, she explained, "Because hell is where I spend most of my life." The affirmation that Jesus is God incarnate means that there is no experience so dark that God does not share it. The familiar words of the old spiritual "Nobody Knows the Trouble I've Seen" are gathered up into a larger reality: God not only knows the trouble we have seen but, in Jesus, God has experienced it all with us. Jesus is indeed "Immanuel," another name that came to be associated with messianic expectations, a name that means "God with us." Through the hell of internal anguish and the high water of external disaster, God is still with us.

Jesus Helps Us Approach God

In Jesus, God not only approaches us, but we are also given a way to approach God. To demonstrate this unique aspect of our inheritance from Jesus, we must first consider the understanding of God that

Jesus himself inherited. According to the book of Exodus, when the people of Israel were still in exile in Egypt, God encountered Moses and commissioned him to bring news of deliverance to the Hebrews and asked Moses to lead that triumphant parade himself (Exod. 3).

Before Moses answered, even before he learned all the details, he quite naturally wanted to know the name of the one addressing him. Besides, if he had God's name, he could use that to prove to the people that he had seen God—a preposterous claim at best, one that was bound to be received with skepticism and scorn. But if he knew God's name, that would help. After all, no one had ever known God's name before. In fact, no one before Moses had dared ask. But Moses did not let that stop him. He rushed in where even God's own angels tread lightly: "If I go to the people and tell them God has sent me, and they ask, 'What is his name?' how shall I respond?"

Moses got an answer—of sorts. He did not get a name, exactly, but God did say, "I am who I am," which was about as hard for Moses to comprehend as it is for us to translate. In Hebrew, the phrase is spelled YHWH, without vowels, so that it was not only difficult to understand but impossible to pronounce. And that was just the point: the God who appeared to Moses was too great, too magnificent, too distant, too incomprehensible to have a name that could be pronounced.

Once a person knows your name, he or she has a certain power over you. Consider how, when you hear your name on the street, it is almost impossible not to turn around, even if you are quite sure that you are not the one being called. If God's name were generally known by all, imagine how often God would have to turn around. And to have someone's name is to limit that person in some way. When somebody calls me "Martin," it's limiting because it means that I'm not Jack or Bonnie. I am not wind or stream or love. I am merely all the limited things that are "Martin." To name is to limit in a way that does not make sense in any reference to God, who is without limit, who is all things. We do not have words that are big enough, all-encompassing enough.

So God simply responded to Moses, "I am who I am," a word that could not be pronounced, since no word without vowels can be pronounced. When we call God "Yahweh," we are adding the missing vowels, making the name pronounceable again, something the Hebrew scribes would never do. This tendency held true throughout Hebrew tradition, although as time went on, the Jews did use other words to signify God that came close to a name, such as the word *Elohim*. Nevertheless, though God was thought of in personal terms, God was perceived as distant and unapproachable, beyond human grasp and human words.

Into this world and tradition Jesus came, turning this understanding on its head. Jesus not only dared call God by name, but he used an intimate term of endearment. Jesus called God "Abba," a word that is commonly translated "Father," but would more accurately be rendered "Daddy" or "Papa." When Jesus addressed God as "Abba" he was saying something revolutionary, something that is often lost on us because it has become so familiar. To say that Jesus's referring to God as "Abba" would shock the people of his day is an understatement. It was enough to make them shudder and duck for fear of the consequences.

Jesus's familiarity with God was more than a shock, however. It was also remarkably good news, not only because Jesus did not get struck down in his tracks for addressing God in a bold and familiar way, but because it somehow seemed fitting. Jesus did not hesitate to call on God: he turned to God daily, even hourly. His intimacy in his relationship with God was without precedent. His relationship with God was characterized by the kind of care, love, and familiarity that is known only in families, and only in the closest of families at that.

This was good news, not because Jesus had this relationship with God but because, through Jesus, *we* are invited to have this kind of relationship with God as well. We are all given the privilege. God has a name that draws us close. We are invited to approach God in this way, to call on God without hesitation as one who is ever near and wants to be ever nearer. God is not only approachable but actually longs to be approached. According to John, through Jesus we have been given nothing less than the "power to become children of God" (John 1:12).

In this context we need to grant that some serious problems arise when we refer to God as "Father." For instance, for some the word "father" has associations that make it difficult to respond to the idea of God as a loving presence. Then there is the fact that, by referring to God only as "Father," we seem to imply that God is male. To be sure, the exclusive use of male imagery in reference to God not only gives us mistaken images of God, but has also been used for centuries to help prop up male authority. It is important to remember that Jesus spoke at a time before these concerns were raised and that none of these implications was intended. Indeed, in the words of the old hymn, "Time makes ancient good uncouth." We might even conjecture that, if Jesus were alive today, he would share our concerns about exclusively male imagery in reference to God, and he would help us find suitable alternatives. Living in our time, without such assistance, we attempt to respond to these concerns without sacrificing the important inheritance we have from Jesus, the revolutionary notion that we can have a personal relationship with God. However we choose to negotiate our way through the thorny issues of language, the promise to which we lay claim through Jesus remains: the uniquely intimate and profound relationship that Jesus had with God is available to us as well. Not only did God approach us in Jesus, but through Jesus we are invited to approach God in a new way.

Jesus Shares God with Us

Through Jesus, then, we are given the assurance that God understands our lives, and we are drawn into a personal relationship with God. But there's more: through Jesus we are also given a unique way to understand God.

After the Exodus from slavery in Egypt, while the Hebrews were still wandering in the wilderness, Moses pitched a tent he called "the tent of meeting," and there Moses and God would chat (Exod. 33:7). Moses was still not given the privilege of calling God by name, and there was still that unbridgeable chasm between the majesty of God and this mere human being. Nevertheless, there was also something like intimacy in their conversations because "the Lord used to speak to Moses . . . as one speaks to a friend" (33:11).

Fragments of those conversations are also offered in Exodus. God had already promised that the Hebrews would be led into the Promised Land, that they would forever be God's people. Moses then asked for more: "Show me your ways, so that I may know you and find favor in your sight." And God replied, "My presence will go with you, and I will give you rest." Moses shot back, "If your presence will not go, do not carry us up from here" (Exod. 33:13-15). Roughly translated, Moses was saying, "Hey, you had better go with us, because this is not the kind of journey we would make on our own!" Then God, like a parent who succumbs to the entreaties of a child, said, "I will do the very thing that you have asked" (33:17).

By any measure, it was a remarkable conversation, the kind of open, easy exchange one might expect between two people who know each other very well. Moses was traversing new territory here. No one before him had been granted such intimate access to God. But, rather than shrink from the encounter, Moses went one step further. He said, "Show me your glory, I pray" (33:18), that is, "Let me see you. Show me the essence of your being."

God responded: "You cannot see my face, for no one shall see me and live" (33:20). Then God instructed Moses to go to the cleft of a rock. God told Moses that, before God's glory passed, the cleft would be covered by the divine hand. Then, once God had passed, the hand would lift for a moment and Moses would see, not God's face, but God's back. Just a peek, mind you, a glimpse and nothing more, for anything more would destroy Moses as surely as an ice cube hurled at the sun.

Note the paradox: God spoke to Moses as one speaks to a friend. Yet Moses was given only a sliver of a glance of God's back. To Moses, the chosen leader of the chosen people, God was unspeakably close; yet, even to Moses, God remained unimaginably distant—and it was like that in their closest encounters. But then we confront Jesus. In Jesus, the majesty of God is undiminished, yet the closeness of God is experienced in new and startling ways. Jesus is the fullest expression of God's power and glory, but Jesus is also Immanuel, "God with us," as close as our own lives, as familiar as the way home. By sending Jesus, God seems to say, "I will come to you in the person of a simple carpenter. He will encompass the dimensions of eternity and yet he will be as close as your elbow. And through this one you shall see me and not die. You will live to tell the story and live as you have never lived before." In other words: in Jesus, God turned around and we could finally see that face.

We might explain the mystery of how Jesus reveals God to us by saying that Jesus is God-like. But the reverse is even more profoundly true: God is Jesus-like. It is through Jesus that we can know what God is like. Through Jesus, we are given a means to understand the ways of God that would be unavailable to us without Jesus. And this is no mere glimpse of God we are offered. It is a picture of God that we can continually turn to. By observing the ways Jesus responded to those who had been cast off by life, we can understand God's special care for the outcast. By hearing about the ways Jesus healed the sick, we can discover that our God is the kind of God who can put together the broken pieces of our lives. By observing the ways Jesus forgave the very ones who rejected and betrayed him, we can realize how far God will go to embrace us with forgiveness. By studying the ways of Jesus, we need not wonder what God would have us do because we can endeavor simply to do what Jesus did.

According to ancient history, King Croesus of Lydia once summoned the philosopher Thales in order to ask, "What kind of God is God?" Thales deliberated for what seemed a very long time, and he finally had to admit that he could not answer the question. Many years later, the early Christian scholar Tertullian said that that incident was an example of the world's ignorance without Christ. "The wisest man in the world could not tell who God is," he wrote, "but the most ignorant Christian knows God and can proclaim him to others."

It is important to note, however, that the very nearness of God we encounter in Jesus is not always welcome. Most people do not have any trouble believing in God—that is, if the concept of God remains vague enough. A recent survey revealed that 95 percent of Americans believe in God. We can explain this finding only when we grant that believing in God is rather easy. Without Jesus, the concept of God can remain just that—a concept. Such a view of God becomes little more than what someone described as "a sacred blur." We can refer to God and still sound merely theological, without severely compromising our worldliness or sophistication. But there's more: such a comfortably vague concept of God does not require much from us. We not only have little sense of what this God is like, but also few clues about what this God might expect of us.

If we recognize God in Jesus, however, that distance is no longer possible. The sacred blur is brought into stark, startling focus. What was once comfortably vague is now uncomfortably clear and close. Many Christian traditions, including our own, often seem to speak more easily of God than of Jesus. Perhaps this stems from the difficulty we have believing everything claimed about Jesus. Perhaps we tend toward more general talk about God because we cannot bring ourselves to believe the peculiar notion that God was—and somehow still is—uniquely present in a common first-century Jew. But I think the opposite is often true. Our uneasiness with Jesus may not derive from our doubt that God was in Jesus in a unique way; rather, it may flow from our suspicion that it may be true after all. If it is true, then we must confront God and confront ourselves more fully, and who feels entirely prepared for that? If it is true, then we can no longer nestle in the comfort of vagueness. If it is true, then all of our sophisticated speculations about God become irreverent.

Karl Barth was not only perhaps the most influential theologian of the twentieth century, but also one of the world's great minds. His magnum opus, *The Church Dogmatics*, is a huge and intricate work that is widely considered one of the most complete and profound summaries of Christian theology in all of history. Near the end of his career, Barth was asked by a student to summarize what he had said in his multivolume work, the product of a lifetime of scholarship and reflection. Barth thought for a moment and replied, "Jesus loves me, this I know, for the Bible tells me so." What an embarrassingly simplistic thing for a sophisticated scholar and worldly man to say— unless, of course, it happens to be true. If it is true, it begins to look and sound very much like the wisdom and power of God.

There may be times when we are embarrassed by Jesus, embarrassed to think that the source of all wisdom and power, the very meaning of our lives, the very image of God, can be found in the one whom the world rejects as an obstacle and sheer folly. But that's okay. When we are closest to the embarrassment of it, we may just be closest to the truth of it. To make faith claims about Jesus any easier to understand or accept is to diminish their power.

Instead, we are invited to approach this deep mystery with correspondingly deep wonder. Imagine: with every conceivable and inconceivable means of dealing with wayward humanity at God's disposal, God chose to take on weak and common human life. In Jesus, God eschewed all the tools of power and might in order to share in the life we live, a life of hunger pangs and scorched feet, joy and frustration, salt tears and sweet laughter. This monarch rejected a robe for the most humble garb. He was born in a stable, of all places, in a small corner of a big world. He did not summon the people to his throne, hand down decrees, or issue new laws. Instead, he walked among the people, ate with them, and talked to them in a familiar way that was unbefitting his station. He spoke words of disappointment and shed tears of sorrow. He coaxed and wooed the people as if his (as well as their) life depended on their response. He told stories as if there were no other means at his disposal. He bound the people's wounds and washed their feet as if he were a mere servant. This Jesus could have marshaled the power of heaven and earth, could have rightfully claimed adoration and privilege; instead, he chose to share our weakness and defeat that we might share his power and victory.

This is the Savior, the Promised One? Who would ever believe it? And believing it, who would have it any other way?

CHAPTER 3

The Jesus of the Resurrection

Even the strangest realities can become so familiar that our sense of their strangeness needs to be refreshed, and no symbol is more familiar to Christians than the cross. We are accustomed to seeing the cross displayed in places of worship, and it is often prominently situated outside church buildings because this symbol identifies them as Christian churches. It is found on the covers of hymnals and Bibles and embroidered on the vestments worn by clergy. We make the sign of the cross on the forehead of someone being baptized. Sometimes a cross is worn on a chain around the neck, either as a statement of Christian faith or simply as a piece of jewelry. "In the cross of Christ I glory," Christians sing in one of the many hymns that extol the centrality of the cross in Christian devotion. Everywhere we turn, there is that stark and simple symbol.

But what a strange symbol the cross is. It is strange that a means of execution should become a cherished symbol for those who follow the one who was executed. Its strangeness can be refreshed if we consider that, if Jesus had been executed by other means, Christians today might identify their places of worship with electric chairs atop their steeples. Or they might wear gold nooses around their necks. It is strange that Christians, rather than averting their eyes from such a sight, are invited (in the words of another hymn) to "survey the wondrous cross." It is strange, indeed, that Christians should look at a cross, this brutal instrument of hate and death, and see love and life.

Those who first confronted the reality of Jesus nailed to a cross were not drawn to the sight but repelled by it. Those who followed Jesus thought that he was the one to fulfill the promises offered to Israel, to usher in God's realm, to establish a triumphant reign as God's anointed one. But here he was, so seemingly helpless, dying the death of a common criminal, mocked not only by those who nailed him to the cross, but also by the very ones who hung there with him. In Jesus's death, his followers saw all of their hopes dragged into death with him. They scattered like a flock of frightened birds.

It was only later, on reflection and in light of all that was to transpire, that the followers of Jesus were able to proclaim that it was on the cross, where God seemed so achingly absent and God's ways so thoroughly thwarted, that God was most surely present and God's ways most truly manifest. It was on the cross, of all places, that the dimensions of God's triumphant love were made known. It was not something that Jesus's followers (or anyone else) would have planned. God's ways are not our ways and, if we're honest, we have to admit that we prefer our ways. We would not have had God come in the person of a peasant carpenter. We would have had God enter the human drama in triumph, not submit to the ignominious death of a criminal. But the strange ways of God, once revealed, also have a sense of inevitability about them. Once those ways are revealed, it seems as though there are no better ways, and perhaps no other ways, for God's purposes to be fulfilled.

To understand how the strange ways of God manifest on the cross were also strangely right, we must first recall how God's previous attempts to draw us into faithful relationship seemed to be continually frustrated. We have already considered the covenant God established with the people of Israel. In that covenant God promised faithfulness to the people, but the relationship was to flow both ways: God's promises were specified in the covenant, but God's expectations were also spelled out in the Law. But there was a problem: the people seemed continually unwilling or unable to hold up their end of the bargain. It's true that their disobedience was not always flagrant. For example, they could fulfill the commandment not to kill, but they seemed unable to cultivate hearts that were free from the desire for revenge. Even when they did not steal from their neighbors, they could not keep from coveting their neighbors' possessions. Even the righteous in their midst seemed unable to fulfill the complete demands of the Law. Eventually the Law, which had been offered as a beckoning sign of the covenant promises, became a continual reminder of the failure of the people to act in faithful response to those promises.

It wasn't just that little transgressions added up; worse, the transgressions of the people seemed like symptoms of a deeper condition. It became increasingly obvious that there was a rebellious spirit in humankind that made such misdeeds inevitable, that seemed to cause human spirits always to list toward sin. A human is one creature who, given the chance, will lean away from the light and grow toward the dark. Even if we're not given a chance, we can still usually find a way to make a mess of things. God offers the means by which we can live in communion with one another, yet we consistently act in ways that separate us from one another, from God, and also in some way from ourselves. We can again appreciate the timeworn confession that we are sinners if we recognize that it means just this: we are separated from our brothers and sisters, from God, and from ourselves. Even if the symptoms of this estrangement can be held in check for a time, the estrangement remains, dormant and powerful in the human heart.

It wasn't that the people of Israel did not try. And God demonstrated a continual willingness to forgive the transgressions of the people, to renew the covenant and offer them a new start. Hebrew Scripture is largely a story of God's unwillingness to take no for an answer, and God's willingness to stick by Israel even when the people turned away. Nevertheless, after a time it became clear that something else was needed. The people needed more than to be assured of God's forgiveness yet again; they needed a new way to experience that forgiveness. They needed more than a renewed covenant with God; they needed a new covenant established on an entirely new basis.

The Cross as Forgiveness Manifest

Large and frequent doses of forgiveness are necessary in any enduring relationship, and certainly our relationship with God is no exception. This is why the people held the idea of divine forgiveness, so deeply embedded in Hebrew Scripture, very close. The people knew that, because they could not be counted on to be anything but fickle, they had to count on God's forgiveness if the covenant relationship were to survive. The psalmist gives beautiful expression to this assurance of God's forgiveness:

> The Lord is merciful and gracious, slow to anger and abounding in steadfast love.... He does not deal with us according to our sins, nor repay us according to our iniquities. For as the heavens are high above the earth, so great is his steadfast love toward those who fear him; as far as the east is from the west, so far he removes our transgressions from us. (Ps. 103:8, 10–12)

Jesus also spoke of God's forgiveness, perhaps nowhere more dramatically than in a story recorded in Luke's Gospel (15:11–32). The story is about a son who, after asking for his share of his father's inheritance, spends everything on himself in what one translation calls "loose living," since living merely for oneself is always loose. The son takes up residence in a foreign land, distant and estranged, and then a famine comes. He had wanted to be free, so he had cut all ties. Now that he recognizes that he depends on those ties for his very life, they are severed and cannot be tied back together again. He decides to return home and throw himself on the mercy of his father, and he even rehearses a confession to offer when he gets home.

While the son is still a long way from his father's house—not when he had explained himself, not when he had offered his prepared confession, not when his father was close enough to see his hangdog look of regret—the father sees his son coming and runs to him as fast as his tired old legs can carry him. "What is he doing?" the son has reason to wonder. "Is he going to chase me off the property? Box my ears? Give me a lecture?" Instead, when the father reaches his son, he gives him a forgiving embrace and kisses him—not a perfunctory, thin-lipped kiss, but a real kiss of welcome.

This story is usually called the parable of the Prodigal Son, but it would be more fitting to call it the parable of the Prodigal God. The son was certainly "prodigal"—extravagant and lavish—in the way he "squandered his property." But that was nothing compared to the extravagance of the father as he lavished his love and forgiveness. This story is a dramatic assurance of God's forgiveness. We may take up residence far from home—that is, far from God. We may waste our lives, like pouring water into the sand, and we may experience the famine of the soul. We have no excuses, though we may make some up, because we have nothing to offer except our need, like an open wound. But while we are still far off, God greets us with extravagant forgiveness and welcomes us home again.

So the idea of God's forgiveness was nothing new. It was expressed in Hebrew Scripture and in the teachings of Jesus. However, we know—painfully, from our own experience—that words of forgiveness can fall short. We long to have forgiveness made manifest. Beyond hearing the story of how a father demonstrates unconditional forgiveness of a son, we need to have such forgiveness demonstrated in our own lives. We long for that story to be our story in palpable ways, and that need and longing is addressed in the cross.

When humans had done the worst they could to Jesus, the incarnate God—when all of our betrayals and mockeries were spent, when we left him for dead and simply walked away to resume our lives in the distant lands of our own making—Jesus could have turned away from us or turned the situation around. He could have avoided suffering and death, but instead he chose to endure it all so that we might finally know the depth of God's love. By submitting himself to the cross, Jesus demonstrated just how far God is willing to go to express continued care. When Jesus had experienced the kind of familiar cruelty and indifference to which we often subject one another, he responded in a most unfamiliar way—with forgiveness.

Notice also that this is a forgiveness offered without condition. Jesus did not ask that his persecutors cease. He did not require that they show regret for what they had done. This forgiveness was offered as a free gift; yet, in another way, it was a gift obtained at great cost. It required nothing less than the suffering and death of God's anointed one. In the cross God demonstrated a willingness to pay the high cost of forgiveness on our behalf so that we might receive it as a free gift.

What we have been considering here is known as the "atonement." We commonly use the word to mean "making amends," but the English rendering is revealing: "at-one-ment." We can see this "at-one-ment" in every aspect of Jesus's life, but it is most evident in the cross: in the death of Jesus we are made "at one" with God and drawn into the eternal embrace of forgiveness. What once stood between us is now behind us. The days of separation and estrangement are now over, for now we are "at one" with God. That is the "good" part in Good Friday.

Through the centuries, other explanations have been offered for what God accomplished on the cross. Some use the image of sacrifice. When the New Testament was written, the sacrifice of animals was a familiar part of worship. Animals would be brought to the temple, vested with the sins of the worshiper, and then sacrificed to God as a way to purify the one making the sacrifice. The word "scapegoat" has its origins in this ancient practice. As the image of sacrifice is drawn from the temple, another image derives from the courts. In this explanation of the atonement, God is the judge who demands that we be punished for our misdeeds—that is, until Jesus offers to stand in the dock for us, to take the punishment that is intended for us, even though he is innocent of any misdeed. These images may be helpful if they remind us of our desperate situation and the unreserved love of Jesus for us. It is not the loving God we worship who needs to be changed; it is us. Jesus did not die so that God could forgive us; Jesus died so that we would be able to accept God's forgiveness. Paul's classic affirmation makes this clear: "God was in Christ reconciling the world to himself" (2 Cor. 5:19). It is not God who needs to be reconciled to us; rather, it is we who need to be reconciled to God.

The New Covenant

Jesus's death on the cross not only demonstrated the lengths to which God would go to forgive our old and tired ways; it also established a new way to relate to God. When Jesus gathered with the disciples in the shadow of his imminent death, he took a cup of wine and said, "This is my blood of the new covenant, which is poured out for many for the forgiveness of sins" (Matt. 26:28). It was not a reestablishment of the covenant that Jesus offered, but a new covenant established on a new basis.

The terms of this new covenant were not immediately evident. Again it was Paul, writing several decades after the death of Jesus, who was able to summarize this new way when he declared that the day is over when our relationship with God depends on keeping the Law (Eph. 2:8-10). That day ended with Jesus. No longer are we required to live up to our part in the covenant by fulfilling the Law; no longer are we cut off from God by our persistent inability to do what God asks of us; no longer is our relationship with God dependent on actions that seem simply beyond us. Now our relationship with God is based on faith. In this context, "faith" should not be understood as synonymous with belief. We sometimes use the word "belief" in a limited sense: a form of intellectual assent. Paul uses "faith" in its fuller sense: of living trust. In this new covenant, we are asked to entrust ourselves to Jesus. That is how we are drawn into a living and life-giving relationship with God. We can demonstrate that faithful trust by simply receiving the gift of love and forgiveness that is freely offered through Jesus. Now that this new covenant is not based on fulfillment of the Law, it is no longer limited to the Jews. It is offered to any who have faith in Jesus.

Having made that point, Paul immediately goes on to make a second radical assertion: our faith is not another kind of human achievement. We do not have faith because of our efforts; sometimes we receive it in spite of those efforts. It is a gift. By definition, a gift is something we are powerless to give ourselves: it must be given freely by someone else.

That notion is as difficult as it is important for us to grasp. We cannot hold such an idea in our hearts and minds for very long before we slip back into thinking that a living relationship with God is up to us to achieve. We speak of developing a relationship with God as if we might speak of developing biceps, as though it were something that could be done by establishing a regimen of spiritual exercise and sticking to it. Contrary to this understanding, Paul declares that faith is not an achievement, but a gift. All of our efforts to earn faith are in vain. The great accomplishment of the sheep is not finding the shepherd, but simply getting found.

Ironically, we may be best able to grasp the notion that faith is a gift at those times when faith seems most elusive. When God seems most distant or when we are most aware of God's absence, we know from painful experience that we are simply powerless to give ourselves faith. At such times, we can no more will ourselves into a living, trusting relationship with God than we can will our brown eyes to be blue or make someone fall in love with us through our own effort. Try as we might, it is not possible: blue eyes are not a gift we can give ourselves, nor is the love of another person. Faith is a gift that we can only receive from God in trust and gratitude.

The nature of this new covenant is difficult to comprehend. We have a hard time accepting the implications. Our relationship with God does not depend on anything we do or can do. We cannot earn God's love by doing what God expects. And when we fail to do what God expects, we cannot win God's forgiveness by being good or being remorseful. Even when we respond to God with faith, we do not get any credit for that, because faith itself is a gift from God. It can be difficult to know how to respond to such a gift because our relationships with one another, based as they are on give and take and doing our part, give us no practice for responding to the unconditional love of another.

In fact, we are so unaccustomed to such a relationship that we might draw some mistaken conclusions. When we hear the declaration that in Jesus we are freed from the terms of the old covenant, we might then conclude that we are free to do whatever we please. If God forgives us no matter what we do, why not do whatever we feel like doing? This attitude was captured by the poet W. H. Auden:

"I like committing crimes. God likes forgiving them. Really, the world is admirably arranged."

If we are to avoid such mistaken conclusions, we must recall that the gift of forgiveness may be free, but it is not cheap. After all, it was shared with us in the most costly manner, through the willingness of Jesus to die on the cross. We cannot receive so precious a gift with such calloused hands. Here it is important to recall something we considered with respect to the old covenant: unconditional love does not mean the absence of expectations. Expectations may still flow from unconditional love. In a similar dynamic, forgiveness may not be genuine or complete until it includes expectations, as William Muehl, a professor of homiletics, illustrates:

> When a husband who has strayed from the path of marital fidelity is reunited with his offended wife, he knows very well that he has not really been forgiven merely because the appropriate words of mercy have been spoken. Nor is he likely to be persuaded when his spouse sends him off to the office every morning with protestations of pardon and peace and receives him each evening with reminders that he has been forgiven, has his pipe and slippers and the newspaper neatly folded to the sports section by his favorite chair. Such "reassurances" are as damning as anything hurled at sinful Israel by Jeremiah. Our erring husband knows that he has been forgiven the day his wife tells him to get off his behind and dry the dishes.[1]

The forgiveness offered on the cross is unconditional. It is not dependent on our response. Even if we turn from the promise of forgiveness, the promise remains. Nevertheless, we are invited to receive the gift with gratitude, which is expressed in love and obedience. We are forgiven people, and God asks that we act that way. It is then that we can live out the fullest dimensions of the living relationship that God invites us into.

Imagining the Unimaginable

Let us imagine a wealthy baroness who owns a magnificent estate that includes a stately mansion, as one might expect, but also fertile fields with abundant crops, lush grazing lands for all kinds of livestock, and sparkling streams filled with leaping trout. This estate, in short, has everything that anyone could want or need. The owner of this estate is no ordinary baroness. Instead of running the estate herself, she decides to give it to some of the local peasants to use and enjoy without charge. She instructs the peasants how to make the best use of what she is giving them, and then she departs.

After a time, however, she hears that not all is going well at the estate. The tenants have let the fields go to seed. The mansion is in a state of disrepair. Worst of all, the tenants are continually fighting like children in the back seat of a car, defending their space and threatening one another. Naturally, this causes the baroness great concern, so she sends one of her servants to the estate to see what is going on and to offer a few stern words. When the servant returns, he tells the baroness that the recalcitrant tenants have not only failed to heed anything he has said, but they beat him up and kicked him off the property as well. The baroness then sends another servant on the same mission. He returns in the same condition and with the same story. As we might expect, the baroness has by this time become extremely agitated, and she announces that she will reclaim her estate and throw the rascals out. At that, the son of the baroness speaks up: "Before you do that, let me go to the estate myself. Perhaps the tenants simply need someone to stay with them and show them how to care for this gift and show them how to treat each other. I will live with them as a fellow tenant and show them a better way."

So the son goes to the estate with the blessing of the baroness. But when he arrives, the tenants do not receive him or listen to him. Instead, they take him behind the barn and strip him of his clothing; they jeer at him and beat him. And when they have had their sport, they kill him.

Now, let us imagine how we would expect the baroness to respond to such news. Would she ever forgive those cruel and ungrateful tenants? And let us further imagine that, after this horrible episode, the son somehow could be brought back to life and returned to his mother. Would she ever let him go near the estate again? And if she allowed her son to return, would it be to offer forgiveness for all they had done to him? That is simply beyond the reach of our imaginations. Nevertheless, when we proclaim the resurrection of Jesus, we are saying something just as unimaginable. After we mistreated God's creation, disobeyed God's commands, and rejected God's son and killed him, the son returns, not to condemn, but to forgive. God's forgiveness may have been manifest on the cross, but that was a reality that was hidden in the shadows of that dark day. Good Friday only appears good in the light of Easter. It takes the light of Easter to reveal that what seemed like defeat only three days before actually was victory in disguise.

God Gets the Last Word

When Jesus was crucified, the disciples were a completely dispirited group. They were not eagerly awaiting a time when Jesus would return. They were not looking for Jesus to appear in the shadows, as a frightened child might talk himself into seeing a reassuring presence in his darkened bedroom. No, before his arrest and crucifixion they had anticipated that Jesus would lead them in a glory parade. But when Jesus was captured and killed like any common criminal, they fled. They knew that the people who had killed Jesus would surely kill them, too, if given half a chance. So they wanted to get away—away from the others who would condemn them for their association with Jesus, away from the emptiness that was the only reminder of where faith once had been, away to begin picking up the shattered pieces of their lives, one small fragment at a time.

They hid—out of fear and shame and sorrow—and were huddled in what they hoped would be forgotten rooms, unable to let the world in, for that would be to let in more than they could handle. But we cannot assume that, if given a choice, they would even have wanted to see Jesus again. They could not anticipate that seeing Jesus again could be anything but bad news. Seeing Jesus again would be too frightening, the claim on them too great. So, even when the disciples heard rumors that Jesus was alive again, they hid. They wanted to be left alone for a while, to be left alone by life, and probably to be left alone, most of all, by Jesus.

But then something happened. We know something happened because something unexpected and powerful turned this huddle of dispirited and frightened people into a valiant band ready to dare anything and do anything. Suddenly, unexpectedly, something brought into motion the mighty force that would come to be told in every tongue throughout the world. Something made the disciples leave the dark comfort of that room to proclaim in the light of day: "He lives!" Something they could only describe as Jesus happened to them, and they could no more hold it in than a new mother could hold in the news of the birth of her child, no more than a blind man could ignore the restoration of his sight.

The accounts in the Gospels differ on the particulars. In some accounts, Jesus appeared and then disappeared as quickly as a thought, staying only long enough to impress their souls for all time. Jesus spoke to some; to others he appeared without speaking. For some Jesus could only be described as a spiritual presence, while for others his presence was so real that they could say only that he appeared in bodily form, which can be understood as another way of presenting the striking truth to us who were not there to be struck by the experience, the experience of knowing with wonder and awe that "He lives!" He lives as surely as you or I live, yet in a different way. It was not simply the power of his memory overcoming them, not some generalized sense of the presence of God. It was Jesus, in the midst of them again in a way that was previously as unknown and as unimaginable to them as it is to us.

The Gospel accounts are trying to describe something that is finally indescribable, almost like trying to describe spring to those who have only known winter, or life itself to those who have never lived. The language is evocative, chosen to evoke in us the same reaction they had. It is as if the disciples and Gospel writers were trying to describe music to deaf people, as if they were dancing in the hope that we might catch a small sense of what music is about, for a small sense is still enough. It is as if they were trying to describe a sunset to blind people, so they describe it like a trumpet fanfare and hope we catch a glimmer of the majesty and power of it, for a glimmer is still enough. The Gospel narratives differ in the details, but to the central truth and experience they speak as with one voice: It is Jesus! He lives!

As the followers of Jesus told the story of what had happened to their master, it became clear that this was not a once-upon-a-time story. Rather, they recognized that this was a once-and-for-all reality with implications that stretch farther than the eye could see and are larger than the mind could grasp. Whatever else the disciples would come to understand about what had happened, they knew from the start that the resurrection is not simply about what happened to Jesus; it is about what happens to all who trust in Jesus, and about what can happen to all who claim this story as their own. The resurrection is not simply the assurance that Jesus was victorious over death; it is also a promise that we can share in that victory with him. The resurrection does not mean only that Jesus was triumphant over evil; it also assures us that evil will not be ultimately triumphant in our own lives. The resurrection is a promise offered to all. Saint Jean Vianney said of Easter: "Today one grave is open, and from it has risen a sun which will never be obscured, which will never set, a sun which bestows new life."

In the resurrection it became clear to the followers of Jesus that our God is the kind of God who insists on having the last word. The second-to-last word can certainly be very powerful in its message of despair, estrangement, evil, even death. But our God is the kind of God who insists on having the very last word, and that is always a word of hope, of reconciliation, of healing, and of life. When we await God's last word with confidence, the second-to-last word loses its death-grip on us. Paul declared: "Death has been swallowed up in victory. Where, O death, is your victory? Where, O death, is your sting? ... Thanks be to God who gives us the victory through our Lord Jesus Christ" (1 Cor. 15:54–55, 57).

Jesus as Teacher

Some readers of this chapter and the preceding chapter will find it odd that up until now, so late in the game, we haven't considered the teachings of Jesus. To some, Jesus's teachings seem like the crux of the matter. But in this book Jesus's teaching role seems to be relegated to a rather modest postscript.

In another way, however, it is fitting that we do not begin with the teachings of Jesus or make them central to our considerations. The teachings of Jesus, in fact, are secondary. Those who first committed themselves to the Christian faith did so not because of what Jesus taught, but because of who he was. For instance, it is important and a little surprising to note that Paul, writing in the generation after Jesus, makes only passing reference to the teachings of Jesus. In fact, Paul probably knew less about those teachings than we do. Instead, Paul proclaimed that God fulfilled ancient promises by sending Jesus, God incarnate, that this Jesus was willing to suffer and die on our behalf so that we might be reconciled to God, and that God's gifts of everlasting love and eternal life were ultimately triumphant in the resurrection. That was enough for Paul to know. It is enough for us as well. The crux of the matter must forever be the cross (*crux* means "cross") and what lies beyond in the promise of Easter.

The story of Jesus recorded in the Gospels is properly read backwards. We begin with the resurrection, and then view everything else about Jesus's life and teachings in its light. That's why the Gospels have been called Easter accounts with extended prologues. In some respects, however, Easter seems the least likely place to begin any quest for Christian faith. The faith claims made at Easter are perhaps the most difficult of all to accept. It can seem as if Easter is the advanced course for Christians, to be approached only after completing the introductory courses that deal with Jesus's life and teachings. Begin with the Sermon on the Mount; marvel at Jesus's wisdom; learn from him and become fascinated by his life. If one begins there, perhaps then one will be better prepared to hear this mysterious tale about Jesus coming back from death.

It's interesting to note, however, that the disciples in the early church customarily started their sermons with proclamations about Easter, as if it were the only place to begin. The idea that God could raise someone from the dead would be as difficult for them to believe as it is for us. These ancient people were not gullible or stupid: they had seen many people die, but never once had they seen anyone come to life again. To be sure, there was something in the story to doubt. But there is another way to put it: there was something in the story that reached the deepest regions of their hearts and minds, where both doubt and faith are found.

The place to begin in the life of faith is not necessarily with those things that are beyond the reach of doubt. Realities about which we hold no doubt may not be large enough to reveal God to us. Instead, we begin with the larger realities and deeper mysteries that are open to doubt because they are also large enough and deep enough to reveal something of God to us. In fact, the very doubts we may hold attest to the scale and power of what we proclaim. That is, Easter may be just the place for beginners after all. Perhaps the early church was right to begin precisely here, where the stakes are highest, risking great doubt in order to claim a larger faith.

Without the resurrection, the teachings of Jesus would have become interesting artifacts, even if they had been preserved by previous generations, which is doubtful. There is little in the teachings of Jesus that is radically new. Much of Jesus's teachings have precedents in Hebrew Scripture and can be found in some form or another in other world religions. However, from the vantage point of Easter, the teachings of Jesus do become important, not so much because of what is said but because of who says it. If something is said by an obscure Jewish teacher who lived two thousand years ago, we will hear it one way. If the same thing is said by the resurrected Christ, we will hear it in another way entirely. When a theological student says, "There is eternal life," and Jesus says, "There is eternal life," the statements may be equally true, but we will receive them in very different ways. The former may be an interesting hypothesis, but we receive the latter as an authoritative word.

The stories Jesus tells are gathered up and find their meaning in the larger story of Jesus himself. The teachings of Jesus are important because they help his followers understand how they are to live in the light of his death and resurrection. The teachings spell out the implications of what it means to live on the far side of Easter, where God's loving, life-giving ways triumph. Here, as elsewhere in the Christian life, words and actions reinforce each other in helpful ways. Jesus tells his followers that if someone strikes them on the right cheek, they should turn the left cheek to that person, something that is remembered, and perhaps finally understood in all of its implications, only when Jesus is willing to die on the cross. Jesus teaches that God seeks out those who are lost, then demonstrates just how far such love will range when the risen Jesus finds the very ones who betrayed him to demonstrate the searching love of God. When Jesus anticipates his own death, he declares that he is going to prepare a place for those who follow and will come again to be with them, something that is recalled when Jesus returns, just as he promised.

Jesus is a marvelous teacher, and he is a teacher like no other. Most teachers strive for the day when they will no longer be needed. When first we began learning how to add, we needed our teacher every step of the way. As our skills developed, we relied on the teacher less and less. Eventually, the person of the teacher receded to the extent that we may now have difficulty recalling the name of the one who taught us to add. This is the way with most teachers: they are always trying to work themselves out of a job, striving for the day when they no longer will be necessary, a day when *they* step aside but their teachings remain. In this, the teacher Jesus is different. Those who follow him find that, as they learn from him, they rely on him not less and less, but more and more. Jesus is one teacher who does not diminish in importance as we gain in competence. The more we learn Jesus's teachings, the more we rely on the teacher. We seek to know most teachers so that we might learn their teachings. With Jesus, the opposite is the case: we learn the teachings so that we might come to know the teacher.

Already but Not Yet

Thus far we have considered what God accomplished through the life, death, and resurrection of Jesus: the victory of forgiveness over sin, love over hate, life over death. Through Jesus the world is now a different place; something fundamental has changed. In response, we are invited to live in this different world as changed people. Through Jesus we are invited to live as loyal subjects in nothing less than the realm of God. Nevertheless, even a glance at the human scene or the most cursory survey of our own hearts reveals that something remains undone. In many ways, the world seems to be stuck in the same tired and sorry ways it always has been, and when we are honest, we can see some of those same ways embedded in our own hearts.

There is an "already/not yet" quality to the portion of the divine drama in which we live. *Already* Jesus has established the means through which we are drawn into relationship with God, but *not yet* do we live in complete communion with God. *Already* God has signaled victory over death in the resurrection, but *not yet* have we entered the time when God will wipe away every tear from our eyes, and "death will be no more" (Rev. 21:4). *Already* the realm of God is evident, but *not yet* is that realm fully established.

During his lifetime, Jesus addressed those who have to live in the meantime, the challenging meantime between the "already" and the "not yet." He promised that he would return to complete the job he started. He warned his followers against trying to predict just when he would return, because the exact time of his return is beyond human speculation. Instead, he invited his followers to anticipate that he might return at any time and to live accordingly. By following the example and teachings of Jesus, by redefining our lives in light of the resurrection, not only will we be prepared to live in the promised realm of God when it comes, but we can experience even now some of what life in that realm will be like.

CHAPTER 4

The Continuing Presence of the Holy Spirit

The Holy Spirit is active from the beginning to the end of the biblical drama—at work in the first chapter of Genesis, appearing again in the last chapter of Revelation, and evident often in between. In the biblical story the Holy Spirit always seems to be where the action is and in a very real sense it is the Spirit that is doing the acting: stirring things up, always creating, empowering, and sustaining. Yet, even though the Holy Spirit is one of the main characters in the biblical drama, this same Spirit is often treated like an actress who plays a bit part. For many Christians, this central character can drift into obscurity and sometimes be forgotten almost entirely. If our liturgies reflected our understanding, we might as well be baptized in the name of "The Father, the Son, and Someone Else" or "The Creator, the Redeemer, and the Other One."

The Bible certainly introduces us to the Spirit early and often, but that may be part of the problem: each time the Spirit appears, it can be in such new and startling ways that we may be tempted to ask, "Excuse me, but have we met before?" As the biblical story unfolds, the Holy Spirit's character seems to develop. Or perhaps it would be more accurate to say that our understanding of the Spirit's character develops to the extent that we must add new understandings to the old if we are to get an accurate picture.

At Work from Before the Beginning

We are first introduced to God's spirit with the very first words in Genesis: "In the beginning when God began to create the heavens and the earth, the earth was a formless void and darkness covered the face of the deep, while the spirit of God [or 'wind from God'] swept over the face of the waters" (Gen. 1:1-2). The second creation story relates that "the Lord God formed man from the dust of the ground, and breathed into his nostrils the breath [or spirit] of life; and the man became a living being" (Gen. 2:7).

Christians who read these two passages recognize in them the one they would learn to call "the Holy Spirit." It's true that here, as elsewhere in Hebrew Scripture, the spirit is not yet understood as being vested with personhood. That spirit is not seen as one with, yet distinct from, other manifestations of God, as would become true in later Christian understandings of the Holy Spirit. Instead, this spirit is viewed as an expression of the power of God, the mode of God's creative activity. It is through this spirit that God confers life, establishes order out of chaos, and is able to turn a mud sculpture into a living creature.

In these and other passages, the English words "breath," "wind," and "spirit" are all translations of the Hebrew word *ruach*. The same constellation of meanings is found in Greek, the original language of the New Testament, and in Latin: the Greek word *pneuma* and the Latin word *spiritus* can also be variously translated as "breath," "wind," and "spirit." The challenge of choosing which English word to use in a particular instance is the sort of thing that might make a translator want to take up sausage-making instead.

Translators of the Bible must choose one English word or another to stand in for *ruach* or *pneuma*, but the richness of the biblical understanding of God's Spirit that is found in many passages can be retained only when the single English word that is chosen is read to include the other meanings as well. There are important benefits to understanding the various, sometimes interchangeable, uses of the words *ruach* and *pneuma*. For instance, it helps us to be reminded that the continuing presence of the Spirit is necessary for life to be sustained. If the Spirit were removed, the creature would die as surely as if breath were removed. The psalmist makes this clear when he says to God: "When you take away their breath [or 'spirit'] they die and return to their dust. When you send forth your spirit [or 'breath'] they are created" (Ps. 104:29-30). Examining the relationships between "breath," "wind," and "spirit" reminds us that the spirit can be as gentle as the breath on a mirror or as awesome as a hurricane that lifts a house from its foundations. The Spirit can disperse dandelion seeds, like tiny paratroopers, across a field, or it can cause us to hold onto the deck of a ship for dear life. We do not see the wind at work, but we know it is there because we can see what it does.

Other portions of Hebrew Scripture give additional dimensions to our understanding of the Holy Spirit. It is the Spirit of God that empowers the rulers of Israel. The Spirit was seen at work through specially favored individuals, heightening their natural powers with extraordinary gifts, bestowing them with the energy and ability to do whatever God required of them. Through the power of the Spirit, certain individuals were emboldened in battle (Judg. 3:10; 6:34; 11:29); kings were empowered to lead (1 Sam. 11:6; 16:13); others were inspired to prophesy. The Spirit gave prophets the ability to see the human scene with divine eyes. Ezekiel says: "The Spirit lifted me up between earth and heaven, and brought me in visions of God to Jerusalem" (Ezek. 8:3). Not only did the Spirit enable the prophets to see more clearly than others what was going on; it also empowered them to speak the truth about what they saw, to pronounce God's judgment on the people (Isa. 48:16; Mic. 3:8).

The people of Israel anticipated that this same Spirit would be at work preeminently in the coming Messiah, endowing him with special qualities of wisdom, power, and justice (Isa. 11:1-3; 42:1). But more, they expected that, when the Messiah arrived, the manifestation of the Spirit would no longer be limited to certain individuals. Rather, at such a time the same Spirit that empowered their leaders and inspired their prophets would also become available to the people through God's anointed one. This would be a leader and prophet who would not only manifest the Spirit, but also share it with them.

The Gospel writers saw John the Baptist as a prophet who, like other prophets before him, was inspired by the Spirit. John declared that the ancient hope of a general outpouring of the Spirit was about to be fulfilled. This hope still lay in the future, but John himself believed it to be imminent. John made it clear that he was not the one to bring this all about. As John saw it, his job was to prepare the people by declaring the promise again, then stepping aside when the one who could fulfill the promise arrived. He told the people: "I baptize you with water for repentance, but one who is more powerful than I is coming after me; I am not worthy to carry his sandals. He will baptize you with the Holy Spirit and fire" (Matt. 3:11). In Matthew's account, Jesus appears immediately after John speaks, which is, of course, no mere coincidence.

In a rare display of unanimity, all four Gospels declare that, when John baptized Jesus, the Holy Spirit perched on Jesus in the form of a dove, anointing him as the messianic Son of God, a symbol that may have reminded the people of the dove that came back to Noah near the end of the flood. And just as that dove was the harbinger of the first covenant between God and Israel, so this dove gave a sign of the new covenant that would be established through Jesus. As the Gospel writers go on to recount the story of Jesus's life, it becomes clear that the Holy Spirit was evident in him in new ways. The Spirit did not merely alight on Jesus and then later take wing; rather, the Spirit rested on Jesus with the fullest endowment of divine power. In Jesus, the Spirit was not an impersonal force; rather, it was a manifestation of the personal union Jesus had with God. Yet, even then the promised general outpouring of the Holy Spirit on the people was still in the future. But from the moment the Spirit perched on Jesus, the age of hope had already begun to make room for the age of fulfillment. Already the past was stepping aside so that the promised future could be ushered in.

The Promise Fulfilled

According to John's Gospel, after Jesus concluded his public ministry he spent a considerable amount of time with his disciples preparing them for what lay ahead. What a multifaceted and shifting reality these disciples were asked to comprehend. Jesus first told them that he would be killed, and the disciples knew that this meant that their lives too would be shattered like glass. But then Jesus spoke of his resurrection, and the disciples felt a surge of hopefulness that after separation there would be reunion, and after defeat victory. As if those realities were not enough to comprehend, Jesus went on to say that, after his resurrection, he would leave yet again. This, of course, prompted many questions. What were his disciples supposed to do then? Would it all be over? Were they to return to their fishing boats? If not, where were they supposed to go? And who was in charge now? Were they to survive on memories alone?

As the disciples heard Jesus tell them about all that was to happen, their imaginations raced to keep up with what he was saying. But they couldn't keep up. A multitude of questions stopped them. To listen to the disciples' questions as recorded in John (chaps. 13–16) is to hear familiar questions, the questions of children just before their parents go out the door: Where are you going? Do you have to go? Can't we go with you? When will you be back? Who will stay with us while you're away?

These are plaintive questions, pressing and immediate. Jesus responds that God "will give you another Advocate, to be with you forever. . . . I will not leave you orphaned" (John 14:16, 18). Here John uses a new word to refer to the Holy Spirit: *parakletos* (rendered "paraclete" in English and variously translated as "advocate," "counselor," or "comforter"). A literal translation of the Greek is "someone who is called to one's side." The Holy Spirit, then, is the one who stands by the disciples even after Jesus departs. And the Spirit is a constant and comforting presence for those who follow, an advocate in times of trial, a counselor in perplexity. The presence of the Spirit, so wonderfully manifest in Jesus, would stand by and work through those who continued to follow him after his death and resurrection. As the evangelist John tells it, when Jesus appeared to the disciples after his death, he breathed on them (here again, giving both "breath" and "spirit") and said, "Receive the Holy Spirit" (John 20:22). It was the long-awaited outpouring of the Spirit, once only a fervent hope and now a powerful reality.

Luke tells a different story about how the disciples received the Holy Spirit. According to his account, when the risen Jesus appeared to the disciples, his parting words were: "And see, I am sending upon you what my Father promised; so stay here in [in Jerusalem] until you have been clothed with power from on high" (Luke 24:49). So the disciples waited for what must have seemed an eternity. And that is just what they were doing, of course—waiting for the eternal Spirit to enter their lives, waiting for eternity to break into one of their days, any day now. Then, fifty days after the resurrection, on the Hebrew festival known as Pentecost, when the disciples were all gathered in one place, a mighty wind (or spirit—by now you get the idea) filled the entire house where they were sitting. Something that could only be described as tongues, as though they were flames of fire, rested on the disciples just as the dove had rested on Jesus, and the disciples began to whoop it up. They began talking all at once in different languages. In fact, they were so rowdy, so obviously brimful of *something*, that passersby concluded not only that they had been boozing it up a bit, but that they had been drinking new wine, the stuff that really packs a wallop. The disciples were not drunk, of course. They were not filled with spirits, but with *the* Spirit, the Holy Spirit. But in many ways the gathering did resemble a great raucous party, and the Holy Spirit was the life of the party. It was an unparalleled display of enthusiasm (a word that literally means "having the Spirit of God in you").

In many ways, the book of Acts can be read as an unfolding of the implications of what happened on the day the disciples received the Holy Spirit. It records what the followers of Jesus were able to do through the power of the Spirit. They were joined together in community (which is why Pentecost often is called the "birthday of the church"). They shared all things in common, extending help to anyone who was in need. They boldly declared to those who would listen (and even to those who would not) all that Jesus had said and done. They healed the sick, as they had seen Jesus do and as they had tried (unsuccessfully) to do themselves when Jesus was alive. They received new members into their fellowship through baptism, sometimes thousands in a single day. They were able to abandon ethnic divisions that had been assiduously cultivated over centuries, letting them simply fall away. They traveled to the edges of the known world to share the love of God that had been shared with them.

When Jesus was alive, he told his disciples all that he expected them to be and to do, and there must have been times when the disciples wondered if it were all just a cruel joke. Clearly this motley assemblage was not up to the challenge. Even after all the times they had heard Jesus teach and been exposed to his example, and even given all their best intentions to follow, the disciples were still a huddled and tiny gathering of untutored peasants, fickle in allegiance and timid in spirit. But when they received the Holy Spirit, all of that changed. They became known by the marks of their teacher: boldness, power, wisdom, authority, and love. Although they had once seemed so ill-equipped to carry on the ministry of Jesus, the Holy Spirit now gave them the power to do just that. The followers of Jesus received the Holy Spirit the way a sail catches the wind. It sent them into the world to do what they had been commissioned to do and now were empowered to do.

The disciples came to see such an intimate connection between the risen Jesus and the Holy Spirit he shared with them that they came to call that Spirit "the Spirit of Jesus." Through the Spirit, Jesus himself was with them to the close of the age. Jesus had enjoined his followers to be his heart and hands in the world, and now they were given his Spirit to take up this awesome task.

Luke's two books were later entitled The Gospel according to Luke and The Acts of the Apostles. They are actually companion volumes of a two-volume work: only when they are read together do they give a full account of what Jesus accomplished. Luke declares that, even when Jesus departs, it is still Jesus who is at work in and through the early church in the person of the Holy Spirit, the same Spirit who was at work from before the beginning, but who now can only be understood fully if also recognized as *his* Spirit. If we keep this in mind, we may conclude that Luke's second volume is misnamed. The acts of the apostles, by themselves, don't matter; the apostles alone can do nothing extraordinary. Rather, what is extraordinary is the way the Holy Spirit (a.k.a., the Spirit of Jesus) can be at work through such people. It would be more accurate, then, if Luke's two books were named The Acts of Jesus throughout His Life and The Continuing Acts of Jesus through the Church.

Gifts of the Spirit

Although the followers of Jesus are invited to receive the general outpouring of the Holy Spirit, the Spirit is manifest in specific ways that differ with each individual. "Now there are varieties of gifts, but the same Spirit," is the way Paul put it (1 Cor. 12:4). To some, the Spirit gives wisdom, to others knowledge, to others gifts of healing, to others faith. But "all these are activated by one and the same Spirit, who allots to each one individually just as the Spirit chooses" (1 Cor. 12:11). It is through the Holy Spirit that the power and love of God can be at work through people like us. All of us have experienced times when we were able to persevere through circumstances that by all accounts should have destroyed us. And at other times our stumbling attempts to speak the truth somehow revealed glimmers of a wisdom deeper than we thought ourselves capable of. We are at a loss to explain why. We might speak of these things as a mystery; indeed, they are a mystery, and it has a name: the Holy Spirit.

Creative people often stand in wonder before this mystery, even when it remains nameless. Robert Louis Stevenson commented on his own writing by saying: "The real work is done by some unseen collaborator." Friedrich Nietzsche, the famously vociferous atheist, was forced to admit: "One can hardly reject completely the idea that one is the mere incarnation, or mouthpiece, or medium of some almighty power." The great operatic tenor Luciano Pavarotti attested to this same mystery when he referred to his own voice in the third person.

This mystery may be particularly evident in creative people, but it is manifest in all of us. The Holy Spirit is at work whenever we are able to live beyond our human potential. It is at such moments, when we look at our own actions with a certain incredulous shake of the head, that we are invited to affirm with Paul, it was "I . . . though not I, but the grace of God that is with me" (1 Cor. 15:10). A wick cannot take credit for the flame any more than a cello can accept praise for a sonata. Something else is at work—something beyond the mere instrument that is used. There is something in a word that can dispense a comfort beyond words, something in a simple act of mercy that can make us feel surrounded by love. And that something is the Holy Spirit.

It is through the Spirit that God invites and equips us to be instruments of God's power and love. So Jesus was not merely making a virtue of necessity when he told his disciples, "It is to your advantage that I go away, for if I do not go away, the Advocate will not come to you" (John 16:7). As long as the disciples had a wonder-worker at their side, they did not have to perform any wonders. As long as they were in the presence of the master teacher, they were not equipped to teach. As long as they had the healer with them, they could not assume the role of healers. The disciples could see the power of God that was manifest in Jesus, but for that power to be at work through them, something else was required. Jesus had to leave so that the Spirit could come to the disciples in new ways.

It is through the Holy Spirit that God created the heavens and the earth, and it is through this same spirit that God invites us to share in the joy of creation as well. God not only ministers to a world in need of teaching, healing, and comfort; through the Holy Spirit, God gives us a chance to be teachers, healers, and comforters. We who witness the power of God with amazement and wonder can be all the more amazed and wonderstruck that, through the generosity of the Holy Spirit, that same power can be at work in us—of all people. Imagine! We get to do it now.

The Holy Spirit in Community

The Holy Spirit is not only God within us, but also God between us. The Spirit's true home is community. Also, it is the Spirit who creates community out of mere proximity: that is, the Holy Spirit makes community both necessary and possible: *necessary* because it is only as individuals come together in community that they become a vessel that is fully capable of catching the Spirit, and *possible* because only such a one can bind us together in the strong and tender ways that are beyond our doing. Though the Spirit may be at work in various communities, the church is the community in which the Holy Spirit is called by name, sought in unique ways, and called upon as the source of the community's life.

It is because the Holy Spirit is known in different ways in each life that we must gather in community. To benefit from the variety of gifts that the Spirit confers, we must be in community with others. We have each other because we cannot be all things ourselves. If, for example, a church included only those who had the gift of creative envisioning, there would be no one to take minutes at their meetings. If everyone had the gift of inspired prayer, there would be manifold blessings but nothing to eat at the church potluck supper. If everyone had the gift of song, there would be a large choir but no one to greet worshipers at the door. Spinning out the implications of his image of the church as the body of Christ, Paul puts it this way: "If the whole body were an eye, where would the hearing be? If the whole body were hearing, where would the sense of smell be?" (1 Cor. 12:17). Because no one individual can have all the spiritual gifts, the gifts of others can be gifts to us, but (obviously) only if we are together in community. The various spiritual gifts are given to individuals not merely to benefit other individuals in that community. The gifts are given to individuals for the sake of the community, so that the community itself might be built up.

If the Holy Spirit requires community to be fully manifest, the same Spirit offers what the community requires. It is only through the Spirit that our diversity in background, race, age, taste, and preference can give way to a larger unity. It is only through the Spirit that we can gather with people we did not choose to be with (and under other circumstances might prefer to have nothing to do with) and be bound to them in ways that are as firm as they are mysterious. Of course, it's not always easy to live in community. That's why we need help, the kind of help that only the Spirit can provide. Another way to put it is this: it takes a lot of love, which Paul names in his familiar hymn to love as the greatest of all the gifts of the Spirit (1 Cor. 13). Although this chapter is often quoted in other contexts, such as weddings, it is important to note that it is part of Paul's discussion of spiritual gifts. Paul cites love as the spiritual gift that is given to the gathered community, the church. It is the greatest gift because it makes that community possible.

The Trinity

When I was a freshman in college, I took an introductory course in the history of Christian doctrine, and at the end of term one of the exam questions was this: "According to classic Christian doctrine, which is the correct summary of the Trinity: 'God is one in three' or 'God is three in one'? Explain your choice." I remember approaching that question with unusual trepidation: any misstep might not only be enough to give me a failing grade on the exam, but, as I reflected on my exposure to church history, it might be the kind of response that in earlier centuries could have gotten me burned at the stake. The perils of taking up the doctrine of the Trinity are legendary. In Helen Waddel's novel *Peter Abelard*, the canon of Notre Dame attempts to find damning evidence against Abelard by asking one of Abelard's pupils if he thought that his teacher's latest treatise on the Trinity was heretical. The pupil's response: "Of course it is heretical. Every book that ever was written about the Trinity is heretical, barring the Athanasian Creed. And even that one saves itself by contradicting everything it says as fast as it says it."[1]

As a college student, not having mastered the art of self-contradiction, I chose one of the options provided; it turns out, the correct answer was "both." If the unity of Father, Son, and Holy Spirit is to be maintained, we must affirm that God is "one in three"; but if the integrity of the persons of the Trinity is to be maintained, we must affirm that God is "three in one." Those who are not interested in slicing theological distinctions this thinly can quickly become exasperated by discussions of the Trinity. But the doctrine of the Trinity does have some important things to teach us. One of the reasons that the way people understand the Trinity has been so hotly contested is that the stakes are very high.

One other reason that the doctrine of the Trinity has been subject to such long and lively debate is that the Bible, often called on to referee such disputes, takes up the matter only implicitly. The word "Trinity" is nowhere to be found in the Bible. The standard Trinitarian formula is found only once in Scripture, when the risen Jesus enjoins his followers to baptize "in the name of the Father and of the Son and of the Holy Spirit" (Matt. 28:19). However, the Bible reflects—and Christian experience confirms—a unique understanding of God. In Scripture we find the affirmation that God was truly present in Christ and remains at work in the continuing presence of the Holy Spirit. But how are those persons of the Trinity related? That's a question that Scripture does not address in any systematic way, a question that the doctrine of the Trinity attempts to answer in phrases such as "one in substance, distinct in three persons."

Some people have tried to clarify the doctrine of the Trinity by offering metaphors. But even the metaphors that are most appealing—and in some ways helpful—are not fully satisfying. For instance, Tertullian, an early Christian theologian, described the Trinity as like sun, ray, and light. Others have offered similar images, such as ice, liquid, and steam. To be sure, such images reflect both unity and integrity, and they have a certain intellectual tidiness that is appealing, but what is lost is any sense of personhood, not only for the Holy Spirit but also for the other members of the Trinity.

My favorite contemporary formulation was offered by David H. C. Read, a Presbyterian minister, who explained the Trinity as "God everywhere and always, God there and then, God here and now."[2] But there are also problems with Read's formulation. He maintains the personhood of God, but here the Trinity, particularly the last two persons, can begin to sound like a tag team in which one wrestler takes over as the other gets out of the ring. The image does not sufficiently reflect the unity of the Trinity, the understanding that where one person is present, so are the others.

It may be that such metaphors are not helpful because the Trinity itself is a metaphor, a figure of speech intended to help us grasp a reality that cannot be fully described through more direct means. This means that using other metaphors to describe the Trinity can be a rather tricky business. Using our own metaphors to describe the

Trinity is to merely layer one metaphor on top of another. But there are ways in which the doctrine of the Trinity reveals, rather than obscures, God. For one thing, the doctrine of the Trinity helps us understand that the God we experience in various ways is the same God. This means that Jesus did not appear at one point in history and then disappear again. As one with God, Jesus was there from before the beginning and in some way resides with us still. Some people even see evidence of this understanding in the accounts of creation when God says, "Let *us* make humankind in *our* own image." But in this context either the first person plural is a "royal we" or it reflects the primitive understanding that God was addressing the heavenly court of celestial beings. Whatever the interpretation of this particular passage, the doctrine of the Trinity helps us understand that Jesus, who appeared at a particular point in history, is still somehow present in every time and beyond time. More to the point in the context of this chapter, the unity of God in the Trinity helps us affirm that the same God who is the creator and ruler of the universe can also take up residence in our feeble hearts in the person of the Holy Spirit, empowering our lives with the same power that keeps planets in their orbits. Through the work of the Holy Spirit, the same God who is beyond reach and beyond our imaginations can be as close as our own breath.

Another important affirmation in the doctrine of the Trinity is the personhood of God. God is not an impersonal force. Rather, God is best described using metaphors of personhood and personal relationships. We cannot speak of God as having love, wisdom, or will without implying something intensely personal. This reminder is most important when we approach the Holy Spirit, the person of the Trinity we most often slip into describing in impersonal terms. The Spirit has the integrity of personhood and even what might be described as a character and a personality. That is why the Holy Spirit is not described as an "it" but as a "you." (One thing that can be said in favor of the term "Holy Ghost" is that it retains the shadow of personhood.)

Exactly which pronoun to use when referring to the Holy Spirit is another subject of debate. A suitable precedent can be found for every preference. The Greek word *parakletos* is masculine, the Greek word *pneuma* is neuter, and the Hebrew word *ruach* is feminine. Although we might prefer to choose the feminine to counterbalance the masculine language that predominates in most biblical references to God, it is probably best to find ways in which to discern and express the presence of the feminine throughout the Trinity. No matter what pronoun we may choose to describe the Holy Spirit in a particular instance, it is the personhood of God that we aim to affirm.

Finally, we find in the doctrine of the Trinity an important reminder that our God is a God of community. Trinitarian affirmations are deeply relational, reminding us that those who intend to worship and serve this God cannot do so alone, but can do so only in community—a community that, at its best, reflects the kind of perfect communion that is found in God. To see how to live out our lives as individuals in community and express the unity that is ours, we can look to our God, who does all of these things to divine perfection. The Methodist scholar Leonard I. Sweet has said: "As the Holy Spirit unites us to one another and to God, enabling the divine family to become our family, we find in the divine life a basis for the Christian life that is rich and deep in reconciliation and self-giving love."[3]

Community is essential to our lives because it is an essential part of God. When God looked at the being God created and said, "It is not good that man should be alone," God knew what God was talking about. God would not want to be alone, either, and in the Trinity, God never has to be.

PART TWO

The Church as the Body of Christ

CHAPTER 5

Life Together as God's People

Imagine a group of people gathered to mourn the loss of someone who has just died. At first they are stunned and tongue-tied. Then slowly, like the melting of spring snow, something happens. The mourners begin to talk to one another. They share recollections about the person who has died—recollections of his quirky habits, his favorite moth-eaten sweater, the things he taught, the last words he spoke, the way they felt around him.

In the midst of this recollection, suddenly, silently, the group of mourners is drawn together. They feel a special kind of bond. Then someone molds this feeling into words: "You know, he was a special person. His actions were remarkable, his words memorable. Just talking about him makes us feel closer, not only to his memory, but to one another. Just telling these stories about him does something. This must not stop. It is too important. We must go on telling these stories. Others need to hear them."

Let us further imagine that the person being mourned was a doctor who for thirty years had treated the people of a small town. He was a source of comfort and healing to all who came to him, regardless of their ability to pay. And though he never made a show of his efforts to help, the entire community was inspired by his example of kindness and self-sacrifice. Now he is gone. No one knows what the town will do without him. Then someone suggests that they build a health clinic in his honor. They will carry out his work in his name.

That way, subsequent generations will not only hear about this remarkable man, but they will also benefit in tangible ways.

Some might say that the church is like that: a group of mourners for Jesus Christ who tell the story of his life and, in some way, attempt to carry on his work. But others affirm that the church is much more than this, that something about this community makes it unique. The church is not a gathering of mourners, because Jesus is still alive in this community. When the church endeavors to carry out Jesus's work, it is the Spirit of Jesus himself who works in and through the church. Phillips Brooks has affirmed that "the ever-living Christ makes the never-dying church." By any measure, it is an astounding claim. And the more one considers the church as we know it, the more astounding it becomes.

A Community of Sinners

Finding fault with the church is easier than finding potholes on the streets of New York. The most vociferous critics may be outside the church, but their complaints are echoed amply by those within. Criticisms of the church are so familiar that all can join in the litany. The church purports to be a source of healing in the world, but it cannot even heal itself of rancor and division. The church is a place where people are told that they are accepted just as they are, but those who come to worship dressed in a way that violates the unwritten dress code can become the subject of gossip. The church is so full of hypocrites that a worshiper may nod with approval at a sermon about the ills of racism during worship and then tell a racist joke before leaving the church parking lot. The church may have been founded as a rescue mission for those who are in distress, but church members often treat it more like a club and spend their energies arguing over how the clubhouse should be redecorated. The church, which presents itself as a community in which people encounter one another at the deepest levels, can be little more than a superficial meeting of masks. The church claims to follow the Prince of Peace, but it has often cheered on nations as they go to war.

We could go on. And these are not modern phenomena. The church has always been a source of exasperation, even—or perhaps especially—for those who are a part of it. A medieval manuscript contains this confession: "The Church is something like Noah's ark. If it weren't for the storm outside, you couldn't stand the smell inside."

How are we to respond? By granting that the criticisms are accurate. That is the place to begin. The church is as flawed as its members; it is as imperfect as any human community. This shouldn't surprise us because the church is, after all, a gathering of sinners. There is nothing unusual about that. What sets the church apart is that it freely acknowledges the power of sin, not only in the world, but in itself and its members. Through its creeds and its book, the church advertises itself as a gathering of sinners. Only sinners need apply. Sin is one of the chief qualifications for membership.

If the sinners who make up the church distinguish themselves from other sinners, it is in this way: they are dissatisfied sinners. Their prayers of confession demonstrate that they are not satisfied with themselves any more than they are satisfied with the world around them. They publicly admit that they need to be forgiven, that they seek to change, and that they need help in doing so. A church member once told me, "My friend said that she stays away from the church because it is filled with hypocrites. I told her that I want to be part of the church because I know I am a hypocrite." If church members have any reason to boast, they can boast only of their need. They are set apart not because of what they have or who they are, but only because of what they seek to receive and to become.

The church is uniquely vulnerable to criticism because of the unparalleled scale and scope of what it is called to become. An organization that is charged with something on a smaller scale (such as filling the potholes in the streets of New York) is not as vulnerable. If the task that defines an organization is limited, criticism will also be limited, both because the chances of failure are fewer and because the consequences of failure are not as great. Increased expectation means increased vulnerability to criticism. So when the same flawed, limited human beings who cannot keep potholes filled declare that, through the church, they endeavor to continue the work of Jesus and share the love of God in a hurting world, they become vulnerable to criticism on a thousand scores. Those who stand for more are knocked down all the more. To see just how vulnerable to criticism the Christian church is, we need only consider the range of what it is called to undertake.

Ministries of the Church

The many-faceted ministry of the church is often defined by using five words that derive from the New Testament. Those five distinguishing characteristics, in English and in Greek (the language of the New Testament) are:

- Proclamation (*kerygma*)
- Worship (*leitourgia*)
- Teaching (*didache*)
- Service (*diakonia*)
- Christian community (*koinonia*)

I will examine some of these, particularly worship and service, at greater length in subsequent chapters; but let's take a quick look at all of them here.

Proclamation (*kerygma*). The church is charged with telling the Christian story, both to those who have never heard it before and to those who need to hear it again. When Paul finished preaching in Antioch, the worshipers who shook his hand at the conclusion of the service said, "Please preach that same sermon again next week." What a startling request! No one has ever said that to me. People are usually drawn to the latest. We read today's newspaper with interest; tomorrow that same paper will seem good for nothing but starting a fire in the fireplace. The people of Paul's day were no different: it was a new day and they would ordinarily want to hear a new message. So, what could Paul have said in that sermon in Antioch to elicit such an unlikely response?

Quite simply, he told the story of God's interaction with the world, first through the people of Israel and then through Jesus of Nazareth. Paul spoke of God's faithfulness throughout history, about the covenant God established with Israel, and about how God rescued the people from slavery in Egypt and led them into the Promised Land. He told them that all of history had been a preparation for Jesus's birth and that, when the right time came, God sent Jesus into the world out of God's own being. Paul told the people that, though Jesus was blameless, he was crucified, but the promise of his coming was fulfilled when he was raised from the dead. And in this life is the source and meaning of our own lives. That is the message the people wanted to hear "again next week."

In some form or another, that is the story the church has told ever since. That is the story we have the responsibility to share with those for whom it is as new as today's headlines. And that is the story we gather to hear again ourselves, even though we may have heard it countless times already, so that we can be formed by it. Although the story is not new, it renews us. And we do not tire of it any more than we tire of bread or sunlight, and we need it just as much. We can no more tire of this story than we can tire of the words "I love you," which is the message this story brings: God's love made known to us.

Worship (*leitourgia*). Worship is the central activity of the church. Other ministries of the church flow from worship because in worship we seek and celebrate the presence of God in our midst, a presence that makes all of our ministries possible. In worship the church not only proclaims but also enacts—through song and sacrament, prayer and praise—the story of our faith. The worshiping church engages in an activity that seems odd indeed when judged by the standards of a culture that prizes self-sufficiency. We gather to worship the Creator because we recognize that we are but creatures. We praise the one who reconciles us with God because we confess that we are estranged. We seek the continuing presence of the Spirit because we know we cannot go it alone. We do not worship God because we are faithful people; rather, we worship God to hear about, and in some way be claimed by, a God who is unfailingly faithful to us. (For more on worship, see chap. 7, "The Church at Worship.")

Teaching (*didache*). The church teaches because no one is born a Christian; becoming a Christian requires training. In many ways, the Christian story seems quite odd, and Christians do not deny this. Those who have committed themselves to this story know that no amount of study will make it anything other than odd. But Christians are those who are invited to discover that, even though the story is odd, it is also true. This is not a story that we would have come up with on our own, but that is why we submit to it: it contains a power and wisdom that is beyond us.

Ultimately, however, the church does not teach so that we might assimilate a few Christian ideas. The church teaches so that we might be formed into faithful disciples—that is, so that we might become odd ourselves. To be a Christian entails living a life that does not fit easily into the world around us. It means discovering that we approach life differently, value different things, and affirm different truths. That is why Christians always feel a bit like strangers, even in the most familiar settings. After all, the life of the Christian is no less peculiar than are Christian ideas. For instance, it is odd that we should gather to worship an unseen God when there are many more sensible and practical ways to spend our time. It's also odd that we pray for our enemies, not so that they might repent, but so that they might find God's blessings. Indeed, it's odd that we pray for our enemies as we might pray for our friends. We never would have come up with this way of life ourselves. Learning this Christian way of life requires teaching.

Some time ago a teaching approach called "values clarification" was popular in schools, and also in some churches. Through a variety of exercises, people were encouraged to discover their own personal values. People discovering their own minds and learning to follow their own consciences was a thoroughly sensible approach. But it assumed that values were already there, merely awaiting "clarification." The church, by contrast, assumes that values must be taught. Even the conscience, which sets off inner warnings when we do something wrong, needs to be educated in order to sound its signal at the appropriate times. We are not born with moral sensitivity. That is why G. K. Chesterton concluded that the worst advice we can give people is to tell them to be themselves.

Obviously, this is not the kind of education that can be limited to the classroom. Because the church aims to teach not only a few ideas but also a way of life, every gathering of the church is an opportunity for education. It's true that we learn from Scripture and Christian tradition; but we also learn in the very life of the community, the way we make decisions and the way we respond to the needs of those in our midst and receive the strangers we encounter. In this sense, a committee meeting or fellowship hour can be as important a setting for education as a Bible study class. Whenever the church gathers, no matter the setting, we learn not only a way of viewing the world but also a way of being in the world.

Service (*diakonia*). The church engages in service not because Christians are particularly sympathetic to others, but because it is through service that we respond to the story of what God has done for us all. It is because God has first loved us that we endeavor to share this love with others. Because God has called the strangers in our midst God's own children, we aim to receive them as brothers and sisters. Because God cares for those who are hungry, we feed them. Because God has not forgotten those who are in prison, we visit them. We sometimes slip into thinking that through service we are giving ourselves to others, but we are actually giving God. We give only what we have received.

That does not mean that service is always something grand or glorious; often it is expressed in the smallest ways. Fred Craddock, a renowned teacher of preaching, once said that we sometimes assume that responding to the call to serve is like taking a thousand-dollar bill and laying it on the table: "Here I am Lord. I'm giving it all." In reality, though, God sends us to the bank and has us cash in that thousand dollars for quarters. We go through life spending twenty-five cents here and fifty cents there: listening to the neighbor kid's troubles instead of saying, "get lost"; giving a cup of water to a shaky old man in a nursing home; caring for children in a homeless shelter while their parents look for jobs. Most often, service is carried out in small and simple ways, just as God shares love with us in countless small and simple ways.

In this context, it is helpful to remember that our word "deacon" derives from the Greek word *diakonia*. According to the bylaws of one church I served, deacons were charged with spiritual leadership of the church. At one of the meetings of the board of deacons, someone complained that, instead of being true to this high and momentous charge, they were spending too much of their time delivering food to the homeless shelter and washing dishes after communion. How could they tend to important spiritual matters when they were occupied with such mundane tasks? "I feel like a glorified butler," one of the deacons complained. So we looked together at the book of Acts, where the word "deacon" first appears, and there we discovered that the apostles commissioned the first deacons so that someone could take food to the widows. They were, indeed, butlers, charged with the mundane task of delivering food; but they were also "glorified" because that simple act was an important expression of God's love. In the church everything is turned upside down, and many of our assumptions begin to shake loose. To lead is to be a servant, even as Jesus took on the role of servant, and the greatest honor is not when we are given a gold watch, but rather when we are given a dish towel. (For more on service, see chap. 12, "Doing Faith.")

Christian community (*koinonia*). As we gather in Christian community, we have an opportunity to live out the implications of the covenant that ties us with God and one another. No one can be a Christian by himself or herself. A Christian alone is as useless and lifeless as an ear alone or an arm alone. The Christian faith is a religion of community, first and last. The church is not something we go to, but rather something we are. The simple children's song is a reminder to us all: "We are the church."

When we join a church, we not only commit ourselves to God and Jesus Christ, but also to one another. This is not a matter of some people joining an institution to which others already belong. When anyone joins the church, all its members are joined together. At this marriage ceremony, everyone present gets hitched again. New members join longstanding members, and longstanding members join new members, through vows to worship and serve together as part of the covenantal community.

In some ways this is a reckless thing to do because, even if we do know a little about this God, we usually know even less about the people to whom we are committing ourselves. There are people in the church we would seek out as friends and others whom we would probably have nothing to do with—except that they, too, are part of this community. So now we must listen when ordinarily we might consider walking away. Now we take on the burdens of others that, under different circumstances, we would never agree to shoulder. We endeavor to do all of this—and more—because now we are tied together in this motley bundle we call a church.

I once heard a psychologist say that a church is valuable because it is "a community in which we can learn to stand one another." That may seem like a modest claim, but actually it is something momentous. The Christian community is valuable because there we have ample opportunity to practice the art of receiving strangers and forgiving one another. And if we can learn to accept one another within the church, we can learn to accept anyone. The church that gathered in Thessalonica in the first century was a community that included both Jews and Gentiles. Under normal circumstances, these sworn enemies would not have chosen to associate with one another, but they were thrown together by a common loyalty to Jesus Christ. They did not choose one another, yet here they were together—feeding one another, listening to one another, comforting one another. A remarkable thing. In his first letter to the Thessalonians, Paul commends the church for receiving strangers. It's clear that the members of the church had learned how to receive strangers who came to their church because they had first learned how to receive the familiar strangers who were already part of their church. If we practice the uncommon art of forgiveness long enough within Christian community, forgiveness can mark our relationships outside the church, too.

The church, like a family, is a community in which we have an opportunity to learn how to live with people we did not choose. Our fidelity to those we are stuck with is a powerful reminder of the fidelity of a God who is stuck with us all. In the Christian community we are invited to forgive one another, receive strangers, and care for those we did not choose, because we gather in the name of the God who forgives, receives, and cares for us all. In the first century, a pagan wrote with astonishment, "Behold how these Christians love one another!" At its best, Christian community speaks more powerfully than any sermon.

The church's ministries of proclamation, worship, teaching, service, and Christian community are undertaken not only for the benefit of the church, but also for the benefit of the world. The ways in which this dual purpose is achieved differ in each instance. For example, proclamation can take the form of preaching within the church; but it's called evangelism when the same proclamation is extended into the world. The ministry of service entails both care for one's fellow church members and care for strangers in the world. Even Christian community, which would seem the most inwardly directed of all ministries, is undertaken for the sake of the world as well. Christian community, properly formed and lived out, can provide a welcoming alternative to the ways of a world that often treats people as commodities to be used when it is expedient and ignored when it is not. Indeed, if the church loses sight of its ministry to the world, if it begins to turn in on itself in self-concern, it endangers its very life. Dietrich Bonhoeffer observed, "Unless the church is the church for others, it is not the church at all."

The Body of Christ

When a congregation sets out to call a new pastor, it usually first considers the characteristics it wants in prospective candidates. Typically, a church will say that it wants someone who is a good preacher and teacher, someone who is wise and knowledgeable, a person of discernment, a leader, a sensitive person who can help heal some of the hurts of life, a person with a prophetic social conscience, and someone who can perform miracles (especially around budget time).

Paul lists these same qualities in the twelfth chapter of 1 Corinthians. It's all there. But I'm relieved to mention that Paul does not present these as desirable characteristics of the pastor. Rather, he lists them as manifestations of the Holy Spirit that are found in the members of the congregation. The pastor cannot be all of these things; no one person represents the fullness of Christ. Instead, these gifts are represented within what Paul called the "body of Christ"—the congregation.

Each member of the congregation has a ministry, and each member is equipped with different gifts to fulfill his or her own ministry. In the Reformation, this understanding was expressed in the phrase "the priesthood of all believers." "The mutual ministry of all believers" is another way to put it. Someone who had heard that Quakers have no ordained ministers once said to a Quaker friend, "I hear that you did away with all the ministers." "Not at all," replied the Quaker, "we did away with the laity." Her response captures an understanding that is equally true for us: we are all called into the ministry on the day we are baptized. Ministry is not something a church hires one person to do; it is something that every member of the church is invited to take part in.

The pastor certainly does have a unique role in the congregation, what Paul called "equip[ping] the saints for the work of ministry" (Eph. 4:12). (The word "saints" should not frighten us: in this context it does not denote people of particular piety or holiness, but simply means "the people of God.") Many people assume that the role of the laity is to help the pastor do ministry. In fact, quite the opposite is true: the pastor's unique role is to equip the members of the body of Christ, the laity, to fulfill their ministries. This pastoral role may be fulfilled in a variety of ways, but it is primarily through preaching and teaching that the pastor endeavors to equip his or her fellow ministers. Through these means, and in a variety of settings, the pastor tells the Christian story. The pastor's most important functions are to get the story straight, to be sure that the community does not forget it, and to let the story nourish the ministries of the people.

Most of us tend to disqualify our own gifts and consider them insufficient for ministry. In fact, none of us is qualified. Nevertheless—

miracle of miracles!—God can work through us. This was brought home to me when I led a retreat of church leaders in a congregation I served. We studied the passage in which Paul develops the image of the church as the body of Christ by identifying various spiritual gifts with parts of the body. Then I asked each person to identify his or her particular spiritual gifts with a part of the body. An uneasy silence descended. No one had anything to say. Each one could go on at length about the gifts he or she lacked, but a spiritual gift that might be used in ministry? Who, me?

I could see that this approach was not going anywhere, so I suggested that we talk about the gifts we had discerned in another person. After a brief pause, someone said:

"Liz is an ear. No doubt about it. When my husband died, there was Liz. She sat with me and listened, and through her listening she created a quiet, peaceful place for me to be myself and work through my grief."

"Who, me?" Liz replied. "It wasn't anything. I didn't do anything. I just listened."

"And Dick here," someone else said, "I think of him as a strong right hand. Whenever we go to the homeless shelter, he is the one who hauls everything in and out of the car and stays late to sweep the floor."

"Who, me?" said Dick. "I always do that because I don't feel comfortable doing anything else."

The conversation went on like that for some time. Everyone had a gift. No one was lacking, but most of us were surprised to learn what others saw as our gifts, and even more surprised to learn how others saw those gifts being used in ministry. "Oh, nothing here," we all protested. "No saints. Just a bunch of unqualified stumblers and backsliders." But then we looked again. When we are bound together, we become the body of Christ, the church, strangely equipped for ministry. And no one would have guessed it.

No one has all the gifts necessary for ministry. That is why we have each other. When we consider all that we are called to do as a church—spread the gospel, teach the faith, praise God in worship, comfort the grieving, visit the sick, feed the hungry, clothe those with inadequate clothing, work for justice, and be neighbors to the world—it can seem more than a little overwhelming. No church could hire enough ministers to do it all. And that is good news: it means that all church members get to do their part, to discover and use their own gifts for ministry. This understanding of ministry does limit the role of the pastor. But by limiting the role of the pastor, we can discover the limitless ability of God to work through a community in which each person is encouraged to take up his or her own ministry.

The Church Universal

An individual congregation is a community in which people have made a covenant with God and one another. But the church is more than a single community; it is a community of communities. The covenant extends beyond God and the individuals in one congregation; it is also among churches. Just as within a single congregation we need one another to be the body of Christ, so congregations need one another to fulfill their charge.

There are two reasons that churches covenant with one another in what we call denominations. One reason is practical, the other theological. The practical reason is that there are many ministries a single congregation cannot carry out alone. For example, most individual congregations do not have the expertise and resources to publish a hymnal, design a church school curriculum, or support a seminary. To do anything on that scale, congregations need one another. But the theological reason congregations join together is even more important than the practical one: congregations covenant together to express the overarching unity we have in our common allegiance to Jesus Christ. When we commit ourselves to follow Jesus we commit ourselves to all those others Jesus has claimed, and that extends far beyond those who worship with us at the corner of Elm and Main streets.

Fred Craddock tells of visiting a church in which the stained-glass windows included the names of those who had donated them. Craddock asked his host if the families who had given the windows were still members of the congregation. To his surprise, he was informed that no one in the congregation had ever met the people whose names appeared on the windows of their sanctuary. It seems that the windows had been purchased from a church in a different state when that church, after commissioning the windows, had decided not to build a new sanctuary after all. "We talked about taking the names off," the man told Craddock, "but then we figured that it was important to keep the names. It reminds us that the church is more than just us."

This is an important reminder. The covenant in which we share unites us with people we have not met, people in every corner of the globe, people who differ from us in race, nationality, language, and tradition, but who share with us the one thing that finally matters—a common allegiance to Jesus Christ and a willingness to be bound together in his name. It's certainly true that the church does not always fully express this unity, to our frequent embarrassment and frustration. There are nettlesome divisions both within and between faith traditions. But when we covenant with one another in denominations and seek opportunities to covenant with churches of other faith traditions, we can catch a glimmer of the unity that Jesus prayed would mark his people, a unity that, as elusive as it might seem much of the time, is still ours to claim.

The Church Made Visible

The flaws and divisions that mark the church seem to undercut the lofty claims that are made for the church. Saint Augustine, writing in the fifth century, explained the disparity between what the church appears to be and what it is called to be by saying that there are really two churches: the visible church and the invisible church. The visible church encompasses all the aspects of the church that can be seen—church meetings, budgets, worship services, youth gatherings, fellowship hours, people at their best—and more often perhaps, the visible church is people at their worst, people who are never anything but flagrantly human. The invisible church is God's community in which everyone is united in perfect communion: there are no divisions, and the Holy Spirit blows unimpeded.

From that perspective, every church has both a visible and an invisible dimension. When we are disillusioned with the church, it is because we are seeing only the visible church. When we make great claims for the church, we are speaking of the invisible church. Although Augustine's concept has had considerable appeal through the centuries, there are problems with it. The church certainly does contain both the flaws of something human and the glories of something divine. But when we speak of the visible church and the invisible church as if they were two separable realities, we can dismiss the visible church, with its all-too-visible flaws, too easily. This may lead us to seek a reality that is invisible and a church that is ideal—otherworldly, disembodied, unimpeded by anything human.

For all its appeal, that view would mistakenly imply that the church is most true to its charge and most holy when it is most distant from things human. But those who gather in the body of Christ need to remember that God chose to be embodied in human form in Jesus, who was not some otherworldly presence who maintained divine purity by shunning human limits and human frailty. Rather, God was, in Jesus, human to the bone. In Jesus, God's fingernails got dirty in the grit of earthly life. The same is true of the church, Christ's body: God works in the church in a very earthy, *this*-worldly, human way.

Take a look at Simon Peter. Jesus obviously thinks he is the ideal church member. After all, he gives him the name Peter—that is, "The Rock"—and says, "On this rock I will build my church" (Matt. 16:18). Simon's new name has meaning for us because we think of Peter as the unshakable rock of faith, the trusted disciple, the very foundation of the Christian church. Then we read a story about this same "rock" who, when Jesus is walking on the water, decides he'll stroll out to meet him. As Simon's doubts increase, he sinks like a stone. This same "rock" sleeps like a log when Jesus wants someone to wait with him while he prays in Gethsemane. And when Jesus is arrested this same solid "rock" denies Jesus three times before the rooster crows at break of day.

Is this the ideal church member, the solid rock, on which the church should be built? When we consider Simon in all of his humanity, the name Peter seems more like a cruel joke, like calling an enormous person Tiny. After all, this person is more like mud than a rock. And if its very foundation is no more firm than mud, no wonder the church fails to live up to others'—and our own—expectations. Here we must remember that neither Jesus nor the church makes us any more than what we are. Like Peter, we can fold in on ourselves in self-concern. Like Peter, we can doubt and sink. Like Peter, we sometimes deny Jesus. Like Peter, we are more like mud than a suitable building material for God's church.

And yet, like Peter, on occasion we can find the courage to stand up to the principalities and powers of this world when an injustice is being done, even though our usual way is to avoid trouble at all costs. Like Peter, we can be empowered to greet the people around us as neighbors, even if we have been used to seeing them only as the people around us. Like Peter, we can be sources of comfort and challenge, instruments of healing, and speakers of truth, not by forsaking our humanity but by allowing something of the divine to work through our humanity. God does not make Peter, you, or me anything but human. God does not need to, for the same God who was at work in the human Jesus also seeks to be at work in and through the human church.

So we do not deny the humanness we find in ourselves or see reflected in the church. The miracle of the church is that the work of Jesus can continue in the church despite our human faults and frailties, that something can be at work when we are gathered as Christ's body that is not of our own making. Sometimes two plus two equals five. God can use even mud and dull blocks like you and me to create a structure of beauty and power—the church.

CHAPTER 6

The Church's Book

From the very start, we need to recognize that the word "Bible," which means "book," is misleading. The Bible is not a single book, but more like a library of books. Exactly how many books make up this library called the Bible depends on who is doing the counting. The Bible read by Protestants contains sixty-six books; the Bible read by Roman Catholics (which includes an additional section known as the Apocrypha) contains seventy-three books. Like any good library, the Bible includes books of various literary genres. There are books of history, prophecy, song lyrics, laws, love poems, sermons, legends, letters—and books that combine a number of these genres.

Although the Bible contains many books, it tells one story, the epic story of God's interaction with the people of God—with Israel and with the early church. The Bible is in two sections. First there is the Old Testament. (Christians today often call this section Hebrew Scripture to acknowledge that Jews claimed these writings as their scripture before Christians ever did, and there is nothing old about it to them.) Hebrew Scripture tells the story of God's covenant with the people of Israel. The Bible's second section, the New Testament, tells the story of Jesus and the new covenant that God established with the church through Jesus. In this context, the word "testament" means the same thing as covenant: it signifies a binding agreement (a usage that is preserved in the phrase "last will and testament"). Roman Catholic biblical scholar Raymond E. Brown describes the

Bible as a whole as "the library of Israel and the library of the Early Church."[1]

How the Bible Came to Be

The earliest parts of Hebrew Scripture were probably written about 800 years before the birth of Jesus; the New Testament includes material that, by our best estimates, was written as late as 150 years after Jesus's birth. That is, the Bible was written over a period of close to a thousand years. That amount of time is hard for us to comprehend, so let me propose an analogy. If we were to collect a similar variety of materials written over a similar span of time in England's history, we could include the medieval poem *Beowulf* (written about one thousand years after the birth of Christ), the legend of King Arthur, the Magna Carta, the plays of William Shakespeare, the sermons of John Wesley, James Boswell's *Life of Samuel Johnson*, the poetry of John Keats, the speeches of Winston Churchill, the plays of Tom Stoppard, and the letter an Anglican priest sent to his parish last Christmas. Obviously, a written record that covers such an immense period of time—a millennium—reflects perceptions of the world and (in the case of the Bible) views of God as they evolved from one era to the next.

The Bible, then, did not have a single author; indeed, the biblical material was written by dozens of authors. We know the names of some, but not all, of the authors. There is enough continuing disagreement about the authorship of some books to guarantee an almost inexhaustible supply of topics for doctoral dissertations for many years to come. Some biblical authors wrote just one book, others wrote more than one book, and many wrote only portions of books. And each author naturally wrote in his or her own individual style.

In addition to these authors, countless other people were involved in shaping the Bible. Our Scripture (with the exception of the New Testament Epistles) existed in an oral tradition, sometimes for generations, before it was ever written down. The accounts found in these books were spoken before they were written. Consequently, much of the Bible is a report by someone who heard it from someone else. Living as we do in a time after the invention of the printing press, we are sometimes suspicious of anything that is passed on by word of mouth. We have all played the children's game in which one person whispers something in another's ear, and this is repeated around the circle. By the time the message makes it all the way around the circle, it can be barely recognizable. "I like Sally's new dress" can be transformed into "You have an ugly face."

Even so, cultures that do not rely on the written word do not find the oral tradition so wildly unreliable. We see traces of this phenomenon when we read aloud to young children. They correct us if we change a single word in the reading of a familiar story. Young children carefully tend to the spoken word in ways that diminish after they have learned to read. It has also been noted that those who do not have the gift of sight sometimes hear things that those of us who are able to see can miss. The same dynamic is at work in cultures that do not have written documents. People in such cultures can relate voluminous material with an ease and accuracy that staggers those of us who have come to rely on the written word.

It has been reported that Homer could recite the Iliad, one of his epic poems, in its entirety on successive nights—without variation. Some modern scholars were skeptical that such a feat could be possible. But then it was discovered that poets in remote areas of the Balkan region of Eastern Europe, steeped in the oral tradition, could recite even longer epic poems—and with Homer's legendary accuracy. In certain African cultures, tribal storytellers (called *griots*) can tell and retell stories of similar length without discernible variation. To be sure, the biblical stories could not possibly have passed through so many memories and be retold by so many mouths over so many years without some variation or development. But we should not assume, from the standpoint of our cultural dependence on the written word, that "oral tradition" is synonymous with "inaccurate."

Eventually, the material that was originally passed down in oral form was written down. Those who reworked the oral tradition into written form are sometimes called redactors (from the Latin *redact*, which means "rework"). In some instances, such as the four Gospels, the names of the redactors are preserved; in other instances, including all of the books of Hebrew Scripture, the redactors are not identified. Furthermore, the original manuscripts they worked on have been lost. The papyrus they used has long since crumbled into dust, but before it disintegrated entirely, the manuscripts were copied—and then copied again. Sometimes the copyist would not make any changes to the manuscript; other times, the copyist would turn into a redactor, deliberately reworking the manuscript to clarify a passage or reflect the evolving perspective of the community.

Whoever the redactors of scriptural tradition may have been, in a real sense the whole community was involved in the process. The Bible is the community's book. By choosing to obscure their identity, the authors and the later redactors emphasized that individuals merely gave expression to the voice of the community. Hebrew Scripture was given its shape by the people of Israel, from oral tradition through written documents to their redaction into the form familiar to us today. It was also the community that, over time, received these writings and came to see them as authoritative. The New Testament books were fashioned in a similar way by the early Christian community, the church.

At no point in the process did someone sit down and say, "Today I think I will write a portion of Scripture." Rather, the authors set out to record the community's experience and understanding of God so that such a word might be of continued benefit to the community. Over time, some of those writings seemed to reflect the community's experience and understanding of God so well that they were set apart by the community as sacred: in some way it was God's word to them. For instance, the Psalms were originally song lyrics, the words to hymns used in the temple's worship. They address God in words of thanksgiving, praise, and entreaty. Over time, however, those words that were addressed to God came to be perceived as "God's word" to the people as well.

Eventually, both Israel and the church felt the need to determine which books would be accepted as authoritative. Lists were compiled of books that were considered sacred. These lists are called "canons" (derived from an Egyptian word meaning a "reed used for measuring"): in other words, the books that were accepted into a canon "measured up." For hundreds of years Israel used various sacred writings in worship and only established them in a canon much later, perhaps as late as a century after the birth of Jesus. What we now refer to as the New Testament canon also took time to develop. For example, in the centuries immediately after the death of Jesus, dozens of so-called Gospels were written, and yet only four are now preserved in our canon. In some instances, the reasons for certain books being excluded are rather obvious. In one particular "Gospel," for example, there are many stories about Jesus as a boy. According to this account, at one point Jesus was playing with other children, but when the children began to depart after some childish dispute, Jesus prayed to God, and the children were struck down dead! Although this "Gospel" was circulated in the early church, eventually the Christian community as a whole did not accept its account as authoritative and did not include it in the canon.

Consensus within the community did not always develop this easily, and in some instances it took centuries for individuals and the church to agree about which books were sacred. Some books were collected as early as the first century; but disputes about the inclusion of other books still raged in some quarters as late as the sixteenth century. The canon we think of as the Bible, including the thirty-nine books of the Hebrew Scripture and the twenty-seven books of the New Testament, was finally fixed at the Council of Trent in 1546 CE.

Just Another Book?

The Bible is given a unique place in the life of the Christian community because it is understood to have special authority. The church acknowledges the Bible as not only the best expression of the community's faith but also as, in some way, God's word to the community. The difference between these two approaches to the Bible reflects the difference between what has been called *natural* religion and *revealed* religion. Natural religion begins with the affirmation that God is everywhere and in all things, and it goes on to argue that God can be perceived in all things, without any special aid or revelation. Some who represent this view go so far as to say that, if our perception is properly developed, the presence of God can be discerned in all things with equal immediacy and accuracy. We can learn as much about God from a blade of grass as we can from even the most extraordinary human life. We cannot expect to encounter God any more fully in the life of Jesus than in any other life. In this view, the Bible takes its place on the shelf with all other books and has no special status.

Revealed religion, which includes both Hebrew and Christian traditions, also begins with the affirmation that God is everywhere and in all things. But those who hold this view go on to stipulate that God is not equally perceptible in all things. Instead, God chooses to reveal God's own self more fully in some events than in others, more completely in some lives than in others, and more clearly in some books than in others. Adhering to this view, Jews affirm that God was more abundantly revealed in the Exodus than in their slavery in Egypt. Christians profess that we can learn more about God by studying the life of Jesus than we can learn from the life of our local butcher. Jews and Christians alike hold that we can deepen our understanding of and relationship with God through the books that make up what we call Scripture more than we can through any other book.

God is certainly present and can be encountered in the blade of grass, in the butcher on the corner, and in many books that are not included in the Bible. But if we are to understand how God is present in such things, we must view them through what God has revealed to us in special events, special people, and indeed, a special book. If we are to perceive fully how God is at work in the life of the butcher, we must view his life through the special revelation of God in Jesus Christ. If we understand the ways in which some divine truth is to be found in the words of Emerson or the local newspaper editorial, it will be because we read them in the light of what is revealed in Scripture. So we do not approach all books in the same way. It is via the books of the canon that we determine which other words "measure up."

This special status was not given to the words of Scripture capriciously. When we read the Bible, we are reading the consensus of the ages. It is the testimony of the church's faith that has been developed over centuries. Through many generations, the community we are a part of commends this word to us as in some way God's word to us all. When Huck Finn learned that the Bible story he was forced to learn dealt with characters who had died "a powerful long time ago," he said that he took no stock in dead people. When we vest the Bible with special authority, we are indeed taking stock in the testimony of those who have gone before us, not only those whose stories are recounted in the Bible but also those who have handed those stories down to us. We listen to the Bible with special deference, partly because it comes to us so well recommended by those who have gone before us. After all, they speak from within the ongoing experience of the community to which we now belong. We can listen with equal concern to whatever a particular preacher decides is worthy of our consideration, or we can listen with special care to the story that has been shaped by and commended to us by the community of faith through the centuries.

Each generation can choose to dig its own new wells, but such wells will necessarily be rather shallow. No single generation, acting in defiant isolation, is capable of more. But there is another option: we can dip into the deep wells that were dug long ago by many generations of the faith community. Those who want to drink deeply from a source that could not be reached through our own best efforts will choose this latter option.

Obviously, each generation must claim the biblical story as its own if it is to shape and inform the life of the community or any individual. We do not accept the testimony of previous generations blindly; rather, we accept it because it increases our ability to see what we could not otherwise see. Part of what we see with the Bible's help is that the story it tells is also our story. Harry Truman, when asked why he spent time reading the Roman historian Pliny, replied, "To find out what is going on in Washington." The Bible certainly tells us about what happened long ago to people who have long since departed; but because the same God who was active then is still active, we read it to understand God and ourselves today. A woman once said to a missionary: "It is not I who am reading the Bible. It is the Bible that is reading me!"

We also accept the authority of Scripture not only because it conforms to our experience but also because we experience the power of this word to form us anew. The Bible not only finds us where we are; it also has the power to move us. It is flawed in some respects, as we would expect any human product to be, but it has the power to transform us in ways that nothing merely human has the ability to do. It is when we confront the power of this story that we can be prepared to affirm the underlying truth of it.

Is the Bible Literally True?

Did everything recorded in the Bible happen just the way the Bible says it happened? That's an important question, but we must first determine which parts of the Bible we are referring to. Clearly, some parts were not meant to be read literally. If we were to take a literal approach to every passage of Scripture, we would have to conclude that John the Baptist was speaking literally when he referred to Jesus as the lamb of God. It is quite clear that no one reads every point of Scripture as completely literal.

The first step in determining whether a passage can be read literally is to ask whether the human author intended it to be read literally. As we discovered in our consideration of the creation stories in the first chapter of this book, it is important to ask what form of literature we are reading. We are used to making such distinctions when we enter other libraries. Those who fail to make such distinctions in reading the Bible will be terribly confused and frequently misled. We read a history of nineteenth-century England differently from the way we read a Charles Dickens novel set in the same period. We can learn from both, but we will learn from each in different ways. The British history may present the facts about an era, but the novel can trace dimensions of the same events that cannot be plumbed in any history. Another way to put it is that a book of history may deal in facts, but a great novel deals in truths. The novel is not a failed book of history, and it should not be read in the same way or be judged by the same criteria.

Something does not need to be historically true to be eternally true. Some people have spent a great deal of time measuring the gullets of fish to prove that the story of Jonah inside the whale is historically plausible. But the discerning reader of the book of Jonah will recognize that it is offered, not as history but as a good story in a form that in many respects closely resembles the modern novella. If we understand this, we can call a halt to our fishing expeditions and, instead, settle down to read and appreciate the book for what it is: a wonderful story that has important truths to offer us.

Each literary genre represented in the Bible—from law to legend, poetry to history—has the power to move, inform, and shape us in ways that are peculiar to that genre. A more difficult question awaits our response: Are we to take literally those passages that are not in the form of legend, story, or poetry? Something like that question comes up in two instances. First, we ask such a question of passages that claim to record something that actually happened but which we have difficulty accepting as historical fact. Second, we ask such a question of passages that represent points of view—either about the nature of God or standards of human behavior—that we do not share. There are two different approaches we can take; both are widely represented in the Christian church, and both entail unique challenges.

The first approach is usually called "biblical literalism." A literalist believes that the Bible is without human error, that is, "inerrant." This approach assumes that the words themselves come to us directly from God: God dictated the words, and the human authors were mere stenographers. For the literalist, the job of interpretation is quite narrow. After all, if the words of the Bible are God's words, then the Bible says what it means and means what it says, and everything in it must be understood literally. Furthermore, the moral rules that are represented in Scripture are unchanged. The particular circumstances that gave rise to a particular story or belief account for little, because whatever is in the Bible must be assumed to be as free from the limits of time and circumstance as the God who "wrote" it.

There are real problems with the literalist approach. For instance, are we to believe that Elisha was able to make the iron ax head float in the Jordan River, as is recorded in 2 Kings (6:6)? And do we *need* to believe it? A literalist would say: "Yes. Everything happened just as the Bible says. If we begin to question the accuracy of this story, then the whole authority of the Bible is undercut." Even if our credulity is flexible enough to accommodate such a perspective, we still have to account for the way the Bible seems to contradict itself. As we considered in chapter 1, Genesis offers two different accounts of creation. They are quite different in crucial respects. How are we to account for the differences? The same can be said of the four Gospels: in Matthew, the Lord's Prayer is found in the Sermon on the Mount; in Luke, Jesus teaches the prayer to the disciples after one of them asks him to teach them how to pray. In addition, the words of the prayer as recorded in the two Gospels are different. We could cite countless other examples. Literalists must harmonize the accounts, twisting the narrative so that it will fit within the limits of their approach to interpretation. Because the Bible represents God's truth word for word, any passages that might otherwise be read as reflecting human influence must be explained away.

Likewise, a literalist assumes that every moral law set forth in the Bible must be equally binding on every subsequent generation. A literalist will allow no room for any understanding to evolve over time. Whatever was true at the time it was written is eternally true. Yet, even thoroughgoing literalists who claim to follow this approach often use it selectively. For instance, even those who cite Leviticus to support the position that God forbids homosexual relationships (Lev. 20:13) do not advocate that homosexuals be stoned to death, the punishment that is prescribed in the same passage. They also neglect to mention that some practices that are commonly accepted today, such as planting two different kinds of seed in the same field or wearing clothing that is a blend of two different fabrics, are also forbidden in Leviticus.

Consider another example. It would be difficult to find anything about which there is surer consensus today than that slavery is wrong and irreconcilable with a Christian worldview and way of life. Yet the apostle Paul seems to accept the practice. On one occasion, Paul returned an escaped slave back to his master, with a letter to the slave's owner (preserved in the New Testament book Philemon) giving no indication that he thought slavery was wrong. Elsewhere Paul writes: "Slaves, obey your earthly masters in everything, not only while being watched and in order to please them, but wholeheartedly, fearing the Lord" (Col. 3:22; see also Eph. 6:5). Biblical literalists of previous centuries used such passages to argue that the Bible supports slavery. In our day, with no one left to defend the practice, a literalist must defend such passages by saying that what appears to be the case is not really true.

Literalism may make the task of interpretation easier, but it does so at the expense of the narrative itself, bending it to fit our assumptions about how the Bible came to be. Fortunately, we are able to approach the Bible in a different way, one that avoids the pitfalls of literalism. This second approach was advocated by Karl Barth when he said, "I take the Bible too seriously to take it literally." Taking the Bible seriously means accepting it as being inspired by God and as containing God's word to the community of faith. But taking the Bible seriously also means taking into account the human influences it reflects. The Bible was not dictated by God, but God's Spirit was at work in the ways whereby the narrative took shape. At every point, however, God's Spirit worked through flawed, limited human beings, so in certain respects the biblical accounts are also flawed and limited. There are historical records in the Bible, and some of them may be very accurate, but others may be less accurate. There are eternal truths in the Bible, but there are also perceptions that reflect the limits of the time in which they were written.

Martin Luther concluded: "The Bible is like the manger in which the baby Jesus lay: while it cradles the word of God, it also contains a lot of straw." The straw, of course, is of the human-made variety. But Luther's image is misleading in one respect: we cannot pick out the divine in the Bible as easily as we might lift a baby out of a manger. The divine and the human converge and mingle in the Bible in ways that are not always easily divided. This makes the interpretative task that much more difficult and also leaves it open to abuse. If we cannot read everything in the Bible as literally true, we must begin to make some distinctions. In some ways contemporary Christians are already too well versed in making distinctions for our own purposes. We prefer our religion à la carte: we like to pick out the things that appeal to us, support our biases, and affirm our practices—and leave behind whatever is uncomfortable or challenging. How can we begin to read the Bible with discernment without succumbing to this persistent tendency?

Obviously, we must learn how to read the Bible with skill and care. The call to serious study of the Bible is all the more urgent for those who do not approach it literally. Raymond E. Brown illustrates this need:

> Suppose I were to ask you whether you really think that Washington cut down the cherry tree, or threw a coin across the Potomac, or slept in all the houses in which he is supposed to have bivouacked, you might answer, "Well, I think some of that is legend." How would you then reply if I said to you, "Well, if you begin doubting those things about Washington, how do you know that Lincoln led the Union to victory over the Confederacy, or that Teddy Roosevelt presided over the building of the Panama Canal?" You would soon be forced to recognize that there are different bodies of evidence for different claims and that at times stories about some people are told with a certain legendary atmosphere whereas others are unadornedly factual. The same has to be recognized in the stories associated with the great biblical characters.[2]

It takes time to develop the skills necessary to make such judgments. When we hear a stranger say something, our understanding is limited. But when we hear a friend say something, we listen with greater understanding. After all, we are familiar with our friend's manner of speech. We know more of what she means when she uses certain words or speaks in a certain tone because we can set the words in a richer context. Discernment about the Bible, like discernment about the words of friends, takes time.

Reading the Bible with discernment also requires that we seek guidance from the Holy Spirit. Our study of the Bible is not merely an intellectual exercise; it is a spiritual endeavor. As the Spirit was at work in those who gave shape to the Bible, we, too, seek the Spirit to be at work in our reading of it. The Spirit not only helped get the words on the page, but it can also help us get the words off the page. We must rely on the Spirit all the more when we attempt to derive God's truth for our time from passages of Scripture that may in some way reflect the limited perspectives of the time in which they were written. John Robinson, pastor of the Pilgrims, told his congregation in 1620: "The Lord has more truth and light yet to break forth out of his holy word."

New Testament scholar Krister Stendahl has pointed out that it can take some time for the implications of the truths revealed in the Bible to be fully realized. When Paul said that in Christ there is "no longer slave or free," it came like a revelatory flash. Only hundreds of years later were the full implications of that understanding seen or lived. We must seek the influence of the Holy Spirit if we are to develop in our understanding.

Furthermore, reading the Bible with discernment requires that we make a distinction between individual passages and the overall sweep of the biblical narrative. For instance, when we read the Gospel accounts of the resurrection, we notice that they differ on many of the particulars. Mark records no resurrection appearances and only hints that Jesus would meet his disciples in Galilee. Luke says that Jesus appeared only in Jerusalem, in the upper room, and at the village of Emmaus just six miles away. Matthew says that Jesus appeared to the disciples only in Galilee and on top of a mountain. John says Jesus appeared in Jerusalem in the upper room—not once, as in Luke, but on two occasions separated by a week. John also says that much later Jesus approached the disciples in Galilee, not on a mountain as Matthew states, but by a lake.

How are we to respond these differences in the Gospel accounts? We may dismiss all of the accounts as so irreconcilable that they are worthless. The community that gathered these stories together, however, obviously thought that there was value in preserving all four. Each tells the story in a different way, and each perspective has value.

A mountain can be described from the perspective of north, south, east, and west; the descriptions may differ, but it is the same mountain. When we make room for more than one description, we can see more of the mountain than we could from any single perspective.

We do not need to deny the differences by trying to harmonize the resurrection accounts. But it's important to recognize that, though they differ in some of the particulars, they all point unmistakably in the same direction: though Jesus was killed, he appeared to the disciples and others after his death. That is the central truth to which the Gospel writers testify, and they do so with one voice.

Reading the Bible is a matter of listening both to the individual authors and to the cumulative witness of the story as a whole. I once saw a film of a children's choir singing the national anthem. The filmmaker at first focused on individual children, and it was clear that many of them had the words confused. Some seemed virtually tone deaf. But when the filmmaker had the camera and microphones take in the whole choir, something remarkable happened. The tones were rich, the harmonies lush, the words clear. From that perspective, individual flaws were gathered up into a seemingly flawless performance. To be sure, it is instructive to study individual passages of Scripture. But it may be even more important to consider the overall direction of the biblical story. To paraphrase Shakespeare, the devil may be able to quote certain isolated passages of Scripture for his purpose. But the story in its larger dimensions is surely God's.

Discerning readers of the Bible can expect to encounter passages that simply seem unbelievable. We all have files in our minds labeled "Accepted" and "Rejected." When we read something in the Bible, we usually feel obliged to relegate the item to one or the other file. Sometimes there is not much at stake in whether we believe or disbelieve the historical accuracy of certain biblical accounts. For instance, if it could be proved to our satisfaction that Jesus never walked on water (Matt. 14:22–33), we could put that in the "Rejected" file and still not find our faith in Jesus diminished. Before we file the story away, however, it is important to recognize that it has much to teach us that is not dependent on its historical accuracy. When we read the story with care and receptivity, we will note that the focus of the story is on Peter's struggle for faith in Jesus, something that will be entirely lost if we only concern ourselves with whether or not the account is historically accurate.

Those who attempt to read the Bible with discernment will still have files in their minds labeled "Accepted" and "Rejected." But they will also have a large and active file labeled "Awaiting Further Light." I described the importance of that file in my book *Living Faith while Holding Doubts*:

> Such a file will be filed with all those things that do not yet clearly belong in either the "Accepted" or the "Rejected" file.... Such a file may also include many items that we would be inclined to put in the "Rejected" file were it not for the voices of historic Christian witnesses that seem to be whispering, "Not so fast. You may not fully believe this now, but please trust us enough to put it somewhere where you will be sure to consider it again."[3]

Those who make liberal use of the "Awaiting Further Light" file exhibit humility before the testimony of the community of faith. This does not mean that we must pretend to believe things we don't believe; but it does mean that, at certain points, we take the Bible more seriously than we take ourselves. It means that we remain open to truths that are not entirely encompassed by our own limited perceptions. It means that we freely recognize, along with Shakespeare's character Hamlet, "There are more things in heaven and earth, Horatio, than are dreamt of in your philosophy."[4] Those who make frequent use of an "Awaiting Further Light" file reserve room in their hearts and minds for God's truth to unfold over time.

How to Read the Bible

What follows are some practical suggestions about how to read the Bible. Those who set out to do so reason that it is best to begin at the beginning and read it all the way through. If you do, however, you are almost sure to get bogged down around Exodus 25 or, if you are particularly determined or just plain stubborn, around Leviticus 3. If a person who wanted to learn how to read went to a library, we would not advise him or her to begin with the first book on the shelf. There are better places to begin. Bible readers might begin by reading one of the four Gospels; then they might turn to the Acts of the Apostles and sample a few of Paul's letters—1 Corinthians and Philippians, for example. Circling back to Hebrew Scripture, they could read Genesis, the first part of Exodus, then go on to Samuel and Kings. Readers can benefit, at any point, from dipping into the Psalms. After this relatively brief overview, readers are better equipped to wade into the more demanding sections.

The Bible was shaped in community, is addressed to the community, and is best read in community. Although we can benefit from reading the Bible on our own, the words take on full and vigorous life in their natural setting, the community of faith. It is when we search, affirm, and doubt together that we are best able to discern the word of God.

A good biblical commentary is another way to benefit from the reflections of others. A commentary, like a guidebook, can help us know what we are seeing, point out things we might otherwise miss, and even keep us from getting hopelessly lost along the way. There are many helpful commentaries available.

When we read the Bible, it is important to remember that we are reading a translation. We sometimes forget this simple fact. When the translation known as the Revised Standard Version (1952) was first introduced, it ignited a great debate. One Christian typified a common response when he spoke in favor of the familiar King James Version and against the new translation: "I want to read the words of Jesus just like he spoke them." But every Bible is a translation. Even when we read the New Testament in Greek, the language in which it was written, we are reading a translation of Jesus's words, because Jesus actually spoke in Aramaic. Although we may read the King James Version for the richness of its language, we have to recognize that it was a translation into the English language as it was spoken more than four hundred years ago. For regular study, it is best to choose a more readable translation. Because every translation is an interpretation, it is also helpful to read more than one translation. Shadows retreat when light is shed from different directions. Certain biblical paraphrases, such as Eugene Peterson's *The Message*, can add some spice to our study. Reading the Bible can be like living near the railroad tracks: the sounds are so familiar that we cease to hear them, and even our sleep is undisturbed. When we read an unfamiliar translation or a creative paraphrase, we are more likely to sit up and take notice.

CHAPTER 7

The Church at Worship

I first realized that people differ in their approach to worship when I was a teenager. One Saturday afternoon, a group of us had converged on one of the neighborhood streets. Our talk swooped lazily over a number of subjects until it landed on what we were going to do with the rest of the weekend. One of my friends, a Roman Catholic, said that he was going to go to Mass that night so that he could go to the football game on Sunday. Another boy asked, "Why don't you just skip it? Do your parents make you go or something?"

"No, it's just something we do," he replied.

Then someone else, a boy who did not attend any church, asked what they did in the Mass. The Roman Catholic boy described the worship of his church: the responsive readings from the missal, the Scripture readings, the kneeling for prayers, the homily, the Eucharist. In the spirit of true ecumenical dialogue, I interrupted him to ask, "Isn't it boring?"

My friend replied, "Sure, it's boring." But there was something about the look on his face and the way he replied that said something else: the fact that the Mass is boring is somehow beside the point. It's something you do, that's all, and the question of whether it is boring is about as relevant as asking whether gathering around the family table for dinner is boring or kissing your parents goodnight is boring. It's just one of the things you do. Subsequent conversations with other Roman Catholics revealed more of this same approach to worship that to me, as a Protestant, was quite unfamiliar. They did not attend worship because they felt like it. More strange still, I got the impression that they trundled out of bed on Sunday morning not only because a parent or parish priest expected them to worship, but because they believed that in some way God expected them to do so. Worship is a holy obligation to God. To my wonderment, to them it seemed as simple as that.

I had never heard a Protestant talk about worship that way. Instead, the Protestants I knew spoke of attending worship to find spiritual enrichment or inspiration or practical tools for living. To this day, I get the impression that attending worship, in and of itself, does not count for much with most Protestants. Everything depends on whether, when we attend worship, we find what we are looking for. In fact, if the sermon is long and convoluted, if the choir sings a real clunker of an anthem, and if the prayers are uninspired, the Protestant is tempted to question whether worship was worth attending at all. All too often, the Protestant tendency can be to approach worship as we might a lecture or a movie: if it neither enlightens nor entertains, we might as well have stayed at home.

In the old chestnut of a play *Life with Father*, the central character confides that when he goes to worship he puts a one-dollar bill in one pocket of his vest and a five-dollar bill in the other pocket. During the sermon, he silently challenges the minister to deliver a sermon that will make him reach for the pocket with the five-dollar bill. He was a Protestant.

Danish theologian Søren Kierkegaard uses another analogy. Although many people assume that worship is a performance in which God is the prompter, the pastor is the performer, and the congregation is the audience, it is more properly understood as a performance in which the pastor is the prompter, the members of the congregation are the performers, and God is the audience. *Leitourgia*, the New Testament word for worship, itself clarifies our role (it literally means "the work of the people"). From this perspective, it matters little if the music or prayers please us; it matters a great deal if they please God. Perhaps the question we need to ask is this: How does God feel when our worship is over? Is God inspired?

Worship approached in this way does not need to become some kind of rote, bloodless exercise, devoid of meaning for the worshipers. Rather, it is a kind of sacred irony: when we come to serve God in our worship, that is when we are best served. When we sing our praises to God, our own spirits are refreshed—and in ways that are unattainable when we focus on our own need for refreshment. When we speak to God in prayer, it is as if someone has spoken to us the word we most need to hear. When we offer God our homage and our devotion, we are the ones who leave laden with gifts.

It is not that Protestants are wrong to expect that we will be enlightened or inspired by our worship, but it is a mistake to pursue these goals as if they are the point of worship. When we engage in worship only with an eye toward what we will receive, the sacred irony of worship is reversed: what we pursue becomes that much more elusive. By seeking only to meet our own needs through our worship, we serve neither God nor ourselves.

The German word for worship, *Gottesdienst*, is a word the English language might well be envious of. It reflects an important twofold meaning: humans' service to God and God's service to humans. It is appropriate that both are reflected in a single word, because they are inextricably linked. It is when we come to serve God that we discover the many ways in which we are served. This is how we can understand the otherwise troublesome passages of Scripture in which God enjoins us to worship God: God knows that we need to worship God more than God needs our worship. God wants us to have the gifts that can be received only when we offer ourselves to God.

Novelist Frederick Buechner writes:

Phrases like Worship Service or Service of Worship are tautologies. To worship God means to serve him. Basically there are two ways to do it. One way is to do things for him that he needs to have done—run errands for him, carry messages for him, fight on his side, feed his lambs, and so on. The other way is to do things for him that you need to do—sing songs for him, create beautiful things for him, give things up for him, tell him what's on your mind and in your heart, in general rejoice in him and make a fool of yourself for him the way lovers have always made fools of themselves for the one they love.[1]

Those who have occasion to give a bouquet to a loved one learn that the joy of giving the gift is even greater than the joy of receiving it. Giving the flowers is not a burden; the only burden would be if we could not give them or if the gift were rejected. So it is good news, indeed, that God not only invites our gifts of devotion in worship but also graciously receives them.

The gift we offer in worship is the gift of ourselves; the gift we receive in return is the gift of God's own self. The Westminster Catechism begins by asking, "What is the chief end of man?" It answers, "The chief end of man is to glorify God and enjoy him forever." Because God is someone to be enjoyed, worship can be enjoyable. It is not that we are enjoying ourselves, as if worship were entertainment in a sacred key. We are enjoying God's power and immediacy, enjoying God's complexity and simplicity, enjoying God's love and mystery, enjoying God for who God is.

Those who have carefully honed utilitarian sensibilities are often tempted to ask of worship: What use is this to me? But those who see worship as the opportunity to enjoy God know that worship is about as useful as a circus, or kissing someone you love, or sending a dozen roses, or dancing. To the utilitarian observer, those who worship, like those who get caught up in any other such useless activity, look more than a little foolish. But Buechner is right: "Lovers have always made fools of themselves for the one they love."

How Do We Worship?

Justin Martyr, writing about a century and a half after the birth of Jesus, gives us our earliest complete description of the church's worship:

On the day which is called Sunday, all who live in the cities or in the countryside gather together in one place. And the memoirs of the apostles or the writings of the prophets are read as long as there is time. Then, when the reader has finished, the president, in a discourse, admonishes and invites the people to practice these examples of virtue. Then we all stand up together and offer prayers. And, as we mentioned before, when we have finished the prayer, bread is presented, and wine with water; the president likewise offers up prayers and thanksgivings according to his ability, and the people assent by saying, Amen. The elements which have been "eucharized" are distributed and received by each one; and they are sent to the absent by the deacons. Those who are prosperous, if they wish, contribute what each one deems appropriate; and the collection is deposited with the president; and he takes care of the orphans and the widows, and those who are needy because of sickness or other cause, and the captives, and the strangers who sojourn amongst us—in brief, he is the curate of all who are in need.[2]

A portion of the worship described by Justin—the reading from sacred writings, followed by a discourse based on those writings—was at the heart of Jewish worship in the synagogue, reminding us that the earliest Christians continued for a time to worship in the synagogue. But the very first words of Justin's account reveal that, in other ways, the worship of this new religion represented a radical departure from the Jewish tradition. Justin reports that the Christians worshiped on Sunday; that simple fact, which we take as a matter of course, was actually a radical statement of faith from the adherents of this new religion. Jews worship God on their Sabbath, the seventh day of the week, Saturday. The Jewish Sabbath probably had its historical origins in the Jews' Babylonian exile: their identity as a people was maintained only by their strict observance of this holy day. It is little wonder, then, that the Jews came to affirm that the Sabbath was established by God, as far back as the creation of the world, when God rested on the seventh day.

So when Christians worshiped on Sunday, it was a radical, momentous departure from a deeply rooted practice. Christians worshiped on Sunday because that was the day on which Jesus arose from the dead, on which God acted in the resurrection to create us anew; thus every Sunday worship service is a celebration of the risen Christ. Every Sunday is Easter Sunday, and the entire week shifted so that it might turn on the axis of that singular event. What is perhaps most striking about Justin's description of Christian worship is how remarkably familiar it sounds these many centuries later. The individual elements of worship he describes are still present in the worship of most churches today, and the overall movement of worship is largely the same as well. The order of worship he outlines contains these elements: gathering, reading, sermon, prayers, offering, Eucharist, and the sending forth. Let us consider each one:

Gathering. At first the gathering of the church for worship would seem a simple matter of necessity, not worthy of much comment. But the fact that we gather to worship is significant in itself. We sometimes speak of "going to church" on Sunday morning as if the church has some existence without us, as if it could still be the church if no one showed up. The church, however, is the gathered community of God's people, and Christians cannot worship without gathering communally. Christian worship is not like watching a movie in a theater, where our experience is essentially the same if we watch it alone in an empty theater or get the last seat in a packed house. Christian and Jewish worship is set apart from other world religions in which worship is an individual encounter with God. Our worship requires a congregation. Jesus said, "Where two or three are gathered together in my name, there am I in the midst of them" (Matt. 18:20). It is the gathered community, even if a small one, that is the vessel for the Spirit of Christ.

Christian worship has both vertical and horizontal dimensions: it's true that we gather to encounter God, but we also gather to encounter one another in God's presence. They are simply two dimensions of the same experience. We might prefer to stay home and watch a worship service on television, because it would certainly be more convenient. Not only could we avoid the inconvenience of getting dressed up and traveling to church, but we could also avoid the far greater inconvenience of encountering others—with all of their needs and frailties. But the same people who distract and perhaps annoy us are the very ones whom God has promised to work through and to be present among. It is in the midst of others that we encounter the God who promised to be in our midst.

To experience a worship service, all we need is a television set. But that is about as empty as attending a family reunion or a dance via television. To worship—rather than simply watching others worship—we need to gather with the community of faith.

Reading. Worship in the synagogue, from which our own worship derives, was mainly a matter of speaking and listening to Scripture. And in many respects, the reading of Scripture remains at the center of Christian worship as well. Although we may certainly benefit from reading Scripture silently in our homes, Scripture was originally intended to be read aloud in worship. Scripture's natural home is still within the context of worship. It is a word addressed to the gathered church.

It is telling that the worship of the synagogue originated during Israel's exile. Living as strangers in a strange land, the Jews' very identity as a people was threatened, so they read and listened to stories to remind them who they were and where their true home was. They could see nothing around them to sustain their hope, so they listened to stories about the faithfulness of the God in whom their hope rested.

When we read Scripture in worship, we are doing much the same thing. We, too, live in an alien land where it is easy to forget who we are and where our true home is. We, too, need to be reminded that we are God's beloved and that God, our true home, is forever prepared to receive us, no matter how far we may wander in the meantime. We attend to the stories of Scripture with special attentiveness because we hear other competing stories during the week that attempt to make their claim on us. In the world we hear stories that tell us in some clever new guise that our primary function in life is to be good consumers and other stories that imply that our value is in proportion to our beauty or success. We listen to Scripture to be reminded that the competing stories we hear in the world are ultimately empty and false.

William Willimon, an authority on Christian worship, speaks of hearing a psychiatrist discuss the growing problem of adolescent suicide. One of the psychiatrist's theories for the cause of this disturbing trend was this: "Kids have no history. They therefore have no perspective, no way to take the long view of their problems. When you break up with your girlfriend, this may seem like the end of the world because your world is so small. Problems are magnified and quickly engulf the fragile, insecure personality of the adolescent. In such circumstances, suicide seems the only way out." The stories of Scripture help set our lives in a larger context, a context as large as the eternal promises of God. Willimon observes: "Remembrance gives all of us perspective [from the Latin, literally, 'to see through'] so that we are enabled to see through present events to some larger purpose and meaning."[3] Scripture reminds us that, even when we see no reason for optimism, we need not lose hope because we have not lost God.

We hear the stories of what God did long ago so that we may discern the ways in which this same God is still active. We listen to the scriptural promises so that we may know how the story ends. The biblical story we hear is our story as well: it is the source of our identity, the foundation of our life together.

Sermon. The historic witness of Scripture is always a story "to be continued." If Scripture is the story of what God has done, it is in the sermon that we delineate the ways in which this same story reaches into our own time. Without the sermon, our worship could become another form of escapism into a timeless reality that floats like a dream above and beyond the life we live. But through the sermon, we meet at the intersection of eternity and the present moment. That's what Karl Barth had in mind when he suggested that a preacher needs to work "with the Bible in one hand and the newspaper in the other."

A sermon needs to be grounded in both Scripture and in the life of the community of faith. When the connection between Scripture and sermon is severed (as it seems to be all too often) the sermon is reduced to an edifying discourse in which the preacher speaks on whatever is of concern to her at the moment and offers her own perspectives on the subject. But the sermon is not the preacher's opportunity to offer a few comments on life, because, left on our own, we have precious few insights to offer. Rather, the preacher's task is to trace the implications of the scriptural story and to set that story in the context of the ongoing life of the community of faith. The sermon is clearly different from a lecture on the Bible: a sermon does not endeavor to speak *about* the Bible but instead endeavors to speak *from* the Bible. It always follows the implications of Scripture, no matter how far-flung, and never wanders so far that it is out of earshot of the scriptural word.

It is equally important that a sermon be grounded in the life of the community, so it is fitting that most sermons are given by the local congregation's own pastor. After all, the sermon is not some general and disembodied religious discourse; it is a particular word to a particular people. The one who preaches the sermon is the same one who earlier sat beside those who were confined to a hospital bed, who joined the youth group on an outing, and who met with a couple trying to mend a frayed and fragile marriage. The sermon may take its final form in the pastor's study, but it has taken shape all week long, in every encounter, in the midst of lives that are shared, and as the pastor asks, "What might the scriptural word have to say to these people I care so much about at this point in our life together?"

Preaching is not a mere intellectual exercise. Discipleship is a demanding journey of the whole person, so the preacher endeavors to provide sustenance for both the head and the heart. The goal of the sermon is not to teach us about Jesus but to equip us to follow Jesus. A sermon can sustain and equip us in various ways: by comforting us in the ways we are afflicted and afflicting us in the ways we have become too comfortable, by helping us see how far the implications of the scripture reach and how close to home they touch down, by enabling us to see the world in new ways and reminding us of old truths we may have neglected, by telling the stories of our lives and the story of God and by pointing out the places at which they converge. In the sermon, the old, old story is renewed once again in the here and now of our lives.

Prayer. We come to worship with the same request the disciples addressed to Jesus: "Teach us to pray." We want to know, not only how to pray, but also what to pray for. It is telling, then, that in Justin's outline of early Christian worship, prayers are offered after the readings from Scripture and the sermon. In a very real sense, it is only then that we know what to pray about. We may bring some prayers with us to worship, but other prayers will take shape as a response to what we have heard in Scripture and the sermon. I have heard it said that a good sermon should make us desperate to pray. Thus, after hearing testimony to God's goodness, we respond with prayers of praise. After recognizing again the dimensions of our need, we respond with prayers of petition. After being reminded of God's hopes for a hurting world, we respond with prayers of intercession. Paul confesses that "we do not know how to pray as we ought, but that very Spirit intercedes" for us (Rom. 8:26). Through worship we submit to the tutelage of the Spirit, inviting the Spirit to shape our desires and give form to our prayers.

It is also worth noting that the people pray immediately before bringing their offerings to the table. Both are ways in which we are invited to make offerings of ourselves in response to the God who has offered us so much.

In the worship Justin described, all stood together to offer prayers. In many churches today, the main prayer in worship is spoken, not by the people, but by the pastor, and so it is called the Pastoral Prayer. But it is decidedly not the "Pastor's Prayer," as if it were the prayer of one person, a prayer to which the rest of the congregation is invited to listen in. Rather, in such a prayer the pastor attempts to speak on behalf of the gathered community. The pastor's task is to gather up the prayers that are nestled silently in the hearts of the people so that those prayers can be given voice. It is a prayer of one voice but many hearts. As we are invited to worship together, so we are invited to pray together—as the community of faith. (For more on prayer, see chap. 10, "Conversing with God.")

Offering. In the worship of the early church, the offering consisted of the people's gifts of bread and wine for the Eucharist. Whatever was not used in the sacrament itself was then distributed, in Justin's words, to "the orphans and the widows, and those who are needy because of sickness or other cause, and the captives, and the strangers who sojourn amongst us."[4]

Today our offerings most often consist of money. The way the offering is received—by passing plates down each pew—sometimes causes people to call it "the collection." But the offering is not simply a matter of "passing the hat" so that the church can pay its bills. Properly understood, the offering is an important and integral part of worship. Having received the gifts of God in worship, we are invited to respond with our own gifts, our offerings of prayer and material goods.

Other religions reflect a distrust of anything material, but Christianity does not. After all, the God we worship came to us in material form in the person of Jesus of Nazareth. God did not seek to help us escape from the world; God chose to transform our lives in the world. It may surprise many to learn that Jesus talked more about money than he did about any other single subject except the realm of God. He talked more about money than about God, more about money than about love, more about money than about moral principles. But, of course, when he talked about money, he was talking about all of those things as well. Jesus consistently pointed to the everyday stuff of life as we know it—seeds, birds, children, money—to demonstrate the ways in which God can be revealed and at work through them.

The offering provides an important link between our lives in worship and our lives in the factory, office, or field. What we pursue all week long, the result of our labors, has a place here—at the altar. We speak of "making a living." It is here that we offer that "living," our very lives, to God as an act of worship. We make an offering of money not because money should not mean anything to us, but because, God knows, it means a great deal to us. An offering of money is an offering of ourselves.

Eucharist. We have already noted the ways in which Christian worship derives from the worship of the synagogue. The Eucharist, however, traces its origins back to another locus of Jewish worship—the dinner table. In Jewish tradition, every meal has religious significance. It is at table that people are bound to God and to one another. Of course, the Passover is the most important meal in the worship of Israel because it is there that the Jews recall and celebrate their Exodus from slavery in Egypt. According to Luke, it was this meal that Jesus shared with the disciples before his death, what we have come to call the Last Supper.

During the first fifteen hundred years of Christian history, the Sunday worship of the church included both preaching and communion. After the Protestant Reformation, however, these two pivotal elements of worship were often divided, almost as if they were divvied up in a divorce settlement. Most Protestant churches tended to focus their worship on the sermon, and they celebrated the sacrament only on occasion. After the Reformation, Roman Catholics continued to celebrate the sacrament every Sunday in their worship, but they relegated the sermon to a minor role. We can be grateful that today that trend seems to be reversing, as both Protestants and Roman Catholics have begun to reclaim the unity of word and table. After all, the two complement each other, much as the words "I love you" and an embrace complement each other. Through the sacrament, we receive a tangible expression of God's love and are nourished in ways that enable us to respond. Without the sermon, there is a danger that the sacrament will float out of its sacred context, becoming a gesture in search of meaning. Without the sacrament, there is a danger that the sermon will engage only our minds, becoming an idea in search of embodiment. The two belong together.

People sometimes suggest that the sacrament of the Lord's Supper should not be celebrated so often that it ceases to be special. But that is a bit like saying that families should not eat together so often that their dinners cease to be special. Sometimes we do things — gather around the family table, gather around God's table, worship — week after week as we patiently wait for the Spirit to infuse our common activities with an uncommon grace.

Sending forth. Before we depart, we receive a blessing, a promise that the same Spirit of God who gathered us as a congregation and ministered to us in our worship will also accompany us as we part. Our days are filled with little rituals of parting. For the most part, we do not give them much thought, such as when we turn out the light in our office and head home for the day. But there are other times when our parting is momentous, such as when we send a loved one on a long and difficult journey or leave a husband's side before he is to be wheeled into surgery. It is then that our parting, tinged with sweet sorrow, points to the sacredness of leave-taking. We say goodbye, a word that means "God be with you."

That is the blessing we receive at the close of worship as well. "God be with you" because, though we do not know what challenges await us in the week ahead, we know that we will need the continued presence of God if we are to confront them faithfully. And "God be with you" because, though we have been strengthened in this time together, we now go our separate ways—with the benediction, the "good word," that we give each other as we part. At the conclusion of our gathering, we seek a final blessing so that we may be equipped to share the love of God that has been shared with us in our worship. That is, after all, why we come to worship. It is not for a brief escape from life or an isolated encounter with God. Rather, we gather as a community of God's people to praise God for who God is, to feast on the presence of Jesus Christ and learn from Jesus, and to be infused with the continuing presence of the Holy Spirit so that we may fulfill the ministries to which God calls us in the world.

Worship as Ritual

The elements of worship outlined by Justin remain largely unchanged more than eighteen centuries later. The same stories are told, the same hymns sung, and our prayers include familiar phrases. We are sent on our way with the usual blessing. At times there is little that is special about our worship, and we can feel as though we are just going through the motions. But even at such times, our worship is not fruitless. The Christian apologist C. S. Lewis observed that, when we carry out religious duties, we are like people digging channels in a waterless land in order that, when the water finally comes, it might find the channels ready.

A routine becomes a ritual at the point at which something of the sacred is revealed. That usually requires many repetitions, which may be why we keep so few rituals in our day. We are impatient; we have so little time. Rituals, however, are not merely discovered or created—they are cultivated. So we can expect that there will be times when our worship will seem like an empty routine because sometimes it is just that, a routine that is as empty as a cup is empty, waiting to be filled. But if we wait with patience, there will be other times when the most adventurous encounter will take place in this setting that is as familiar as our own backyard. It is at such times that we leave worship with Jacob's astonished words on our lips: "Surely, the Lord is in this place; and I did not know it. How awesome is this place! This is none other than the house of God, and this is the gate of heaven" (Gen. 28:16–17).

CHAPTER 8

Baptism with Water and the Spirit

This is how William Willimon describes a baptism in a typical American church in the late twentieth century:

> A young mother phones the church office and asks to have her new baby "done" next Sunday. One of the baby's aunts will be in town that weekend and it would be nice to have her there. The pastor hesitates for a few moments before responding, since he only sees the baby's mother in church occasionally and has yet to meet the father whom the mother describes as "not the church going type." But, since everybody will be in town this weekend and since the pastor feels that he could not begin to explain to the couple why he feels uncomfortable baptizing their baby, the pastor agrees to "do" the baby during the next Sunday's service.
>
> "We're already having a rather full service next Sunday because we're in the middle of our fall stewardship emphasis and the choir has planned two anthems. Maybe we ought simply to do it after the service rather than unduly prolong things," says the pastor. "Oh well, we can wedge the sprinkling in during the first part of the service—before the baby gets restless. You bring her down Sunday."[1]

Baptism was not always done this way. Hippolytus, who lived in the third century and was known as the "chief of the bishops of

Rome," gives a full description of baptism in the early church that reveals some of the differences. Those desiring to be baptized would spend three years as catechumens (that is, "hearers"), during which time they would be guided through an arduous process of instruction and examination. During this period, the primary emphasis was disciplined training into the ethical expectations of the church. It was assumed that entrance into the church necessarily involved a change of lifestyle and behavior. Candidates had to show evidence of conversion (literally, a "turnaround").

During this period, catechumens were allowed to attend the first part of Sunday worship, in which the Scripture was read and the sermon was preached, but they were dismissed before the Lord's Supper, and they were not allowed to pray with the faithful. Almost three years later, catechumens were examined. This examination was not a matter of providing right answers, but of living righteous lives. The elders of the church were interested in knowing if the catechumens were sharing with those in need, visiting the sick, and in other ways fulfilling the demands on those who would follow Jesus. Those who passed the examination were admitted as candidates for baptism.

A few weeks before Easter, the instruction turned from moral instruction to teaching about the gospel. Having been attracted to the life exhibited by those who followed Jesus, the candidates were now invited to drink deeply from the same source. It was a period of intense preparation. They were led in the study of Scripture and explanation of the Apostles' Creed. They fasted regularly. On Good Friday the candidates entered a strict fast that did not end until Easter morning. On Easter Eve, they kept an all-night vigil and received final instructions.

When the sun rose on Easter morning, the candidates were led one by one into a specially designated baptismal room. After one final renunciation of Satan, the candidates were invited, at long last, to enter the deep and still waters of the baptismal pool.

"Do you believe in God?" a deacon of the church would ask.

"I believe in God, the Father Almighty," the candidate would respond, and would then be pushed by the deacon into the enveloping water. Then a second question was asked:

"Do you believe in Jesus Christ?" When the candidate responded, "I believe in Jesus Christ, his only Son our Lord," he or she would again enter the water. Then a final question: "Do you believe in the Holy Spirit?" After the candidate's response, "I believe," he or she would be submerged again.

After emerging from the water, the candidate would be anointed with the "oil of thanksgiving" and would be ushered into a hall where he or she would join the assembled congregation. The bishop (or "overseer") would offer a prayer over the candidate and then introduce him or her to the other members of the church, proclaiming, "Greet your new sister [or brother] in Christ." Then, for the first time, at long last, the candidate would be allowed to join the congregation in exchanging the kiss of peace, in praying, and in celebrating the Eucharist—acts from which the candidate had been excluded until that moment.

The point of juxtaposing these two pictures of baptism—the ancient and the contemporary—is not to suggest that we should try to re-create the baptismal practices of our ancient forebears. While Willimon's depiction could be criticized as being little more than a caricature of modern attitudes toward baptism, something is revealing here. By viewing these two pictures side by side, we cannot help but wonder if something of the meaning and significance of baptism has been lost along the way. Indeed, in recent years the Christian church has been rediscovering some of the deep and manifold dimensions of this sacrament.

What Is a Sacrament?

Before we consider the sacrament of baptism in more depth, it would be helpful to consider what we mean by the term "sacrament." It would be difficult to improve on the classic medieval definition of a sacrament as "a visible sign of an invisible grace." A sacrament is a communal act of the church through which God's love is made visible. Such uncommon love is made visible through the common stuff of life. In baptism, the love of God is made visible in something as common yet precious as water.

The origins of baptism are not entirely clear. We know that some-one named John baptized Jesus when he was an adult, and we can assume that the practice probably did not originate with the one who came to be known as John the Baptist. Although we do not have any records of Jewish baptisms in the first century, we know that the Jews did eventually baptize converts, and it is unlikely that they would have adopted a solely Christian practice. Therefore, like the Lord's Supper (and, indeed, like so much of what we think of as Christian tradition), baptism probably has its origins in Jewish practice. Jewish baptism was reinterpreted and given a central role in the life of the church because Jesus himself was baptized. It is the baptism of Jesus in which Christians are invited to share.

Churches in the Reformed tradition recognize two sacraments: baptism and the Lord's Supper. In recognizing those two, we are not declaring that those are the only ways in which God's love can be made visible. Rather, such designation reminds us that these are the two rites of the church that Jesus himself instituted by his partici-pation in them. We have no record that Jesus himself baptized any-one else; but we do know that he was baptized, and that in his final commission he told his disciples to "go ... and make disciples of all nations, baptizing them in the name of the Father and of the Son and of the Holy Spirit" (Matt. 28:19).

When we try to use words alone to describe the meaning of bap-tism, we find that we are attempting the impossible. The nature of a sacrament is such that words alone are never sufficient. The dancer Martha Graham once completed an inspired performance and was approached backstage by an admirer. "Miss Graham," she said, "that dance was wonderful. Can you tell me what it means?" "Honey," Gra-ham replied, still out of breath, "if I could tell you I wouldn't have had to dance it." The same could be said of a sacrament. If words alone were sufficient, the sacrament would not be necessary. The nature of a sacrament is such that nothing can convey its meaning as well as the sacrament itself. It's true that words as well as acts are used in performing a sacrament. But neither words nor acts can stand alone. In a sacrament, words and acts work together to help us express and experience the deeper spiritual realities that cannot be plumbed fully with words or acts alone. The New Testament writers use a variety of ways to describe what happens in baptism. No one image is sufficient, but considered together, they trace some of the dimensions of what is revealed and offered in the sacrament itself.

Baptism as Union with Jesus Christ

Water is such a rich symbolic image because it can mean different, even paradoxical, things. For instance, water is a sign of life. Water that covers a parched field brings life. Even a child who pauses to drink from a hose in the back yard on a hot summer afternoon knows that we cannot go long without water. Indeed, nothing can live without water. But water can also be a source of death. Water that is welcome on a dry and crusty field can rise to the point that it becomes a dangerous flood, covering the earth in a smothering blanket. The same child who needs a drink of water to continue her play will be warned about playing too close to the lake.

The water used in baptism contains both dimensions—the threat of death and the promise of life—but in a special way. In baptism, Christians share in the life, death, and resurrection of Jesus. Paul expressed these dimensions of the mystery of baptism to the Christians in Rome in this way:

> Do you not know that all of us who have been baptized into Christ Jesus were baptized into his death? We were buried therefore with him by baptism into death, so that as Christ was raised from the dead by the glory of the Father, we too might walk in newness of life. (Rom. 6:3-5)

In baptism we are bound to Jesus in such a way that we die with him and rise with him. This understanding has many implications. For instance, the promise of baptism is not that our lives will be free of burdens. Rather, in baptism we are invited to share in the life of Jesus, which was ultimately triumphant, but not before he encountered tremendous burdens of suffering, and even death, along the way. The life of a Christian, then, is nothing less than the reenactment of the death and resurrection of Jesus. Baptism is a way of binding our lives to the life of Jesus so that his story can become our story.

What comes first in baptism is God's action. It is God who unites with us, and not we who unite ourselves to God. In the baptism of infants, this may be especially clear. Before the infant knows how to call on God, God provides for the child. Before the child recognizes that this collection of strange faces is the community of faith, God welcomes the child there. Even before the child understands the name of Jesus, the child is bound to him. Although the primacy of God's action in baptism may be clearest with a child, it is no less true in the baptism of an adult. Baptism is a way of signifying God's claim on us, and it is not dependent on any response from us. Before we have any opportunity to demonstrate our love of God, God offers unconditional love to us.

It is in baptism that God makes a claim on us by binding us to Jesus. The rest of our days are an opportunity to live out the implications of our baptism, to learn who we are already through baptism, people who are marked indelibly by the sign of the cross. That is, by baptism we are made into Christians and then spend the rest of our lives learning to live the Christian way of life. The promise offered by God may or may not be fulfilled in our lives, but the promise remains.

Since it is God's gracious action that is foremost in baptism, no one need be baptized more than once. God's promise, once given, need not be repeated. Martin Luther, in a moment of despair, reminded himself: "I am baptized, and through my baptism God, who cannot lie, has bound himself in covenant with me." What God has promised will not be taken from us. Our baptism is active and powerful even if our lives carry no visible sign of the waters that have marked us. That is why Luther was also able to affirm that "there is no greater comfort on earth than baptism."[2]

Initiation into the Church

Baptism is a rite full of promises. It starts with the recognition of God's promise of faithfulness to the one who is baptized. If that one is an infant, the parents promise to raise the child in the Christian faith and the fellowship of the church. An adult who is to be baptized will promise allegiance to the God we know as Father, Son, and Holy Spirit, and will further promise to serve that God through the church. The church, in turn, promises to receive and nurture the one who is baptized so that the promises made in baptism may be fulfilled within the community of faith. That is, through baptism we are not only bound to God but also to one another.

Of all the promises that are offered at baptism, in our time this last promise is the one that is most often misunderstood, sometimes lost entirely. People sometimes request a "private" baptism, as if baptism were something that is between one person or one family and God. Or, even if a baptism is performed as a part of corporate worship, the congregation sometimes is treated like an assembly of interested but distant spectators. These practices obscure an important aspect of baptism—that it is, among other things, initiation into a community of faith. It has been observed that "a Christian alone is a contradiction." Baptism asks the church to make a vow: "Do you who witness and celebrate this sacrament, promise your love, support, and care to the ones about to be baptized as they live and grow in Christ?"[3] To be baptized without the church's full participation makes about as much sense as having a wedding without the groom.

In many ways, the vows made in baptism are similar to the marriage vows. In baptism the church promises to be faithful to the one baptized—"in sickness and in health, in plenty and in want, in joy and in sorrow, as long as we both shall live." To be sure, in baptism we do not choose the ones to whom we are bound. But they are called into the church as we were called into the church, and we are stuck with them. We may have nothing in common with one another—nothing, that is, except the only thing that matters, a willingness to follow and serve Jesus and to do so together. We promise our faithfulness to the ones we are stuck with as a reminder of the love of a God who is stuck with us all.

Let us change the metaphor. When someone is baptized, he or she is received into the church as a new child is received into a family, with all the joys and added responsibilities that such a relationship entails. And the family we are received into encompasses the whole Christian church. People will sometimes say, "I was baptized Roman Catholic," or "I was baptized in the United Church of Christ." But no one is baptized in the name of the Roman Catholic Church or the name of the United Church of Christ. Rather, they are baptized in the name of Christ into Christ's church universal. To be baptized is to be received into Christ's family, which includes Christians of every belief and practice.

Although I would not want to diminish the importance of the vows that parents make in baptism, the promises made by the church take precedence. In baptism, we are called to recognize that our true family is not the one into which we were born, but the one into which we are initiated, the church. In this family, water is thicker than blood. John Westerhoff has summarized this understanding by saying, "In baptism our parents give us up for adoption to the church."

These may sound like stark words to those of us who are used to thinking of baptism as a rite for the biological family in which the congregation plays the role of an audience. We might wonder how many baptisms would be performed if churches and families fully realized the implications of their promises. The baptismal waters are deep indeed—and not without threat. But there is a great, enfolding promise here as well. After a baptism in one church I served, someone in the congregation said to me, "You know, by the time you finished, I thought that if you needed to hand that child over to me to raise, it would be all right." It was certainly a rare response, but she is one person who knew what she was doing when she participated in the baptism of that child as part of the community of faith.

Christians who lived in other times and places did not need to be reminded that the vows of baptism carry a high price and a decisive break with old allegiances. For instance, those who lived in imperial Rome knew that to call oneself a Christian was a momentous thing, that to be baptized in the name of Christ and initiated into the church was to be set apart from the world. It meant, among other things, claiming an allegiance that could get you killed as an enemy of the state.

But things are different for us. A form of nominal Christianity has so permeated our culture that we do not always recognize what a momentous and powerful thing it is to be baptized in the name of Christ. Why does the church need to emphasize that baptism is initiation into a distinctive community of faith, or to take upon itself the nurture of someone into the Christian faith, when that community is so closely allied with the surrounding culture? In imperial Rome, Christians knew that if people were going to learn the Christian story and experience Christian community, it would have to happen within the church, because it surely wasn't going to happen anywhere else. In imperial Rome, Christians also received continual—and sometimes difficult—reminders that they had joined a distinct community that was set apart from the culture at large. In America, far from feeling set apart, most Christians are able to just blend in. In our culture, therefore, it is especially important that we be reminded of the fuller implications of the vows we make in baptism.

We may marvel that the Roman Christians were willing to risk their lives for their faith. But in a different way, we also risk our lives when we seek to be baptized. And we do nothing less than risk the lives of our children when we baptize them. We may not fear the civil authorities, but, though we are free to entrust our lives or our children's lives to anyone or anything, we risk turning to Jesus and saying: "We are yours. Our children are yours. Let us be baptized in your name. May we bear the sign of the cross forever!"

New Birth

Another important aspect of baptism is expressed in the image of new birth. Baptism is a return to the womb, a chance to start over again. As once God "knit me together in my mother's womb" (Ps. 139:13), in baptism the torn fragments of my life are knit together yet again. We approach the water of baptism as if we are returning to the life-giving waters of the womb, to receive the gift of life. When we emerge from the womb, dripping and blinking, we take on the family name. When we emerge from the baptismal waters, we are named and claimed by God. In baptism, besides receiving our "given names," we also take on the name of our new extended family, the name "Christian." Of course, God is at work in both of our births, but in baptism God offers the gift of a birth that is continually renewed.

The image of new birth may seem to hold less power for those who are still fresh from their mothers' wombs. That is, we may wonder what such an image means for those who are yet infants. When, as a pastor, I met with a family about the upcoming baptism of a child, the part of the baptism service that always elicited the most questions was the affirmation that baptism offers new life and forgiveness of sins. What point is there in offering new life to a child whose old life is still quite new? Why talk of forgiveness of sins in reference to an infant, who has not yet had any opportunity for sin?

We can have such questions answered only by remembering that baptism is a one-time gift that extends through time, not only back into the past, but also forward into the future. Its promise reaches from the day of baptism into all of our days. The gift of new life may not mean all that much to an infant, but in time it will; and when that time comes, the gift will still be there, as fresh and new as the day it was offered. Likewise, we may not see that an infant has any need for forgiveness. We see no evidence of sin in the child. But it's there all right, a tiny hidden seed, even from the beginning. And one day, when the need for forgiveness becomes evident, the baptized person can recall the continually renewed promise of baptism that was offered one day when the child seemed not to need it and is still present when he or she needs it most.

It is no mere coincidence that in baptism we recall the legend of Noah and the flood. Both baptism and the flood involve water, of course; and they both remind us that all of us stand in need of God's cleansing. In the age of Noah, God became discouraged because "the wickedness of humankind was great in the earth, and . . . their hearts [were] only evil continually" (Gen. 6:5). Noah and his family were spared because they seemed like decent folks, caught up in a violent world they did not create. So when they were safely aboard the ark, God sent a flood that immersed the whole world in a cleansing bath, so new life could begin in the watery womb called earth.

When the flood was finally over, this little family, this last little remnant of the human race, left the ark. While they were still wobbling around on their sea legs, God said: "I am establishing my covenant with you," that is, "I am committing myself to you. I am going to stick with you no matter what. And, as I am my witness, I am never going to do that again. In fact, I am going to give myself a reminder of my promise. I am more sick of violence than anyone, so I will be the first to lay down my arms. I am going to hang my bow in the sky. It will arch across the heavens. You will call it a 'rainbow.' I know there will be times when you will disappoint me again, and I may even be tempted to send another flood, but when I gather the clouds together, this bow in the sky will remind me of this promise. It will be like a string on my finger to remind me, only more beautiful, and you will be able to see it, too."

In baptism, God again says, "Let's start over, but this time let's do it one person at a time." In the flood God confronted sin by threatening death; in baptism God confronts sin by offering new life. We can now wade into the same waters that, according to the legend, swept away our ancient forebears because Jesus has gone before us and calls to us: "Come on in—the water's fine. It has been blessed by my presence. The seed of violence and corruption may still be in your heart, God knows. But if I am there also, I will prevail. My forgiveness is more persistent than anything you can do. Go wherever you will, do whatever you will, try as you might to abandon me—I will never leave your side. You are mine."

When we emphasize the importance of baptism as a symbol of new birth and forgiveness, troubling questions sometimes arise: What about those who are never baptized? Are they outside the circle of God's care? Is someone who dies before being baptized denied God's forgiveness? Those who work in hospital nurseries are accustomed to requests for "emergency baptisms" from anxious parents who do not want a sick child to die before receiving the benefits of baptism. It is important here to be reminded that baptism is not some form of magic. It is a visible sign of an invisible grace. To say that baptism is a visible way in which God's love is expressed and experienced does not mean that God withholds such love from those who are not baptized. God's persistent love is not so easily thwarted. Baptism is an important way, but it is not the only way, through which we can experience that love.

Reception of the Holy Spirit

On the day of Pentecost, when the gift of the Holy Spirit was manifest so powerfully and mysteriously, many bystanders asked Peter how they should respond. Peter replied, "Repent, and be baptized every one of you in the name of Jesus Christ so that your sins may be forgiven; and you will receive the gift of the Holy Spirit" (Acts 2:38). In this rite full of promises, we are offered the Holy Spirit as a continuing presence in our lives. In Genesis we read that, in the beginning of creation, the Spirit of God "swept over the face of the waters" (Gen. 1:2). At Christ's baptism, the same Spirit descended on him like a dove, and in some way it does in each baptism.

It is through the gift of the Holy Spirit that God can be at work in our lives. God not only acted in dim history, but through the Holy Spirit is also acting today. God not only created the world, but through the Holy Spirit can also be a creative presence in our own lives. God is not only distant and awesome, but through the Holy Spirit is as close as our own breath. All of this is part of what it means to receive the Holy Spirit at baptism.

What we speak of as the gift of the Holy Spirit is actually many gifts. This is reflected in the many names used in Scripture to describe the Holy Spirit. The Holy Spirit is called the "Counselor," teaching us and leading us to a faithful and abundant life; the "Comforter," picking us up when we fall and quieting our restless hearts; and the "Spirit of Christ," the agent of Christ's continuing presence in the world and in our lives. The Holy Spirit is also the active agent at work in the church, informing and enlivening the life of the community of faith. When people are baptized, they are received into the church as full of promise, the many-faceted promise that derives from the promise of the Holy Spirit. (For more on the Holy Spirit, see chap. 4, "The Continuing Presence of the Holy Spirit.")

Some traditions, often called "Pentecostal" traditions, distinguish between baptism with water and baptism in the Holy Spirit. They recognize two kinds of baptism, one with water and one with "fire and the Holy Spirit." In most Christian churches, however, we understand baptism as a unified event in which the Holy Spirit is active, sweeping over the face of the baptismal waters, descending like a dove, infusing our lives in subtle and powerful ways.

Baptism and Confirmation

Baptism and confirmation were not always divided. The term "confirmation" originally referred to the bishop's anointing and laying hands on candidates after they had been baptized. First the candidates were baptized. Then they were brought to the bishop to have their baptisms confirmed. Later, when bishops became overseers of multiple congregations, people were baptized by the local priests, and only later were these baptisms confirmed by the bishop when he visited the local parish. The medieval church made confirmation a separate rite and, in some instances, a sacrament in itself. It was reserved for the time of "discretion"—that is, for the age when children are able to make faith declarations for themselves. Protestant Reformers expanded this understanding and approached confirmation as an opportunity to instruct Christian youth. They devised catechisms through which youth could memorize the basic tenets of the Christian faith. Those who successfully completed their study could have their baptisms confirmed. Eventually, confirmation became the means through which one was received into full participation in the life of the church.

This history (which is more complex than a brief summary can indicate) has created a number of unintended and unfortunate results. When baptism and confirmation are viewed as distinct rites, the meaning of both baptism and confirmation are compromised. For instance, we might wonder about the status of those who have been baptized but not yet confirmed. When baptism and confirmation are divided, baptism can become a kind of provisional act conferring a brand of halfway membership. But James White, an authority on Christian worship, insists: "When God acts, it is not halfway or preparatory. God's acts are unqualified self-giving."[4]

Likewise, when confirmation is understood apart from baptism, the emphasis is mistakenly placed on a confirmand's qualifications rather than on God's unqualified gift. In such an understanding, confirmation becomes an intellectual exercise to test a candidate's grasp of a body of knowledge. Again, White describes the confusion that developed: "The sacramental sense of laying on of hands as a gracious act of God became dissipated in favor of a graduation exercise."[5] Perceiving confirmation as a kind of graduation has some common and unfortunate consequences. For one thing, church members often cease formal study of the Christian faith at the time when they are best able to understand and appreciate it in its fuller dimensions— that is, when they enter adulthood.

In some Christian traditions, infants are not baptized. Such traditions baptize only those who can make the baptismal vows for themselves through what is sometimes called "believer baptism." In such traditions, the role of confirmation is subsumed in the sacrament. Nevertheless, infants are not left totally without the benefits of some initiation into the church. They are offered to God while parents and congregation make their vows through a rite of "dedication." In other traditions, infants are baptized, and then they are confirmed at the age of discretion, often at young adolescence—that is, roughly at the age when their counterparts in other traditions are baptized as believers. Something can be said in favor of both traditions, but certain theological cracks develop in both as well. As a general rule, the traditions that practice believer baptism struggle to explain the meaning of the rite of dedication, while the traditions that baptize infants struggle to explain just what confirmation means.

One thing unites us all. Both responses are ways in which we act out the understanding that there are at least two passages that need to be ritualized within the life of the church. One is the passage into life and life within the church. The other is the passage into adulthood as a believing Christian. In some traditions the former passage is ritualized through dedication, in others through baptism; in some traditions the latter passage is ritualized through baptism, in others through confirmation.

The practice of infant baptism makes clear that we are welcomed into the church, not because of our faith, but because of God's actions. In baptism we claim not that we have grasped God, but that God has taken hold of our lives. We put our trust not in our love of God, but in God's love for us. We baptize any who stand in need of God's grace. There is, therefore, no right time to be baptized. God's unqualified gift, of which we stand in need at every hour, is available to us at any hour. Children and their grandparents can be received into full membership in the church through the same baptism because we all stand before the baptismal waters as newborn children of God.

In this understanding, confirmation becomes yet another occasion for all the members of the congregation to affirm their baptism, to rejoice in the baptismal promises, perhaps made long ago, to recommit themselves to continued growth into full Christian faith and discipleship, and to stand together as a company of people who are all marked with the sign of the cross. There may be particular times in the lives of individuals or the life of the church when it seems particularly appropriate to join in affirmation of our baptism. That is, there are still good reasons for inviting young adolescents to affirm their baptism through the rite of confirmation. But, just as there is no one right time to be baptized, there is no one right time to affirm our baptism. As we stand in constant need of God's grace, we are offered continual opportunity to affirm the baptism that extends such grace to us.

CHAPTER 9

Eating at Christ's Table

When private remembrance seeks expression, it is usually in the form of words. We talk about those we remember, but our talk is not only a way of releasing our memories, not simply a matter of opening the cage for our memories and letting them fly on the wings of words. Rather, talk enlivens our memories, making them all the more real and all the more ours.

We talk of those we have known, not just because we remember them, but also in order to remember them more fully. Do you remember the way she would peer over her glasses when she was doing needlework? Or how she could never tell a joke without laughing before she got to the punch line? Remember that ratty old sweater he used to wear? Or how he used to gather us in the kitchen when he was cooking because he was always more interested in talk than in food? Or how about that story he used to tell about the dog and the porcupine? How did that go again?

Memories in stories, memories in words—that is much of what the Christian faith is. Do you remember what Jesus said? Or how about the day he was sitting by the well? These are memories that are given expression in words, memories given continued life through words and shared with us so that we, too, might share in the remembrance. Yet if memories are deep, and if they have a hold on us in a powerful and personal way, they will soon be beyond the power of words to express, even as the most profound experiences in life are beyond the reach of words. If our memories are powerful, they simply outgrow words, and we long for something more than a story, something that looks and feels more like life itself. Beyond reading the travelogue, we want in some way to make the journey again. We want to do something.

In this connection, I think of fishing, of all things. For me, a person who usually strives to use my hours productively, fishing is a most improbable way to spend an afternoon. But fishing means something special to me because I used to fish with my father. Now everything about it reminds me of him: the sound of the tackle box when I carry it, the smell of the box when I open it, the distant splash of the lure after a long cast, the intent fisherman's stare at the surface of the water. One day, soon after my father's death, I took an afternoon off and went fishing. I could have spent the afternoon talking about my father, telling stories, reading old letters. But in some mysterious way, this was something more. Words are not always enough. Do this in remembrance. Do this because you remember. Do this in order to remember.

Memorial Meal and More

When Jesus gathered with his disciples for a meal in the upper room of a friend's home, they were mindful of the mighty events swirling around them that evening, and they had a sense of foreboding about the future. But they also gathered out of a remembrance of things past. According to Luke, it was a Passover meal that they shared, the traditional Jewish commemoration of the deliverance from slavery in Egypt.

At the Passover feast, a child asks the elders, "Why is this night special above all other nights?" The father responds with words of remembrance:

We were Pharaoh's slaves in Egypt, and the Lord our God brought us forth from there with a mighty and outstretched arm. And if the Holy One, blessed be he, had not brought our forefathers forth from Egypt, then we, our children, and our children's children would still be Pharaoh's slaves in Egypt.... And the more one tells the story of the departure from Egypt, the more praiseworthy he is.

Then the gathered family members remember by doing. They pass bitter herbs to remember the bitterness of slavery. They eat lamb in haste, as though they are fugitives on the run from their pursuers. They break unleavened bread, like the bread that was packed for the journey—before it had a chance to rise. Every element of the meal prompts memories of the Exodus, and the table is a place to remember.

It was this Passover meal that Jesus shared with the disciples, setting it in the context of God's saving history and adding a new chapter by saying that, from now on, part of what will be remembered is this very night (the Last Supper). From now on, those who gather around this table to remember God's loving acts will always remember Jesus and the particular ways Jesus revealed this same God to them. I think Jesus knew how important it would be for the disciples to have something more than stories. Jesus wanted to give them something to do in remembrance. And what Jesus chose was a meal, a simple meal, something they had shared many times and would share many times after Jesus was gone. By choosing such an everyday event, Jesus gave his followers ample opportunity to remember. This was also a way of reminding them that he would be with them throughout their days, even the most mundane of Thursdays, through the most simple and common of activities.

As Jesus's old friends gather, joined by other friends, even joined by you and me, all can remember by doing: remember the way the bread crumbles when it is broken; remember the warmth of sitting shoulder to shoulder with those who share the meal; remember the glow of the lamp, the tang of the wine. Do this in remembrance of me.

Many people throughout Christian history have seen this as the power in the sacrament of Christ's table: a memorial meal given its power through the power of memory. Remember what Christ said and did. We have many words for this sacramental meal, and this fact in itself reveals our understanding that the sacrament has many dimensions. Although different terms can be properly used, each one emphasizes a different dimension of the sacrament, another dimension of understanding, reminding us that no single designation can completely capture its meaning.

The Eucharist

We often say that we celebrate the sacrament of Christ's table. But what does the word "celebrate" usually connote? We celebrate a birthday with a festive dinner, colorful decorations, and heaps of laughter. We celebrate a victory on the playing field with locker-room hoopla and popping champagne bottles. We celebrate an anniversary with a toast and a smile of remembrance. We celebrate Christmas with songs sung heartily, even if not well. And through these and other celebrations, there is a sense of gratitude that spills over into thanksgiving, and a joy that often mocks our attempts to remain dignified—that is, we have fun at celebrations.

In most of our churches, our celebration of the sacrament of Christ's table differs from others we are familiar with. We do perform this sacrament with a keen sense of ceremony, which is a part of all celebrations, even the most raucous. But there the similarity between this celebration and other celebrations seems to end. In contrast to our other celebrations, the celebration of this sacrament in most churches ranges from muted to grim.

In a way, of course, this is easy to understand. Part of what we remember around the table are the solemn events surrounding the Last Supper. And that can and should be cause for some serious reflection. *Last*. It is a serious word under any circumstances—and especially so here. Our minds race with the implications. This was the last supper before Jesus was betrayed—betrayed by a friend, betrayed for money—a betrayal that led to his death, an ugly death, a death of hope and of goodness, and the death of us as well. We remember all the ways we would have betrayed Jesus and do still betray him in our own lives, killing him in our own ways, as surely as any person who is denied or ignored is in some way killed.

If people unfamiliar with Christian practice were to walk into one of our churches while we are celebrating this sacrament, they might conclude that they have stumbled in on a wake. The people are deep in thought, heads bowed, faces signaling remorse mixed with something resembling shame, as we pass the bread and wine without looking one another in the eye. And the stranger to this tradition would not be wrong. In a very real sense, that is what we are doing: it is, in part, a kind of memorial service in which we are remembering the death of Jesus.

Another reason for the dour looks on people's faces is that they can feel unworthy to approach this table. And in a way they are right: none of us is worthy. We have no claims on the gifts of this table. But in another way this attitude misses the whole point of the sacrament. It is not about how good or bad we've been; rather, it is about God's goodness. When we are invited to this table, we may ask the host, "What may I bring?" But the answer is always the same: "Nothing but yourselves." It's a come-as-you-are party. We may assume that we need to bring our best selves or not come at all; instead, we are invited to bring our true selves, just as we are, because God supplies the rest. We come to the table not because we have perfect lives to offer, but because we are all too aware of our imperfections and seek to have our lives transformed.

We might hesitate to come to the table because we have denied Jesus in our own ways; but then we recall that Jesus invited Peter to the table. We might think that our doubts disqualify us, but then we remember that the promise of the table was extended to the likes of Thomas. Everyone who sat at the Last Supper with Jesus was unworthy in his own way. That has not changed. But Jesus's invitation hasn't changed either: it is still extended to the unworthy, and that means there is a place set for us.

Our celebrations of this sacrament, it's true, are in part a solemn commemoration of Jesus's Last Supper. We take our place at the table of betrayal and death. But that is not the end of it, not by a long shot. There are times when it is neither advisable nor possible to imagine ourselves at the table on that fateful night. We close our eyes to imagine again being in the dark, but the light is so bright that we can still see it. After all, unlike the disciples who were present on that occasion, we know how the story ends. It ends not in defeat but in triumph, not with Good Friday but with Easter. The meal itself was transposed from a minor key to a major key when it was celebrated with the risen Christ. Sometimes we cannot begin to pretend that we do not know how the story ends. At such times, the sacrament becomes a resurrection meal.

The evangelist Billy Sunday used to say that most Christians have just enough religion to make themselves miserable. By that he meant that we have just enough religion to know how much we fall short, how often we stumble, how continually we betray God. But to end there is not only tragedy, it is heresy, for it ignores both the end of the story and the point of the story, which is that our God is the kind of God who always insists on having the last word. We celebrate at this table because the Last Supper was not the last word.

One of the terms we use to describe the sacrament of Christ's table reminds us of the celebratory aspect of the sacrament: the word "Eucharist," which means "thanksgiving." The term derives from the thanks Jesus offered to God before breaking the bread at his last meal with the disciples. Halford Luccock, who taught homiletics at Yale Divinity School for many years, was commenting on this name for the sacrament when he wrote:

> Death might be outside the door, but God was inside the door. Jesus's reliance on his [God] was so complete that there was no occasion which did not call for thanksgiving. Where trust like his prevails, one can be thankful in any amazement.[1]

So the word "Eucharist" not only connotes the words Jesus said, but also the attitude he demonstrated—an attitude of thanksgiving. Under the circumstances, that was striking indeed, for Jesus gave thanks even as he was facing the worst that life has to offer. Thanks for the company of the table, which includes his friends and also God, who is not only inside the door but also residing in his heart. Thanks for a life that, despite all the trials and inconsistencies, is still uncommonly good. Thanks for the promises of God that will not go unfulfilled.

Communion

If creatures unfamiliar with our way of life were to observe our strange human ways, I think one of the things that would strike them as most curious about us is the way we share meals together. Much of our lives we share around dining tables. We may sometimes eat a quick sandwich in our office to save time or run off to the nearest fast-food restaurant for a simple refueling, but mostly we seek out one another at mealtimes. People who live alone often report that eating alone is the hardest thing of all. Those who travel extensively in their work report the same thing. I know that when I go into a restaurant alone, it feels great to be able to say, "I'm going to be joined by a friend in a moment," and there is a feeling of emptiness if I have to say that I am eating alone that day.

I once worked with a man who always said at lunch time, "Well, it's time to tie on the old feedbag," which sounds about as solitary as you can get. Nevertheless, I soon realized that this was his way of invitation. He was inviting those around him to tie on a feedbag with him so that he would not have to eat alone. After all, at a meal we can be nourished by so much more than food. See whether any of these additional invitations sound familiar.

- "It's been an age since we've seen each other. Why don't we get together for lunch next week?"
- "Our anniversary is coming up. Let's say we make reservations at that new restaurant."
- "We want to welcome you to the neighborhood, so we thought we'd have a few people over to our house for dinner."

In all of these instances, food and physical nourishment are certainly not our primary objective and need. We seek and expect so much more. For reasons that may never be entirely clear, we feel closer to one another while eating. In this sense, every meal is a communion, a communion with one another that is unlike what we experience through any other activity.

It seems fitting that, in that ominous hour before being betrayed,

Jesus said, "I have earnestly desired to eat this Passover with you before I suffer." Let's sing a grace together once more. Let's talk about the events of the day—as well as of things eternal—once more. Let's laugh at Peter's tall fishing tales and feel ourselves shoulder to shoulder just one last time—as close as we can be. Jesus earnestly desired this kind of closeness and communion with the disciples.

In a passage early in the book of Acts, Luke gives us a few snapshots of the early church. His description is so brief, and his tone so matter of fact, that it is easy to miss the full impact of what he is reporting. Some of what he describes seems familiar and not too earth-shattering. He says that the apostles taught the people, they had fellowship, and they prayed together. Then, in quick succession, Luke observes three startling characteristics of the early church in that same matter-of-fact manner. For one, he says, "many wonders and signs were done through the apostles." That is, miracles were performed by the apostles, and people were healed by them. In the very next verse he says that the members of the early church had all things in common. That is, they sold their possessions and goods and distributed them to anyone who had need. The third wondrous characteristic of the early church is that members ate together: "Day by day . . . they broke bread at home and ate their food with glad and generous hearts, praising God" (Acts 2:43-47).

What we have here is a record of the first church potluck suppers. ("If your last name begins with A–L, bring a loaf of bread; if it begins with M–Z, bring a jug of wine.") Now, to us that may not sound very startling. A shared meal? It's a simple thing. But Luke mentions it as one of the miracles of the early church, a sign of the very presence of God. He does so because the early church was made up of people who normally would not have anything to do with each other. They were slave and slave owner, Jew and Gentile, male and female, tax collector and pillar of the synagogue—all sharing the intimacy and familiarity of a dining table. They did not choose each other, but God chose them all and called them to the common table. They had nothing in common except the only thing that matters, a common allegiance to Jesus Christ. It is a powerful witness that was not lost on Luke.

Something like that still happens every time Christians gather around Christ's table. It is still a sign and a wonder that the broken and scattered pieces of humanity are able to commune with one another. I was particularly struck by this one Sunday. As I stood at the communion table and invited the congregation to join in the sacrament, I noticed, scattered about the sanctuary, a mother and the boy who had just gotten her daughter pregnant, a divorced wife and husband, a doctor and the patient who was threatening to sue him for malpractice. At this table, those who have little in common are invited to share this common meal, those who would otherwise prefer not to have anything to do with one another eat together. It is not normal; actually, it's quite startling. It is as peculiar as the ways of Jesus, whose meal this is. The brokenness of our lives may remain, but in this meal we are invited to offer our brokenness to the host of this meal, the one who was willing to share our brokenness that we might know healing and wholeness.

Though the sacrament we sometimes call communion is more than a mere meal, it is also that. It is around a communion table, like the other tables around which we gather, that we confront our most basic needs. For one, we need food. Frederick Buechner observes: "Man does not live by bread alone, but he also does not live long without it."[2] It is around a dining table that we actively recognize our need for the blessings of God's earth, as symbolized by the bread and cup. It is here that we also confront our tenuous, human vulnerability, for without these God-given gifts of food and drink, we will surely perish.

But no less than food, we need one another. We need to have times when we are gathered together. It is this aspect of the meal that is highlighted by the term "communion." In some way, we are communing with God—God's Spirit enlivening our hearts. But we are also communing with one another. The communal aspect of this meal can be easily lost, especially in those places of worship where we are served the elements as we sit in rows of pews. When the pews of a sanctuary are all set in the same direction, our celebrations can easily lose this communal aspect and become what I have come to think of as worship in an elevator. Everyone in an elevator faces the same direction, and no one dares look at another. A friend of mine used to refuse to play along with this unspoken elevator etiquette. When he got into an elevator, he would face the back. He would look people in the eyes and smile at them. His behavior made the other people in the elevator nervous: you are not supposed to do that in an elevator. When you come into a place where pews are bolted down and all facing the same direction, you can get the idea that you're not supposed to look at each other there either, even when celebrating something called communion. In such settings, we resemble more the unrelated and isolated parties sitting at a lunch counter, looking straight ahead, not needing to—indeed, not being able to—look into the faces of those around them.

In one church I served, when we first started passing a loaf of bread in addition to the precut cubes of bread during our communion service, I noticed that the loaf would often come back untouched. At first I chalked it up to the force of habit. But then one day I decided to watch people receive the elements, and I observed another reason: it is next to impossible to tear a piece of bread off a whole loaf unless someone holds the plate for you. Holding a serving plate for the person next to you is something we do naturally around a dinner table—but not, it seems, in the pew. I think the reason is that, in order to do so, we would have to look at—and perhaps even say a word to—another person. In other words, holding the plate for another person would interject an unfamiliar communal aspect to our communion, like facing the wrong direction in an elevator.

Sometimes the elements of the sacrament are laid on an altar. When an altar is used, we are reminded of the great costliness of Christ's sacrificial life. As lambs were once brought to an altar to offer to God, now the one John the Baptist called the "Lamb of God who takes away the sins of the world" (John 1:29) is sacrificed on an altar for the sake of the people.

When communion is celebrated at a table and people are gathered around it, a different dimension of the sacrament is revealed. Sitting shoulder to shoulder, they are reminded that communion is, in part, communion with one another. An individual supplicant may approach an altar, but a table can be spread with food and still seem empty if it is not encircled by a community of people. A table invites us to take our place with others. Around the table of communion, we are reminded that the Christian community is not a loose gathering of individuals approaching God in one another's presence. Rather, we are more like the family that has been invited to share our lives around the dinner table. When we take our place at such a table, we discover that we are drawn together with sisters and brothers, some of whom we have yet to meet. The very symbols we use remind us of this: "The wheat that is gathered to make one loaf and the grapes that are pressed to make one cup remind participants that they are one in the body of Christ, the church."[3]

The Lord's Supper

Through the centuries, there have been people who have testified that something else is at work in this simple meal, something beyond the power of memory to bestow, something more than an opportunity to commune with the family of faith. There is an additional dimension to this sacrament, a mysterious something extra. Some depart from Christ's table and report that they have been fed, as if by a feast, though the table is only set with a few crumbs of bread. Some proclaim that they have had their spirits soaked with the spirit of Jesus Christ, though there is hardly enough in the cup to quench a common thirst. If the word "communion" emphasizes the horizontal aspect of the sacrament, reminding us of the ways it draws us toward one another, the term "Lord's Supper" emphasizes the vertical aspect of the sacrament, reminding us that we are drawn into the living presence of Christ. People have come to the table to remember a presence and remember a relationship. But there's more: people have found at that same table an opportunity to experience a presence and enter into a continuing relationship.

Many attempts have been made to explain this mystery. As careful and learned as these explanations may be, none of them is entirely satisfactory. The early church simply affirmed that the risen Christ was with them at their celebrations of the Lord's Supper, but during the Middle Ages there were laborious attempts to explain how and when Christ was present in the sacrament. It was during that period that complicated philosophical theories such as transubstantiation were offered. Transubstantiation is the belief that somehow the very substance of the bread and wine is transformed into the substance of the flesh and blood of Christ, even though the outward appearance of the bread and wine remain unchanged. The medieval church began to affirm that, when the priest lifts the host and says, *Hoc est corpus meum* ("this is my body"), the bread is miraculously transformed into the physical presence of Christ.

Protestant Reformers, while they affirmed Christ's presence at the church's celebrations of the sacrament, were disturbed by such interpretations. To them, such interpretations reduced the sacrament to alchemy, a form of sacred magic. The Reformers were also concerned that such an understanding of the sacrament led many of the faithful to avoid the Lord's Supper out of fear that they might somehow desecrate the body and blood of their Savior. Today there seems to be wide consensus in both Protestant and Roman Catholic circles that the manner and means of Christ's presence cannot be captured by one or another explanation. Christians today seem to agree on this: Christ's presence is real in this sacrament, but the manner and means of that presence may remain mysteries to us forever.

The ways in which Christ is present at this meal are not mysteries in the same way that a magician's pulling a rabbit out of a hat is mysterious. If we were to examine a magician's hat and insist that he repeat the act again without his cape, then we might very well understand how the feat was accomplished. But the mystery that is present at Christ's table is forever beyond the reach of analysis and explanation. It is more like the mystery of love. Where does it come from? How is it sustained? How does it sustain us? We will never fully know, but the power is no less real because we are unable to explain it. It is nothing less than the mystery and power of Jesus, made real and made available to us. John Calvin summarized his understanding of Christ's presence in the Lord's Supper by saying, "I would rather experience it than understand it."

In our cerebral approach to religion, we often assume that the most important religious truths can always be reduced to words. But, just as an art critic once observed about great art, the part of the sacrament that really matters is the part that will forever remain beyond the reach of explanation. Part of its importance comes from the fact that it takes us where words cannot go.

There are times when we can be particularly grateful that the presence of Christ is not something that can be grasped only by the intellect, that such a presence can be experienced by other means. A woman suffering from Alzheimer's disease who cannot hold a point in a sermon long enough for it to make any real difference can still hold the cup of blessing to her lips and receive the presence of Christ. A child for whom theological explanations are as incomprehensible as molecular biology can still receive the blessings of this table. (It is ironic that some churches deny children any participation in the Lord's Supper. They are asked to sit through twenty minutes of the verbal aspects of worship, which are largely beyond their grasp; then they are dismissed before the real action starts, the Lord's Supper, an aspect of worship that they can understand.) William Willimon observes:

> Unfortunately, in our abstracted, verbal, word-oriented culture, we often overlook the power of the symbolic. Sometimes Protestants say, "The bread and wine of Holy Communion is *only a symbol* of Christ." Only a symbol? Talk of this kind implies that there is something more than the symbolic—namely, the verbal or the literal. But the point I am trying to make is that the literal and the verbal are not *more* than the symbolic, but *less*. It would be more accurate to say that something was *only a word*, for words are often intangible, abstract, vague, and generalized. Words themselves are symbols—somewhat abstracted, intangible symbols.[4]

The story of Jesus is one of God made palpable, a God who was not content to remain distant and abstract, but instead chose to share the common stuff of our days and to be tangibly present in our lives. Leo the Great once said that it "makes conspicuous" Christ's presence among us. Most of the time, the presence of Christ surrounds us and infuses us as imperceptibly as water surrounds and infuses a fish.

Without the tangible gifts of bread and wine, we can remain unaware of the presence that is there all along. How is Christ present in this meal? We cannot fully know. What we can do is seek the mysterious blessings of this table and receive the palpable gifts of a palpable God.

PART THREE

What Is Promised, What Is Required

CHAPTER 10

Conversing with God

Prayer is often difficult. But that doesn't mean that prayer is complex, or that it requires great skill and knowledge, like learning how to play Chopin or to solve problems in calculus. Rather, prayer is a relatively simple activity. So prayer is both difficult and simple. In fact, as I hope to demonstrate, one of the reasons that prayer is so difficult may be because it is so simple.

The Simplicity of Prayer

In the Sermon on the Mount, Jesus addressed the subject of prayer with a few brief teachings and an example, the accumulative effect of which was to underscore the simplicity of prayer (Matt. 6:5-13). Jesus's teachings could have been introduced with the beginning sentence of Dr. Benjamin Spock's famous book on child-care: "You know more than you think you do."[1]

Jesus starts by saying that when we pray we should not be like those who love to stand and pray in public places to be admired for their prayers. One reason for this counsel is obvious: those who like to pray in public often seem to be looking over their shoulders to see who besides God might be listening. It would seem strange to overhear a person talking at length and with obvious care on the telephone if she had first neglected to dial anyone's number—unless, of course, her whole intention was to be overheard. Prayers that are spoken in public can easily become just that: less to be heard by God than to be overheard by fellow human beings.

Such prayers are not only directed to the wrong party—to men and women rather than to God—but the content and manner of expression of such prayers will be changed as well. When we pray to be overheard, simple prayers are not impressive enough. Instead, we feel the need to "pretty up" (to use my grandmother's expression) our prayers so they might sound pleasing to the human ear. I am painfully aware that ordained ministers, who are often the ones called on to offer public prayers, can sometimes mislead people about the nature of prayer by always trying to offer beautiful prayers, as if God will hear our prayers only if we fill them with well-turned phrases and poetic images.

This might also explain why so many of us are reluctant to pray out loud in a public setting. We feel that we do not have the technique down, as if the language of prayer were a foreign one that we had not yet mastered. Rather than embarrass ourselves, we ask to be excused. That was the case during the Constitutional Convention of 1787. When the delegates confronted the barriers of hardened disagreement, Benjamin Franklin proposed that they seek divine guidance by opening the sessions with prayer. The delegates rejected his proposal, not because they did not believe in prayer, but because they did not have enough money to hire a chaplain. No prayers were offered because no one present felt sufficiently fluent in the foreign language of prayer.

Note that the boldness of the hypocrite's prayers in Jesus's teaching and the reluctance to pray on the part of the delegates to the Constitutional Convention spring from the same misconception that there is a special language and technique to prayer, that prayers must be properly expressed to be acceptable. The only difference is that the hypocrite thought he had mastered the language of prayer, whereas the delegates thought they had not.

When Jesus offered his example of prayer, the prayer we call the Lord's Prayer, it was brief and simple. It was not the kind of beautiful prayer that would impress human listeners with its theological profundity and poetic imagery. The language that he used was not the language of the temple, but the language of the people. This is sometimes lost on us because we only have the words of the prayer in translation. Consider the word "hallowed" in "hallowed be thy name." I cannot remember ever using that word in any other context, except perhaps in a song that, if I remember correctly, praised the "hallowed halls" of my alma mater. Most of us simply never use the word, so we come to think of it as part of the special vocabulary of prayer, even though it can be properly (and much more simply) rendered as "holy" or "honored."

Then there are all those "thou's" and "thy's." Some people prefer to use these terms for addressing God as a way of expressing special deference. We should note, however, that the words come from an old translation (the King James Version) that dates back to an era in which the pronouns "thou" and "thy" were as familiar and down to earth as our words "you" and "your." The form of address that Jesus used was as informal and familiar as any available to him, as informal and familiar as we might use to address a friend on the street or in a market.

In translation, we begin the prayer, "Our Father. . . ." This may sound like a formal manner of address, but the word Jesus actually used was much different. He began his prayer by saying *Abba*, an Aramaic word that is more akin to "Daddy" or "Papa." It was a familiar form of address that one might hear from an infant because it resembles the early gurgling sounds that precede speech. In a sense, then, Jesus is saying that even infants who have not yet learned how to talk have sufficient vocabulary to address God in prayer.

The ease and familiarity with which Jesus approached God in prayer was so striking to his contemporaries that even Paul, who probably did not know the full Lord's Prayer, had heard the startling fact that Jesus had called God *Abba*. To Paul, this was a sign that, through Jesus, we are invited to a new and intimate relationship with God. In our time, we are rightly concerned about any implication that God is male. But when Jesus used the term *Abba*, it was not his way of establishing the gender of God. The important aspect of such a designation for Jesus—and the thing that so impressed Paul about the way Jesus addressed God—is that it affirms that God is personal rather than impersonal, close and trusted rather than distant and unapproachable. The late Presbyterian minister George Buttrick insisted: "The fact remains that we can hold no comradeship with an abstract noun."[2] Jesus invites us to use the language of familiar relationships in our prayers.

There is certainly a place for beautiful prayers; within the context of worship, for example, such prayers can sometimes better coax from our hearts the simple prayers that nestle there. But they can also be unhelpful if we begin to see them as models that must be followed in our own prayers, or if we somehow conclude that God's heart is only opened by thoughts that are well-expressed or needs that are carefully presented. That's one reason Jesus advises us to pray in private—not because religion is an essentially private matter, but because praying in private helps us avoid the temptation to "pretty up" our prayers. Alone, we are less likely to shape the form and content of our prayers by making them sound "prayerful."

The Subjects of Prayer

If we already know the language of prayer, the proper subjects of our prayers are equally at hand. We can look far and wide for the subjects of prayer and come back empty because the proper subjects of prayer were closer than we dared look—as close as our own hearts. Centuries ago, Cato the Censor gave this advice to a Roman advisor: "Stick to the point, and the words will come." And that is good advice for those who would like to learn to pray. But what is the point of prayer? Whatever is in our hearts—whatever needs, whatever joys, whatever confessions, whatever frustrations. Clearly, we can no more run out of such raw material for prayer than we can run out of thoughts.

The French author François Fénelon, writing in the seventeenth century, put it well:

> If you pour out to God all your weaknesses, needs, and troubles, there will be no lack of what to say; you will never exhaust this subject; it is continually being renewed. People who have no secrets

from each other never want for subjects of conversation; they do not weigh their words, because there is nothing to be kept back. Neither do they seek for something to say; they talk together out of the abundance of their heart—without consideration, just what they think.[3]

Seen that way, prayer is the heart's ongoing conversation with God, which will free us from the notion that every word must be carefully weighed and presented. God is not concerned with the words we use. We can let participles dangle, and leave sentences incomplete. Indeed, some of the most powerful and profound prayers are those that have no nouns, but rather consist only of urgent verbs such as "help," "listen," "heal," and "forgive." If we use the language of the heart, we may even abandon words entirely and instead simply open our hearts and invite God to take a tour of all that resides there—the half-formed thoughts, the elusive longings, the inescapable yet undefinable sense of need. Paul affirmed that when words elude us, inarticulate sighs can be offered to God as a prayer: "For we do not know how to pray as we ought, but that very Spirit intercedes for us with sighs too deep for words" (Rom. 8:26).

Conversing with the One Who Accepts Us

Understood in this way, prayer is rather simple. It is ongoing conversation and communion with one who knows us very well. Yet this may be one reason prayer is often difficult—precisely because it is so simple. It is always difficult to be open to another, to let ourselves be known. We would prefer to carefully monitor what others see and know about us. We who are often self-conscious to be caught wearing a bathrobe or with our house a mess are certainly reluctant to open our untidy hearts to examination. And when the one we are open to is God, there is no way to engage in the kind of carefulness we usually prefer.

Facing God means, for once, facing ourselves. Opening our hearts to God means confronting all that resides there ourselves. And who is fully prepared for that? This is another reason we sometimes take refuge in formal prayers. It is a way of trying to maintain distance—distance from God and distance from the reality of our own lives. Jesus offers us a way to move beyond this reluctance and open ourselves to God in prayer when he says, "God knows what you need before you ask" (Matt. 6:8). That is, when we pray we are merely recognizing what God knows already and realizing that God has already accepted those prayers. God invites us to share, through prayer, this perception that both we and our prayers are acceptable.

In the Academy Award–winning movie *Marty*, Ernest Borgnine plays a homely butcher in his late thirties who lives with his mother in Brooklyn. He spends his Saturday evenings standing around with his friend Angie.

"What do you feel like doing, Marty?" Angie asks.

"I don't know, what do you feel like doing?" Marty replies. And the conversation never goes much beyond that. Marty is uncomfortable around women and clams up because, in his own words, he is just "a fat, ugly man."

One night Marty goes with Angie to the Stardust Ballroom, where a stranger offers Marty five dollars to escort home the stranger's unattractive blind date. Angie assumes that Marty will turn down the offer, describing the woman as "a real dog." But Marty turns down the money and approaches the woman. The two dance a bit, and then Marty walks with her to the bus stop. When they reach the bus stop, Marty and the woman keep on going because they are lost in conversation. The woman listens attentively and with appreciation. Sensing this, Marty is a flood of words: he talks about his work, his worries, his family, his hopes—thoughts he has never expressed, and some he has expressed but that have never been fully heard. Occasionally, he interrupts himself by saying, "Gee, I just can't stop talkin'. I'm going to let you talk now." Then the woman says something that triggers a new thought in Marty, and he is talking again. The woman smiles until Marty stops himself again. "Gee, there I go again! I just can't stop talkin'. What is this?"

What this is, Marty, is the easy flow of conversation with someone who accepts you—fat, ugly man that you are.

God has heard our prayers before we speak them and has already accepted those prayers and accepted us. But when God knows our prayers before we speak them, we are left with an obvious question: If God already knows everything we'll say, what is the point of prayer?

Consider this comparison. A couple has been married for years. In spite of all they have been through together (or perhaps because of all they have been through together), they still love each other. Then one night, over coffee and dessert, the husband is obviously disturbed about something. The wife knows to wait. Whatever it is, it will come out eventually. And sure enough, he blurts out, "You know . . . it occurred to me today that you never tell me that you love me anymore."

The wife responds, "Oh, you know I love you, very much."

"Yes."

"Then why do I have to say it?" she asks.

"Because it makes a difference. I need to hear it even when I know what you are going to say before you say it. And maybe you need to say it."

God knows our prayers even before we speak them, but it is still important for us to say them. It makes a difference. Speaking the words themselves creates tender ties. Words of love are never unnecessary, never redundant, and neither are words of prayer. A silent understanding cannot replace a loving exchange of words. There is no limit to what we can offer to God in prayer, but our prayers usually consist of five elements: praise, confession, thanksgiving, petition, and intercession.

Praise

Through praise, we acknowledge the greatness of God and delight in that greatness. Many of the Psalms erupt with resounding praise:

> Bless the Lord, O my soul,
> and all that is within me,
> bless his holy name.

Bless the Lord, O my soul,
   and forget not all his benefits—
who forgives all your iniquities,
   who heals all your diseases,
who redeems your life from the Pit,
   who crowns you with steadfast love and mercy,
who satisfies you with good as long as you live
   so that your youth is renewed like the eagle's.   (Ps. 103:1–5)

Such praise does not merely express gratitude for the gifts of God (which is called "thanksgiving"), but it also expresses gratitude for who God is. Certainly, such praise is often prompted by appreciation for something God has done or given. But praise does not end there. According to C. S. Lewis, "Praise says, 'What must be the quality of that Being whose far-off and momentary coruscations are like this!' One's mind runs back up the sunbeam to the sun."[4]

There is an ancient Hindu prayer that says only, "Wonderful, wonderful, wonderful." This is also the Christian's prayer when he or she catches a glimpse of the majesty of God, a God who splashes a sunset across the horizon or equips a hawk to soar effortlessly overhead, a God who knows us better than we know ourselves and yet—miracle of miracles!—still loves us. A God who did not remain distant but chose, instead, to share our lives of salt tears and sweet laughter in the person of Jesus Christ. Such a God surely prompts our praise.

Many people have difficulty with the idea that God requires our praise. Here again, Lewis is helpful: "I found a stumbling block in the demand so clamorously made by all religious people that we should 'praise' God; still more in the suggestion that God Himself demanded it. We all despise the man who demands continued assurance of his own virtue, intelligence or delightfulness."[5] Lewis goes on to explain how he came to understand the impetus for praise differently:

I think we delight to praise what we enjoy because the praise not merely expresses but completes the enjoyment; it is its appointed consummation.... It is frustrating to have discovered a new author and not to be able to tell anyone how good he is; to come suddenly, at the turn of the road, upon some mountain valley of unexpected grandeur and then to have to keep silent because the people with you care for it no more than for a tin can in the ditch; to hear a good joke and find no one to share it with (the perfect hearer died a year ago). This is so even when our expressions are inadequate, as of course they usually are.[6]

We praise God, then, not only because we enjoy God, but in order that our joy may be complete.

Confession

"Love means never having to say you're sorry." That line, from a popular movie of my youth, looked great on a movie poster. It's an attractive sentiment, but it's also dangerously misleading. The truth is that love means having to say you're sorry—a lot. No loving relationship is maintained over time without ample doses of forgiveness, and our relationship with God is no exception.

Confession closely follows praise in our prayers because it is when we have encountered the holiness of God that we also encounter our own unholiness. It is as we praise God for who God is that we recognize again who we are—people in need of God's forgiveness.

In confession we invite God to join us on a tour of our hearts and minds, to survey what is there. If our inventory is honest, we will notice many things that we might prefer not to see: careless words that were spoken, and needed words that went unspoken; things we have done that we cannot look at and other things we have done that we cannot avert our eyes from, try as we might; all the personal little failings and all the ways in which we have contributed to the larger ills of society. Such an inventory adds up quickly, but it still does not provide the complete picture, because these individual sins are but symptoms of a deeper condition: our rebellion against God and our resulting alienation from God and other people. So confession is not only a matter of being forgiven for particular sins. Through confession we also seek a restoration of relationships, with God and with other people, that whatever stands between us might now be put behind us.

People sometimes speak of a need to forgive themselves for something they have done. But, alas, that is not possible. Frederick Buechner reminds us that you can no more forgive yourself than you can sit in your own lap. So we do not seek to forgive ourselves; rather, we make our confessions so that we might receive forgiveness from God and in the hope that we might come to share God's point of view. If confession is difficult, receiving forgiveness can be even more so. Among other things, it entails giving up our own view of ourselves in deference to God's point of view about us. We may view ourselves only as flawed and frail creatures who seem consistently unable to live up to God's expectations and our own intentions. George Orwell observes, "Every life, when viewed from the inside, is a succession of failures." But God declares that we are forgiven people. Receiving God's forgiveness requires enough humility to trust God's promises more than our own perceptions. Whether or not we can forgive ourselves, we are forgiven people after all.

Some congregations no longer include a prayer of confession in their worship because the practice is considered too "negative." They contend that people have enough difficulties in their lives without the church adding to the burden. Instead, they "accentuate the positive" and talk about possibilities and "human potential." Obviously, there is no room in such a view for confession, which reminds us of the very things we are trying to avoid. We may attempt to ignore the negative and accentuate the positive about ourselves by avoiding confession, but surely any pagan can do that. In fact, pagans have no other choice: they have no one else to trust in. Because they do not believe in a God who forgives, they have a desperate need to believe in the basic goodness of humanity. Either most people are basically good, essentially noble, and caring, or there is nothing left but despair.

Christians, however, can afford to be realists. We are free to face the truth about ourselves: good and bad are inextricably intertwined within us. Sometimes we act nobly, but even then our motivations can be mixed. When given a chance, we mess up; sometimes, even when we're not given a chance, we mess up anyway. That is, Christians can be realists enough to say with Paul: "All have sinned and fall short of the glory of God" (Rom. 3:23). Christians can be hopeful realists: we are free to be realists because our hope is in God. It's not that we have stopped being sinners, but that God has accepted us, sinners though we are. That's the only realistic thing that can be said—but also the only hopeful thing.

In a culture that does not recognize the reality of sin, guilt feelings are a problem to be avoided at all costs. But Christians know that sometimes it is good to feel guilty, because sometimes it's simply good to face the truth. There can be something wonderfully freeing in being able to say what we may have known all along—that not all is right with us. Refusing to look at this truth, being unable or unwilling to confess our sins, only ends in repression and evasion, and there is nothing exhilarating about that. There is, then, no way to understand the shadowed realities of so much that we see in our world and in ourselves. The world leaves us with a gnawing restlessness about ourselves and seemingly no place to turn. Christians, however, can turn to God with our confessions because we are assured of God's forgiveness.

Thanksgiving

Thanksgiving does not come naturally to us. People usually assume that what they have is the result of hard work or the luck of the draw. Some even claim that they are self-made men or women. We have a sense of entitlement and assume a right to our share of the world's goods (and perhaps someone else's share as well). The holiday we call "Thanksgiving" is often reduced to nothing more than a celebration of consumption as we eat and drink even more than usual.

Christians, however, proclaim that we are not self-made, that everything we are and have is a gift from God. Prayers of thanksgiving are opportunities to recognize God as the giver of life and all that is life-giving. A prayer of thanksgiving offered before a meal is often called "grace," a word that refers to something we can never achieve but can only be given. When used in this setting, the word "grace" reminds us that, even though we may have purchased the food at the store with "our own" money, it is a gift from God.

It is telling that those who have much are most likely to boast that they are self-made. This reveals the irony that continuous bounty, not scarcity, is most likely to discourage thanksgiving. When God's blessings are numberless as the sands, we usually do not get very far with our counting. Often it seems that the more we have, the more likely we are to say, "Thanks for nothing." The implications of thanksgiving are greater when we have much. The stakes are that much higher: there is more to protect. Those of us who have much and desire much have a greater need to isolate ourselves from the realization that ultimately we have nothing, that everything is from God and is God's. What does this imply for us as people who live in a privileged country at a privileged time in history? How can we offer prayers of thanksgiving when we are surrounded by bounty?

Prayers of thanksgiving, like other prayers, are enlivened if they are specific and concrete. It is not always helpful to thank God for "all we have." Our limited imaginations cannot grasp it all. As God blesses us in specific ways, so our responses must be specific. In our prayers of thanksgiving, we remember the particular gifts of God and offer them back to God in gratitude. The occasions for thanksgiving are everywhere: the feel and smell of the soil on the first day in the garden; the person who knows just how to tell you that you are doing something wrong; the first snow of the season; the last snow of the season; hot pastrami on rye; a person who has approached a seat of power to plead the cause of those who have been cast off by life; the soothing pulse of a hot shower; a Chopin waltz; a day with much to do; a day with nothing to do; the moment you observe your child across the room and somehow know that she is going to make the transition into adulthood. The possibilities are endless—as endless as the gifts of God.

So a prayer of thanks may begin with an inventory of what we have been given. It is important to note, however, that in the New Testament the same Greek word (*charis*) that is sometimes translated as "thanks" is also sometimes translated as "grace." The word may define an act of giving or an act of receiving: if giving, the word means "gift or unearned favor"; if receiving, the word is best translated as "gratitude." Before meals, some people say "grace" and others offer "thanks." It is the same word, *charis*, in both instances.

This is very revealing. We know that, in unhealthy relationships, gifts are sometimes given for the purpose of getting a desired response from the recipient. Apparently gracious acts can degenerate into a way of saying, "I did you a favor, so now you owe me thanks." In healthy relationships, by contrast, there is an easy flow between giving and thanks, grace and gratitude. In such relationships, neither gift nor thanks is prompted by expectations but freely offered. Both gift and thanks respond freely to one another in an endless echo of grace. We receive a gift in the same spirit in which it is given: it is all grace. We may even lose track of where it begins and where it ends. That is the spirit in which Christians are invited to offer their prayers of thanksgiving.

Here we come upon an irony: by continually expressing thanks, we can come to be thankful. We offer thanks day in and day out, in season and out of season, perhaps at first just to get the feel of it, then, after a time, because we feel it. Sometimes, especially at first, we do not offer our thanks to God because we are thankful. Rather, we offer our thanks so that we might someday *be* thankful. Sometimes words of thanks need to be on our lips before (by some slow and largely imperceptible process) they can take up residence in our hearts.

In our own simple way, we seem to have some understanding of this. We say to our children, "Say thank you to the gentleman" or "What do you say to the nice lady?" We continually prompt, coax, urge, even demand that thanks be offered. Perhaps we are reminding our children (and ourselves) to articulate our thanks because we have some dim understanding that it is by continually offering thanks, whether we feel like it or not, that we might eventually take our part in the easy flow of gift and thanksgiving.

Petition

We are also invited to bring specific requests to God through what are called "prayers of petition." Such prayers can reflect the range of things that concern us, from the obviously significant to the seemingly mundane. Some people feel that they must limit their petitions to those that are worthy of God's attention. Others contend that we should not approach God with requests for material things. Jesus showed no such concern. The prayer Jesus taught his disciples included a request for "daily bread." It seems a small request to bring before the God who must keep the stars in their orbit, and certainly it is of a material nature. But God recognizes that such concerns often occupy us. There is no point in offering a prayer that dwells on purely spiritual matters if we spend the rest of our day trying to figure out how to get bread on the table. Our prayers fall lifeless at our feet if they do not reflect the real concerns of our lives.

Many of our daily concerns, of course, are not worth dwelling on, and many reflect an unbecoming materialism, but it is often only in prayer that we can recognize this. Prayer can have a winnowing effect on our desires. We need not limit the requests we bring to God to those things that are worthy, because it may be only by bringing them to God that we can discern what is worthy and what is not.

Jesus suggests that one of the most important things about praying is to keep at it. In one parable, Jesus says that prayer is like knocking at a friend's door at midnight to borrow some bread. The friend does not leap out of bed at the prospect of helping. So you have to make a real pest of yourself and keep knocking. When the friend finally pulls himself out of bed and stumbles down the stairs, there is no question that he will give you whatever you ask, if only to get you off his back: "I tell you, even though he will not get up and give him anything because he is his friend, at least because of his persistence he will get up and give him whatever he wants" (Luke 11:8).

This parable is not suggesting that God is a sound sleeper or a grouch. It is not that God must be badgered into answering our prayers. Rather, it is counsel to us to pray with the kind of persistence we would use to rouse a friend from deep slumber. Elsewhere Jesus says, "Is there anyone among you who, if your child asks for bread, will give a stone? Or if the child asks for fish, will give a snake? If you, then, who are evil, know how to give gifts to your children, how much more will your Father in heaven give good things to those who ask him!" (Matt. 7:9-11). Jesus counsels persistence in prayer because it is by keeping at it that we can come to want our prayers answered as much as God wants to answer them. George Buttrick has observed, "There are gifts which earthly parents cannot wisely grant their children until they ask for them."[7]

To say that God answers prayer is not the same as saying that we always receive what we are asking for. Prayer is not like saying magic words that will produce a rabbit out of a hat every time they are spoken. Morton Kelsey reminds us that "God is not a cosmic bellhop," obediently jumping to do whatever we ask. Answering a request is not the same thing as granting a request. There are, after all, many ways in which a request can be answered. One can answer by saying "yes," but one can also answer by saying "no." And, as every parent knows, one often replies, "We'll see."

To be sure, even our most heartfelt prayers are not always answered in the way we would like. Sometimes, when God does not seem to be giving us what we're asking for, perhaps God is giving something else. Jesus's prayer in the Garden of Gethsemane reflects this understanding. Jesus knew how he wanted things to turn out. He began his prayer by asking that he be spared the pending betrayal and death: "Remove this cup from me." He then followed that petition with another: "Yet, not what I want, but what you want" (Mark 14:36). Although Jesus was specific in his request, he recognized that God might have other plans. He had confidence that his prayer would be answered, even though he knew that his request might not be granted.

Obviously, the distinction between prayers answered and requests granted is probably not enough to console the man who is continually pulled into the yawning darkness of alcoholism in spite of his impassioned prayers for help. And such a distinction will seem strangely moot to the woman whose desperate prayers do not seem even to delay her eviction from her apartment. Whether these are examples of unanswered prayers or denied requests, the outcome is the same. We can understand those whose experience leads them to conclude that, at the very least, God does not answer all prayers. When we confront the scope of misery in some lives, we can only grant that there are times when God seems not to answer some prayers.

Whether those prayers are answered in ways we cannot discern is, of course, impossible to say. When we pray, we are on the shores of mystery, and from that vantage point there is no way to measure its depths. Nevertheless, part of the mystery that we can acknowledge, if not fully understand, is that God does grant some of the requests that are made in prayer. There are times when our persistence is rewarded, and our petitions are granted in ways that defy any explanation, except this one: God does answer prayer.

Intercession

When we consider intercessory prayer, the mysteries we encounter in prayers of petition are only deepened. After all, when we pray for ourselves (petition) the answer is often evident, in part, in our own actions. In the examples above, if the alcoholic man prays for release from his disease, God may respond by helping him admit that he is powerless over alcohol, the first step of twelve-step sobriety programs. God may answer the prayers of the woman who faces eviction from her apartment by granting her the courage and resourcefulness to find another home. But in intercessory prayer, we approach God to intercede on behalf of someone else. It's true that, in some instances, those who bring such prayers to God can also become the instruments through which those same prayers are answered. For example, a friend may pray for the recovery of the alcoholic man and through those same prayers become equipped by God to help the man confront his disease.

Nevertheless, we are invited to intercede through prayer in instances when no other kind of intervention is possible. We are encouraged to pray on behalf of those who live on the other side of the world, for those whose lives do not touch ours in any discernible way. Jesus counsels that we should pray behind closed doors. But if we never opened the door to rejoin the world, would our prayers have any effect? Is there any point in asking that our prayers be answered when we are unable to be part of the answer in any other way?

If we need proof that not every request made in intercessory prayer is granted, we need look no further than the daily newspaper's account of the latest war or famine. But there are other times when, as in prayers of petition, our requests seem to be granted. There is certainly always an alternative explanation. Perhaps the remission of a friend's cancer had nothing to do with your fervent prayers on her behalf, even if her physicians can only call it "miraculous." Perhaps the hostages were going to be released anyway. How can we know that it was our prayers that made the difference? C. S. Lewis draws a comparison from our relationships with other people:

> Our friend, boss, and wife may tell us that they acted because we asked and we know them so well as to feel sure .... But notice that when this happens our assurance has not been gained by the methods of science. It is born out of our personal relation to the other parties; not from knowing things about them but from knowing them.[8]

Those who have come to know the God who is always up to something good in the world also come to believe, without irrefutable evidence but with unshakable conviction, that many otherwise inexplicable events demonstrate the mysterious power of intercessory prayer. Our lives are inextricably intertwined with the lives of God and our neighbor in ways that we cannot fully grasp. Buttrick puts it this way: "God rests our neighbor's good upon our toil and thought. Why not upon our prayers? Apparently there are some gifts which God chooses to give through love's labor and planning—and prayer."[9]

So we are invited to collect our prayers from far and wide and offer them to the God for whom nothing is distant. One can view the newspaper as a daily prayer book delivered to our doors. Indeed, living in an age such as ours, there may be no other way to read the newspaper than to see it as an occasion for prayer. As we read each story, we can invite God's Spirit to touch down and pray that the power and love of God might be let loose. And, since we do not live entirely unto ourselves, we can offer ourselves as instruments of that same Spirit. We can, as Augustine advised, pray as if everything depends on God, and act as if everything depends on us.

Prayer as a Way of Life

Praise, confession, thanksgiving, petition, and intercession. These are not techniques to be isolated and mastered as much as they are elements of an ongoing conversation with God. The apostle Paul enjoins us to pray without ceasing. Whatever else this might mean, it certainly means that prayer is to be woven into the fabric of our lives. When we begin to pray, it can feel as awkward as conversation on a first date. As with any developing relationship, it takes time. We may pray infrequently because, we complain, God seems distant, when God may seem distant, in fact, because we pray infrequently. Orthodox Archbishop Anthony Bloom observes:

> We complain that He does not make Himself present to us for the few minutes we reserve for Him, but what about the twenty-three and a half hours during which God may be knocking at our door when we answer "I am busy, I am sorry," or when we do not answer at all because we do not even answer the knock at the door of our heart, of our minds, of our conscience, of our life. So there is a situation in which we have no right to complain of the absence of God, because we are a great deal more absent than He ever is.[10]

Through prayer we are invited to consciously share our lives with God, to tell God whatever concerns us or delights us, the things we have done wrong, who we wish we were. We are invited to commend to God's care the ones we look at across the breakfast table and the ones who are across the globe, the people we love and the people we have a hard time loving. We are invited to share what is most important in our lives so that God's life might be shared with us.

CHAPTER 11

Resurrection to Eternal Life

A boy's play stops suddenly when his ball falls near a dead sparrow on the lawn.

Family and friends huddle around a newly dug grave, a gaping gash in the earth that is a reminder, as if they needed one, of the fresh wound in their hearts.

A phone sounds the ominous ring it seems to reserve for the middle of the night, and a woman gropes for the receiver in the dark with an instant and powerful dread.

The daily newspaper sits like a grim messenger at the front door, waiting to remind us, through accounts of famine in Africa, war in the Middle East, and death in our neighborhood, that we are surrounded by death and that it will not always remain outside our door.

It is at such times that the question that is never far from us appears again. It is a question that has been taken up by philosophers in every generation; in one way or another, it has made philosophers of us all. Life does not let us escape this question because it concerns what is clearly inevitable. What happens to us when we die?

Convictions Based on What We Know about Ourselves

Christians are not alone in affirming that there is life after death. But the basis for that belief is quite different for Christians than it is for other people. People sometimes affirm a belief in some kind of afterlife on the basis of their experience with individuals. It is not difficult to understand the reason for this confidence. We often have a sense that the sum of personhood is more than a mere body, even more than a body energized by a mind. This may especially be the case when we have observed someone's life and death at close hand. Dr. Elisabeth Kübler-Ross, the author of *On Death and Dying*, confessed that, before she started working with terminally ill patients, she had always been skeptical about any claims concerning life after death. But as she worked with more and more dying patients, she became convinced that death does not put an end to us. She reported that, when you are with someone who is alive in one moment and dead the next, the body looks like an old overcoat that has been cast off at the moment of death. At such moments, even a scientist like Kübler-Ross, who has been trained to believe only those things that can be observed and proved, knows beyond a doubt that something of the individual lives on.

As a pastor, on frequent occasions I have also been with individuals at the moment of death. I, too, can attest that when you are with someone who is dying, it can feel as though you are in the presence of someone in labor, as if the one who is dying is struggling to give birth to new life, his or her own new life, that will arrive at the point of death. I can echo the testimony of those who have said that, when you see someone who has just died, it can feel as though you are looking at a piano after the pianist has left to play another instrument.

Our conviction of life after death often arises from our observations of the life and death of another. But we can be led to the same conclusion when we consider our own lives. Many poets, our pioneers of the inner life, have reflected this understanding. We have, in the words of William Wordsworth, "intimations of immortality." Walt Whitman shared this credo: "I know that I am deathless. / I know this orbit of mine cannot be swept with a carpenter's compass."[1] On what basis does Whitman "know" that he is deathless? He knows it as well as he knows himself, because he senses within himself an eternal spark that cannot be confined to the span of his earthly life.

In recent years, some people have interpreted the accounts of those who have been clinically dead and then were revived as confirmation of their "intimations of immortality." Dr. Raymond Moody's book on the subject, *Life after Life*, became a worldwide bestseller. In that book Moody chronicles the experiences of a hundred and fifty patients who had been clinically dead but then continued to live and were able to describe their experiences.

Despite some individual differences, these accounts agree in many respects. With striking frequency, the patients report that at the point of death they hear the doctor declare them dead. They have the sensation that they are moving through a long, dark tunnel. After that, they find themselves separated from their own bodies. They can observe their bodies from outside or above. They then discover that they possess a new and different body with new properties and powers that is very different from the body they left behind. Moody goes on to report other common elements in the experience of one man:

> Others come to meet and to help him. He glimpses the spirits of relatives and friends who have already died, and a loving, warm spirit of a kind he has never encountered before—a being of light—appears before him. This being asks him a question, nonverbally, to make him evaluate his life and helps him along by showing him a panoramic instantaneous playback of the major elements of his life. At some point he finds himself approaching some sort of barrier or border, apparently representing the limit between earthly life and the next life. Yet he finds that he must go back to the earth, that the time for his death has not yet come. At this point he resists, for by now he is taken up with his experiences in the afterlife and does not want to return. He is overwhelmed by intense feelings of joy, love and peace. Despite his attitude, though, he somehow reunites with his physical body and lives.[2]

One cannot help but be intrigued by such accounts. On the central elements of the experience, there is a remarkable degree of agreement. For a Christian, it is striking how closely these accounts reflect biblical imagery. Not only do they seem to be descriptions of a life beyond death, but the God figure is described as light—and yet a light bestowed with personality. Those who die assume a new and different kind of body. There is a final accounting, a kind of judgment. And there is reunion and an intense sense of joy, love, and peace that is not found in our ordinary lives.

As remarkable as these accounts may be, however, we must be careful to note that they cannot be called eyewitness accounts of life after death. Although each person lost vital signs and was declared dead, each was resuscitated within minutes. That is, they may have been clinically dead but, as Moody himself points out, not a single individual in his study died in any strict or final sense. The people he examined may have experienced dying, but they did not experience death—a critical distinction. Dying is the way, whereas death is the destination. And none of those interviewed had reached that destination we call death.

Convictions Based on What We Know about God

These accounts from those who have hovered for a time at the border of life and death are certainly intriguing, and in some ways quite compelling. They seem to confirm what we may sense about ourselves and others: that death does not put an end to us. But the Christian affirmation of life after death does not issue from human intuition, nor is it founded on what we have experienced of human life or on what we believe about ourselves. Rather, it is based on what we believe about God. We believe that our God is a God of justice, and yet justice seems thwarted in this world. We believe that our God is a God who keeps promises, and yet those promises seem to be unfulfilled during the days of our lives. We believe in a God who cherishes each individual, and yet, if there is no afterlife, our fate will be an anonymous oblivion.

The first stirrings of a belief in life after death (evident in Hebrew tradition) is found in the book of Daniel and arose at a time when the people saw no other way that God's promises could be fulfilled or that God's justice and love could be revealed. It was a remarkably late development, evidenced only in the latest scriptural traditions. Before that time, Jews showed no belief in a life after death. It's true that we can trace images of resurrection through Hebrew Scripture, such as in Ezekiel's famous vision of the reanimation of the dry bones, but in such instances the images are clearly metaphorical and do not refer to a literal life after death. There are also frequent scriptural references to *Sheol*, the shadowy underworld where all the dead reside. But *Sheol* is not a place where a life after death is lived: no fellowship with God or with one another exists there. It is a shadowy, ghostlike existence, a place of perpetual darkness and silence, of powerlessness and oblivion. *Sheol* is the place where the elements of creation are now absent. It is characterized by the absence of light, the absence of community, the absence of God—in short, it is a place where life itself is absent.

For most of their history, then, Jews held no belief in an eternal life in the positive sense of the term. With remarkable consistency, they concentrated on the present world, without demonstrating much concern with what was understood as a dismal, dark, and hopeless hereafter. According to Hebrew tradition, it is within history that God acts, and it is within history that an individual's life continues. If anything of the individual lives on after death, it is only through the ongoing life and memory of God's people. This is far from a mere process of biology. This continuity is only possible through God's continuing presence. It is not just any community that lives on, but God's covenantal community. So it is that Abraham's dying act was to give instructions that his son Isaac was not to take a Canaanite wife but to marry a good Jewish girl. This eleventh-hour concern over his son's marital status may seem strange to us, unless we remember what was involved: the perpetuation of Abraham's life through the continuity of the community. In short, Abraham was insuring that he would live beyond his death.

But something even more important than the destiny of an individual was at stake. Nothing less than the efficacy of God's promise was on the line. God had promised Abraham a new land in which God would dwell with Abraham and his people. Now that Abraham is breathing his last breath, the promise can only be fulfilled through the ongoing life of the Hebrew people. And through the centuries, the descendants of Abraham were sustained by the belief that God's promises were not defeated but only awaited fulfillment in history, a history they would never live to see, but a history in which they would share as part of the continuing life of the community.

It is significant that the only unambiguous reference to the resurrection of the dead in Hebrew Scripture was written at a time when the very life of the people was threatened. It is found in Daniel, which was written in the second century before Jesus's birth, making it among the last portions of Hebrew Scripture to be written. It was a time when the Hebrew people were suffering under the violent rule of a Hellenist despot who sacked the temple in Jerusalem and prohibited Jewish worship. The righteous suffered, and many people were martyred. The anguished question arose: Are the righteous to go forever unrewarded and God's people crushed before God's ancient promises can be fulfilled? Daniel's answer was a defiant "no." Even if Israel is destroyed and all the faithful killed, God will raise the dead at the end of history. When that happens, God will settle old scores. The faithful, who waited in vain for the fulfillment of God's promises during their lifetimes, will take part in that fulfillment in a new life that God will bestow. God's justice demands it.

We have not experienced the particular threats that enveloped the Hebrews so ominously at that time in their history. But we know what it is like to live in a world in which justice seems thwarted. In many settings, and in various ways, crime *does* pay, and so do oppression, prejudice, and greed. When Gloucester in Shakespeare's *King Lear* takes in the injustices of the world, he declares: "As flies to wanton boys, are we to the gods; they kill us for their sport."[3] It is a grim view of God and God's justice, but we might be drawn to the same conclusion—if this life were the only life there is. The French existentialist Jean-Paul Sartre concluded: "If there is a God, He is a scoundrel." We would have reason to share in his dark declarations if the world as we know it were the only court of justice, if there were no life beyond this one. Because justice is not experienced by all of God's children on earth, eternal life becomes morally necessary. A just God who reigns over the rank injustices of this life is a contradiction that is resolved only by the belief in a life beyond death. When William Gladstone endured a crushing defeat, he declared before the House of Commons, "I appeal to time!" Those who believe in a just God are invited to take up this cry when injustice seems to go unanswered. The time to which we appeal is beyond our earthly time, when God's justice will reign and God will resolve the contradictions we experience.

If, as Christians affirm, God cares for each unique individual in a uniquely individual way, then God will not carelessly throw each treasured individual into oblivion. One might imagine a child tossing out a toy she's lost interest in. But we are not God's toys. We are God's children. God can no more be indifferent to our destiny than a mother can forget the name of her own child. To believe in eternal life, then, is not to believe in something in addition to believing in God; it is to believe in this kind of loving God. There is another way to put it. If we believe in God—a God of justice rather than indifference, a God who fulfills rather than taunts, a God who loves rather than torments—then eternal life is simply too good *not* to be true.

From Expectation to Fulfillment

Those who turn from Hebrew Scripture to the New Testament will notice a dramatic new development. The hope of eternal life, a mere grace note in Hebrew Scripture, becomes a dominant theme echoed in every corner of the New Testament. Toward the end of Hebrew Scripture, Daniel speaks of the resurrection of the dead as a potential that will be realized at the end of time. By contrast, the New Testament resounds with the startling affirmation that, in the resurrection of Jesus, the potential became actual, the future arrived ahead of schedule.

Once again, the very justice of God is at stake. God's righteous son must be vindicated and raised in glory if God's justice is to prevail over humankind's version of justice. The justice of humans was brutally manifested in the crucifixion, but God's justice prevails in the resurrection. The resurrection also provides palpable affirmation that

God's love is not compromised by death. Even when we turn from God's promises in disobedience and violence, the promises remain. Easter is God's insistence that God will have the last word.

If the Easter stories were only accounts of what happened to one isolated individual, we might respond with great wonder and awe, an appropriate response to a divine sleight of hand. But it was clear to Christians from the beginning that their fate was bound to the fate of Jesus, that the story of Jesus's resurrection was also their story. Those who follow Jesus are invited to share in his life. When we die, we die the death of Jesus. And because our lives are bound to the one who was raised from the dead, we anticipate our own resurrection with confidence. Christians do not begin with some general belief in the reality of eternal life that makes the story of Jesus's resurrection more plausible. Rather, we begin with Jesus's resurrection, as implausible as it may seem at times. It is an event that Christians are invited to greet as both implausible and true. It is because of the power of this implausible truth about what God has done on Easter that we have confidence in the reality of an eternal life for us all. (For more on the resurrection of Jesus and its significance, see chap. 3.)

When people die, it is not natural for them to live again. That is why the Christian understanding of eternal life is not captured by the word "immortality." If human beings were created immortal, then we would live forever as a matter of course; it would be part of what it is to be human. The term "resurrection" (meaning "raising up") makes clear that this eternal life in which we are invited to share is all God's doing. Contrary to the old hymn, we do not have "eternal life, implanted in the soul." Eternal life is not part of human nature; it is only a result of God's act of raising us.

What Kind of Afterlife?

Christian Scripture gives precious few details about the nature of the afterlife. "Raising up" and "resurrection" are metaphorical terms, the same as would be used for awakening and rising from sleep. But what is this resurrected life like? The New Testament authors say very little in response to such a question. They demonstrate a scrupulous reluctance to describe the nature of the afterlife. It's true that certain Christians have attempted to provide some of the details that are missing in the scriptural accounts. For example, in *The Pilgrim's Progress*, John Bunyan describes his last sight of the sojourners Christian and Hopeful in this way:

> And lo, as they entered, they were transfigured, and they had raiment put on that shone like gold.... I looked in after them, and behold, the city shone like the sun; the streets also were paved with gold and in them walked many men, with crowns on their heads, palms in their hands, and golden harps.... There were also of them that had wings, and they answered one another without intermission, saying, "Holy, holy, holy is the Lord."[4]

Bunyan's work, written in 1678, greatly influenced conventional pictures of heaven, but the images are much too literal and elaborate to be found in the words of Scripture.

At one point, the Sadducees pressed Jesus for details about the afterlife (Matt. 22:23–33). The Sadducees were a conservative Jewish sect that rejected the belief, growing within other segments of Judaism, that the dead would be raised at the end of history. The Sadducees questioned Jesus in an attempt to demonstrate the absurdity of any belief in a life after death. If a wife had seven husbands, they asked, and each of them died, who would be her husband in the resurrection? Definitely a thorny question. Jesus responded by saying that it's a problem only if we imagine our future life to be just like this life. But the afterlife will be different, he said, unlike anything we have yet experienced. We will be like angels.

When Paul received a question from the church in Corinth about the nature of the afterlife, he responded, in part, like this: Our life on this earth can be described as a seed of wheat. When we die, it is like a seed buried in the earth. That buried seed will rise again, not as a seed, but as something new and different, a shaft of wheat (1 Cor. 15:35–44). The authors of Scripture, in general, seem more concerned with who, rather than what, is beyond the grave. They affirm that we die into the eternal presence of God. We can certainly experience the presence of God in glimpses and intimations during our lives; but after death we will experience God in a sure and immediate way that is not possible in this life, a presence that is unmistakable and intimate. Furthermore, we will be individuals, and we can expect our individuality to be retained in the afterlife; we will not be simply folded into some kind of oversoul. Roman Catholic theologian Hans Küng says: "We do not enter into God—as Indian thought suggests—like a drop of water into the sea, if only because a human being is not a drop of water and God is more than the sea."[5]

Paul insists that we will be raised with a body, even as Jesus was raised with a body. This can seem like a strange notion to those who have been influenced by the idea of the immortality of the soul, a concept that can be traced back to the philosophy of Plato. But Jewish thought does not divide people into separable parts. Body, mind, and spirit are one and indivisible. The soul is not the essence of the individual, because the individual is all of one piece. Without a body, we would not be who we are. The notion of a disembodied soul was foreign to Paul, steeped as he was in Jewish thought, because such a notion seemed to compromise the integrity of the individual.

Even so, Paul is quick to add, this body will be unlike any we know or can fully imagine, just as Jesus was raised with a body that was different from the body in which he lived his earthly life. Paul called our resurrection body a "spiritual body" (1 Cor. 15:44), a term that still leaves a lot of questions unanswered but makes clear that we will remain distinct individuals, with individual histories and personalities.

If God preserves the individual after death, we can expect to encounter others after our death. Jesus said to the thief who was crucified with him, "Today you will be with me in paradise" (Luke 23:43). Admittedly, this is difficult to picture. In making such affirmations, we are once again reaching beyond our ability to fully picture or imagine what it will be like. For instance, if my father is there, how old will he be? Or, how can the woman who had seven husbands possibly sort out all the interwoven relationships?

I have come to some partial understanding of this by comparing it to my memories of Christmas celebrations. When I recall any particular Christmas celebration, a large assortment of people show up and the tenses get all confused. My father is there. My Aunt Tudy is there, as she was every year after her husband died. My grandmother is there, sitting quietly in the corner, taking so long to unwrap her gifts that the children take naps before she is finished. In addition to these three—who have all died in the past decade—my mother, my brother and sister and their families, and my wife and I and our children, are somehow all there in this Christmas of my memory. Aunt Tudy takes my daughter Alanna in her lap to tell her a story, even though Aunt Tudy died before Alanna was born. My father delights in the antics of his grandson Todd, as surely as he would have if he had ever lived to see him. My grandmother's memory, which escaped her entirely in her last years, is restored at this Christmas, and she is once again able to tell the story about how my grandfather courted her for only ten days before proposing marriage. And somehow my grandfather himself is there as well, although he died several months before I was born.

In this Christmas of my memory, all the broken and scattered pieces of life are put together in ways that were never possible in any "real" Christmas. When I try to assemble a memory of some Christmas past, I believe that I can catch a fragmentary glimpse of the afterlife. In the afterlife, as in these jumbled Christmas memories, people are united with God and reunited with one another. The tenses are confused, which is another way of saying that we are freed from the limits of time. Death will no longer have the power to separate the generations. Distances will be transcended and differences reconciled. That is, we will be together in ways that are impossible in this life—and that we can only barely approach in our dreams.

It's true that we don't know just what this promised resurrected life will be like. We are assured that God will be there, and we will be there as individual personalities. But perhaps that is enough to know, enough for us to respond to in wonder and trust.

Heaven and Hell

We are all familiar with traditional images of what happens when we die. According to these images, when we die we face an eternal fork in the road, with two divergent ways that lead to two very different places. One road ascends to a place of light, of bliss and communion with God, a place called heaven; the other road descends to a place of darkness, of torment, of fire—a place called hell, where God is absent. When we die, God (the perfect judge) determines which road we must take and whether heaven or hell will be our home for all eternity.

These images can be so firmly planted in our minds that we might be surprised to see how tenuously they are rooted in the words of Scripture. Traditional pictures of heaven and hell owe more to works of literature such as Dante's *Divine Comedy* and John Milton's *Paradise Lost* than they do to Scripture. That is not to say that there is no trace of these images in the words of Scripture. In the most striking example, Matthew records that Jesus told a parable in which, on the day of judgment, he would "separate people one from another as a shepherd separates the sheep from the goats" (Matt. 25:32). To the sheep he will say, "Come, you that are blessed by my Father, inherit the kingdom prepared for you from the foundation of the world" (25:34). To the goats he will say, "You that are accursed, depart from me into the eternal fire prepared for the devil and his angels" (25:41).

However we are to interpret this parable, the images it evokes do not dominate the words of Scripture, contrary to what traditional images of heaven and hell might lead us to believe. Jesus was not a hellfire-and-damnation preacher. More often, the final judgment is pictured as the fulfillment of our own choices. If we have sought communion with God during our lives, we will experience that communion at death. If, by contrast, we have sought to distance ourselves from God during our lives, after death we will be allowed to live with the consequences of that choice. In other words, judgment is something we pronounce on ourselves. For example, in one parable Jesus likens God's realm to a great banquet. Many who are invited simply choose not to attend. Clarence Jordan, New Testament translator and Georgia peanut farmer, comments:

Jesus was trying to show that the kingdom of the new order, this family of the Father, is like a big family gathering around the table, eating together. It's fellowship. It's fun. It's feasting. It's joy. It's life. It's beauty. But there is also a tragedy involved. There are some people who choose not to attend. Jesus' picture of going to hell was not being sent to a place of torment, but just being left out of the joy of the fellowship.[6]

The eternity of hell's punishment (summarized in the words Dante says stand at the entrance of hell: "Abandon hope, all you who enter here") is most difficult for us to reconcile with the image of God as a God of grace and forgiveness. Küng puts the matter starkly: "We must be clear about what this means: a human being, perhaps because of a single 'mortal sin,' damned forever, unhappy forever, tormented forever. A human being, perhaps a great criminal, but nevertheless a human being, without a prospect of any kind of redemption, not even after thousands of years."[7]

Such a judgment, more severe than any human judge would pronounce, seems to contradict the theme that dominates Scripture and is found countless times in the words of Jesus: our God shows special care to the least, the last, and the lost, not on the basis of their goodness, but on the basis of God's mercy. It's true that the brutally simple images of God's eternal reward or punishment meted out on the basis of how we live our earthly lives do grab our attention. That may be part of the point: we are reminded that the decisions we make and the behaviors we adopt in this life are not trifling matters. Even on the most commonplace of Tuesdays, in the most mundane decisions, we are toying with eternity.

Nevertheless, when we cling to such images too closely, they seem to limit God's gracious ways of dealing with us. Doesn't it stretch credulity to affirm that, during this life, God uses every means to woo us and draw us into a loving relationship, but that at the moment of death, all means for doing so have been exhausted? Jordan tells a story that reveals the limits of such a concept of eternal punishment. The story goes something like this: Imagine that a man has led a sinful life and has never given much thought to God. Now he is walking along, taking stock of his life, and he says to himself, "Perhaps I should change my ways and turn my life over to God. Yes, I think I'm ready to do that." And as he continues like this, he crosses a train track. At that very moment, a freight train comes barreling down the track and kills him. Jordan asks if we can imagine God saying: "Blast it! If only that freight train hadn't come along just at that moment, I could have got him!"[8]

Jesus told other parables that remind us that God's grace is not so easily thwarted. He likened God to a shepherd who searches diligently for a lost sheep and does not rest "until he finds it" (Luke 15:4). How long is that? As long as it takes. Jesus goes on to liken God to a woman who, when she discovers she has lost a coin, lights a lamp and gets a broom and sweeps and sweeps and sweeps "until she finds it" (Luke 15:8). Again, how long is that? As long as it takes.

In Paul's letters, these themes are given prominence. He says that God "has made known to us the mystery of his will, according to the good pleasure that he set forth in Christ, as a plan for the fullness of time, to gather up all things in him, things in heaven and things on earth" (Eph. 1:9-10). Elsewhere, Paul declares with equal boldness: "For God has imprisoned all in disobedience so that he may be merciful to all" (Rom. 11:32).

We may have limited choices in relation to God—we may choose to accept God or reject God—but that does not mean that God is limited to the same choices in relation to us. We do not know how God will eventually draw us all into full communion. God has many ways to woo us. Certainly, some of those ways are not limited to our earthly lives. Even though our experience is bounded by birth on one end and death on the other, we should not assume the right to limit God's work to the same arena.

When I once made that point in a sermon, someone who had served in World War II was incensed: "Do you mean I will have to share eternity with Hitler?" he asked. "I want no part of that!" That response reveals an assumption that the Hitler with whom he would share eternity would be the same murderous Hitler he had known in this life. But after experiencing the purifying, redeeming presence of God, even the most degenerate of us can be transformed. So yes, after death we may share communion with Hitler. But that Hitler would not be the tyrant of human history; he would be the transformed Hitler of divine eternity, redeemed by the love of a God whose searching love is not limited by the span of our earthly life and who will not rest until we are found.

Heaven and hell, then, are not two different places. Rather, when we die, we all die into the eternal presence of God. Some will experience that as heaven and others as hell. If we have spent our lives serving, obeying, and praising God, when we die into the eternal presence of God, it will be the fulfillment of our desire. What we have longed for all our lives, communion with God, will be ours, and we will know the bliss we associate with heaven. If, instead, we have spent our lives scoffing at, disobeying, and denying God, when we die into the eternal presence of God, it will be a very different experience. To face the God whom we have disobeyed and denied, and to face in God's presence the truth about our own lives, is to know some of the torment and remorse we associate with hell.

A friend once told me that her understanding of divine judgment would be to have friends, family, and God all in a screening room showing a film of her life—her actions, her words, her thoughts—and those present would be asking, "Barbara, you did this?" and, "Barbara, you said that?" It is a sobering image, but I think an apt one. It contains some of the elements of Jesus's parable of the rich man and Lazarus (Luke 16:19–31). During their lives the poor beggar Lazarus waited outside the gate of the rich man's house hoping for a scrap of food. The rich man ignored Lazarus, their lives separated by a wall of stone and a still more impenetrable wall of indifference. Now, after death, they are together in the same place. But for each it is a very different experience. Lazarus is nestled in the bosom of Abraham, but the rich man is in torment because, for the first time, he finally sees the truth about his life, the choices he has made, and their consequences. Carlisle Marney once offered this helpful paraphrase of a familiar biblical passage: "You shall know the truth and the truth shall make you flinch before it makes you free."

To have a clear and searching light on all of our actions, to see them in all of their clarity and consequences for the first time in the pure and purifying presence of God is itself a form of punishment. In his epic poem *The Inferno*, Dante says that in hell the punishment is "the sin itself, experienced without illusion." If we think that this softens the concept of divine judgment, or if we are comforted by it, then perhaps it is because we have yet to imagine fully what it would be like finally to see ourselves without illusion.

If after our deaths we must survey our lives from God's point of view—that is, without illusion—then we are also invited to see, from God's point of view, that we can be made new. We are given the words of Scripture so that we may know how the story ends. The eternal life in which we are invited to share is not just any life; it is the life of the resurrected Jesus, a life that is ultimately triumphant over the torment and estrangement we associate with hell. But we cannot know just how and just when this triumph will be fully and clearly made known in our own lives. God searches for us in ways and at times that are beyond the borders of our imaginations and even beyond the span of our earthly lives.

In the meantime, eternal life is not merely something that will come in the sweet by and by; it is a reality we can catch glimpses of in the here and now. In Christian Scripture, the term "eternal life" is often used in the present tense, as something that can be experienced in this life as well as anticipated in the next. Eternal life connotes depth as well as length. It speaks of the quality of life as well as the quantity. In this life we can experience the kind of communion with God and one another that gives us a foretaste of the perfect communion we associate with heaven. Frederick Buechner offers this comparison:

> This side of Paradise, people are with God in such a remote and spotty way that their experience of Eternal Life is at best like the experience you get of a place approaching it at night in a fast train. Even the saints see only an occasional light go whipping by, hear only a sound or two over the clatter of the rails. The rest of us aren't usually awake enough to see as much as that, or we're mumbling over our nightcaps in the club car.[9]

In the light of the resurrection, we are encouraged to live a life of such depth and breadth and height that it can be called eternal life, offered to us not simply as a promise that awaits fulfillment at the end of time, but also as an invitation that awaits our response here and now.

CHAPTER 12

Doing Faith

According to the book of Exodus, Moses was on the Midian side of Mount Horeb, keeping his flock and minding his business, when God revealed himself (Exod. 3:1-12). And this was no gentle revelation that he could easily ignore. Moses saw a bush that was on fire without going up in flames, and he heard the very voice of God. As if that were not enough for one day, God said to Moses, in effect, "Now that I have your attention, I have an assignment for you. I have seen the suffering of my people in Egypt, and I have heard their desperate cries. Go to them and lead them out of slavery."

One might assume that Moses would not need to be told about the suffering of Israel in slavery. After all, they were his people, too. He knew them well. Indeed, he had once lived among them. There was a time when he had heard their sorrowing cries as surely as God had. But while he was tending a flock on a remote hillside, the cries could be silenced, the horrible sights could go out of focus—even in his imagination. Now, in the presence of God, that blissful distance was no longer possible. On Mount Horeb, Moses saw God; and that was indeed a welcome sight. But, as Moses discovered, to see God is to see other things that one might rather not see. In the presence of God, Moses saw, as if through God's eyes, the suffering of the slaves in Egypt. Their cries now had a sharply focused edge to them again, and he could no longer ignore them. The two revelations—of God and of God's people in need—were one. They always are.

Nevertheless, what God has joined together, we often attempt to break apart. In a variety of ways, we try to separate our devotion to God from service to others. And we are in good company. Even Jesus's most trusted disciples often seemed to miss the connection between the two. In one instance, according to John's Gospel, when Jesus encountered some of the disciples after his resurrection, they ate breakfast together by the gentle glow of a lakeside fire. As others broke off into their own conversations, Jesus turned to Peter and asked, "Simon, son of John, do you love me more than these?" It is *the* question, and Peter thought he had *the* answer: "Yes, Lord, you know that I love you." Then came Jesus's curious reply, an apparent non sequitur: "Feed my lambs."

Perhaps a little time elapsed before Jesus again turned to Peter and asked, "Simon, son of John, do you love me?" Peter thought he had already answered the question, but it did not seem the time to quibble, so again he replied, "Yes, Lord, you know that I love you." And Jesus said, "Tend my sheep."

Then a third time Jesus asked, "Simon, son of John, do you love me?" Peter, a fisherman who was never known for being on an even keel, was angered by the question: "Lord, you know everything, so you have to know that I love you." And again Jesus said, "Feed my sheep" (John 21:15–19).

We are not told if Peter ever got the point. The point is this: the question "Do you love me?" can never be answered fully in words. Saying it three times, elaborating on the depth of our devotion, is insufficient. When Robert Browning asked Elizabeth, "Do you love me?" she responded with her sonnet: "How do I love thee? Let me count the ways." But even when she had finished her beautiful counting, her words fell short of the true language of love.

Eliza sang to the hapless Freddie in *My Fair Lady*: "Words, words, words, all I hear are words. . . . Show me! Show me!" Words of devotion, welcome in some circumstances, can be annoying, even offensive, when they are not accompanied by action. And how do we express our devotion to God? By feeding and tending God's little ones. The God we encounter on the mountaintop is always pushing us back into the valley so that we can care for God's children in need.

Worship as Social Witness

Our devotion to God and our service to others may be as inseparable as two steps of a dance, but it all begins, as it did for Moses and Peter, in an encounter with God. It means that the social witness of Christians begins, not with a protest march or a soup kitchen, but with worship. Jim Wallis, founder of the Sojourners community, relates how he came to this understanding:

> When I was a new Christian, I read something by a monk who said, "Worship is the principal vocation of Christians." I remember disliking what he said. I was concerned about the gospel imperatives of feeding the hungry, clothing the naked, sheltering the homeless, and working for peace in a world at war. My dislike, in hindsight, was based on an inadequate understanding of worship.... I was victim of a trap that continues to confound and paralyze much of the church today. It's the trap of dividing the church between those who regard the gospel as principally spiritual and those who see the gospel as primarily political.... Since the earliest days of the church's life, there has always been an integral relationship between worship and politics. Worship and politics both raise the same questions: Whom do we love most? Where is our security finally rooted? To whom or to what are we most loyal? What finally is our deepest identity? All of these are worship questions; they are also political questions.[1]

The very existence of a community that worships God is itself a form of social witness. Governments have long understood this, and they typically respond to this threat by either attempting to domesticate the church or by trying to wipe it out. After all, those who have erected altars to nationalism, communism, capitalism, or any of the other "isms" that demand our allegiance, cannot long bear the existence of a living, visible, alternative community of faith that worships and responds to the claims of a different God. So sometimes the most effective thing the church can do for the world is to be the church. William Willimon observes:

The Puritans sowed the seeds for the American Revolution—not because Puritans were interested in being revolutionary, but because they proved, in dozens of New England churches, that democracy works for people who are freed by Christ to trust one another. The first Christians turned the world upside down, not by getting a majority of seats in the Roman Senate, but because the Classical World looked at the Church and said, "See how they love one another."[2]

Our encounter with God through worship is not simply a matter of getting our marching orders, so that we might leave knowing how we are to meet the needs of the world. If that were all that were required, then worship would be a simple matter. If we already knew what needs to be done, and we already had the character or strength or whatever else it takes to do it, then worship could be as simple and expeditious as a briefing session. If all we needed was to be informed, then such an approach to worship would be sufficient. If, however, the claims of those in need have a special claim on those who have encountered God; if the virtues required to address human need are cultivated in the community of faith; if more than being informed, we need to be formed into faithful people for the sake of the world—then we will tend carefully to our worship. We can be informed quickly, but to be formed takes much longer. For such a formation to take place, we will have to continually hear the biblical story, pray countless prayers, and sing the same songs of praise over and over again.

When Europeans brought African slaves to North America, they were eager to expose them to the Christian religion. After all, the gospel had civilized the sons and daughters of the slave owners, so why would it not work with these African "savages"? But when the slaves began to meet as a church, they heard what God had told the captive people of Israel: "I have observed the misery of my people who are in Egypt; I heard their cry on account of their taskmasters. Indeed, I know their sufferings, and I have come down to deliver them" (Exod. 3:7-8). And the slaves heard Paul say: "There is neither Jew or Greek, there is no longer slave or free, there is no longer male and female;

for all of you are one in Christ Jesus" (Gal. 3:28). The slaves heard and understood these words time and time again, and the words did not produce the compliant slaves that the slaveholders expected. Instead, this story spread the seeds of hope and the expectation of deliverance.

At the same time, European brothers and sisters began to hear these same words in churches throughout the country and to hear in them the word of God. So the abolition movement began—in worship. It did not happen all at once; rather, it took many years of prayers prayed and Scripture lessons read. But through them all a great power was unleashed, a faithful community was formed, and there was no turning back.

Mother Teresa did not wade into the slums of Calcutta because she thought it was a good thing to do. Rather, first she was immersed in the spiritual disciplines of her church, and in that way built a foundation that maintains her ministries still. The British journalist Malcolm Muggeridge has observed: "Each day Mother Teresa meets Jesus; first at the Mass, whence she derives sustenance and strength; then in each needing, suffering soul she sees and tends. They are one and the same Jesus; at the altar and in the streets. Neither exists without the other."[3] People who were simply well-meaning would have left the Calcutta slums long before. When asked why she had not left, Mother Teresa responded, "Because God told me to go and has not yet told me to leave."

Biographers of Martin Luther King Jr., when writing from a purely secular perspective, are frequently at a loss to explain what motivated and sustained this young African American preacher to withstand repeated violence and death threats in order to challenge the very seats of power in our land. The reason these biographers cannot fully explain King is that what he represented cannot be understood unless we understand the church. One night, when King had received yet another phone call threatening the lives of his family, he was plummeted into the depths of despair. But then, in his words:

It seemed in that moment that I could hear a voice saying to me, "Martin Luther, stand up for righteousness. Stand up for justice.

Stand up for truth. And lo I will be with you, even until the end of the world." I heard the voice of Jesus saying still to fight on. He promised never to leave me, never to leave me alone. No never alone. He promised never to leave me, never to leave me alone.[4]

Martin Luther King Jr. was able to hear that voice one night because he had heard the same words on so many other occasions. Sunday after Sunday, he had been immersed in the story of a God who led Israel out of Egypt and raised Jesus from the dead, a God who is on the side of the weak and sustains hope in circumstances that the world declares hopeless. Through the careful and continual worship of the church, he had heard that story so many times and in such a way that it was not only in his mind but was also stored in the marrow of his bones.

It takes a lot of singing and a lot of preaching for us just to get the story straight. But if, after all the singing and preaching, that story really sticks to our hearts, it makes a difference. We will leave our worship changed. And when that happens, we do not need to be told that we can make a difference in the world or that we need to help God make changes in the lives of others.

Are Christians Any Different?

When we single out worship as the starting point for Christian witness, it doesn't mean that people who worship other gods, or no god at all, are any less sympathetic to human need or any less drawn to meeting that need. People of other traditions can be just as motivated to serve others as Christians are, but Christians are motivated in different ways. Sometimes our compassion seems almost effortless, as if compassion is inescapably part of what it is to be human—a good thing to do. Human compassion can be very powerful. It is the force behind much that is praiseworthy in our world. However, if we respond to human need only because it seems like a good thing to do, eventually a time may come when turning our backs seems like a good thing to do. If we are motivated by our own response to human need, our efforts can become exhausted. When the emotional appeals of the television commercial for the hunger relief agency have been made too many times, or we have walked down too many streets crowded with human sorrow, or when the one we help disappoints us, or takes advantage, or shows not the least sign of gratitude—we may then discover that our compassion is actually quite limited. At such times, compassion no longer seems like an effortless, natural human inclination; it seems beyond the best human effort.

Many people assume that Christians are supposed to care more deeply and to feel more compassion than the rest of the world does. And when we Christians realize, to our continual frustration, that our feelings of compassion have very real limits and that by nature we are as prone toward self-concern as anyone, we can feel as if we have failed. But it is important to note that Jesus does not ask us to care for others, to turn our cheek, to give the shirt off our back, and to give to those who beg because we have compassion. Rather, he exhorts us to treat others this way because God has compassion. We do not care for the poor and pray for our enemies because that's the kind of people we naturally are, but because that's the kind of God our God is. Our God is kind to the ungrateful and selfish and makes the sun rise on the good and the bad. Ever since Jesus came into the world, Paul declares, "we regard no one from a human point of view" (2 Cor. 5:16).

Someone who works in an emergency shelter once told me that he often gets frustrated with those who seek refuge there. They can be difficult, surly, contrary, and ungrateful. In short, they can act very much like people. He frequently feels like lashing out or just giving up, and he has found only one way to transcend these natural human impulses. When he encounters a particularly unlovable person, he reminds himself that Christ died for this person. For this person, the one who makes my life difficult, the one I would rather never see again, of all people! Something like Paul's affirmation was the only thing that kept him from quitting: from now on, "we regard no one from a human point of view."

We Christians do not care for others because we have compassion for them; that compassion is likely to wear out. Instead, we express to those in need the love of a God who cares for each of us—as if he or she were the only one. We do not give the shirt off our back because we are feeling generous, but because we worship a God who showers gifts on us all. We do not offer to help the poor because they are deserving, but because God's gracious love extends to all, even to those who seem undeserving. We do not pray for our enemies in the hope that it might work—that is, because it might make them our friends—but because our enemies are God's precious children. Constant compassion can seem like an impossible task for mere human beings. That's why we have the God we know in Jesus Christ.

From Disciples to Apostles

Worship is the proper starting point for Christian witness—but not the endpoint. Our worship is to be judged by whether we leave our encounter with God changed, whether we see more clearly the suffering of God's people and are better equipped to address that suffering. Jesus used two words to describe his followers. One word was *disciples*, which means "students"; the other word was *apostles*, which means "those who are sent forth." Jesus first summoned people to him so that they might learn from him. But he did not stop there; he then sent them forth—that is, away from his side—into the world to carry out ministries in his name. In a similar way, we are summoned into the church to learn from Jesus. But then, just as important, we are sent forth to complete our calling: we are called into the church and then called to leave the church.

Our ministry to the world begins in the worship of the church, but unless our worship prepares us as people sent forth to do ministry, we will be an absurd spectacle. Jesus says that we will be no better than a spice that is purchased at great expense for the sole purpose of sitting forever on the shelf. We will be like a lamp placed under a bushel, which is as silly as paying huge electric bills only to cover every light in the house with paper bags. Our activities will be as absurdly incomplete as a high school that is so busy with pep rallies that there are never any actual sports events. There is certainly a time for high schools to have pep rallies, but if they do not lead to something else, they are exercises with no meaning. So we respond fully to the call to worship only when we also answer the call to leave worship and go forth to take up our ministries in the world.

When people describe why they come to worship, they often speak of their need for regular refueling. The word "refueling" is not a bad one to describe what happens in worship, but only if it is applied correctly. "Refueling" is not adequate to describe what we seek in worship and the life of the church if it means that we are simply seeking a way to rejuvenate ourselves, to find enough encouragement to face another week. Rather, we come to worship to be refueled for ministry. We are refueled not merely to invigorate ourselves, but so that we can bring the word of life to the world. We come not merely to be encouraged, but to be equipped to serve. We come not so that we might cope with the world, but so that we might care for the world.

The Reach of Outreach

Someone who wanted to follow Jesus said, "I will follow you wherever you go" (Luke 9:57). To say that to Jesus is to say that we are willing to go wherever Jesus is. That is, we are saying that we are willing to go to the near and distant places of suffering in our world, to confront the great and gaping hurts of people in whatever form they might take, to see the many faces of need throughout God's whole world. The man who offered to go wherever Jesus was going ended up not going anywhere with him—that is, after Jesus spelled out the implications of his offer. After all, we have to be especially careful when we offer to go "wherever" with Jesus, because going wherever with Jesus means going wherever God is, and that includes some grim and difficult places.

Andrew Young, former mayor of Atlanta and an ordained United Church of Christ minister, once told the following story. He had tried for some time to lead his daughter in the Christian faith and encourage her commitment to the Christian church, but with little success. When his daughter did eventually join a church, he was pleased.

But while she was in that church, she took an interest in the international housing ministry of Habitat for Humanity, and felt called to become a volunteer in that organization's project in Uganda. This was more than Young had bargained for. He was greatly concerned about having his daughter in what was at the time an unstable and violent country. He confessed with a self-deprecating laugh, "I just wanted to see her settle down and lead a decent Christian life, find a good Christian man to marry. I sure didn't have in mind her going to Uganda." Indeed, we have to be careful when we say that we will go wherever with anyone, especially if that person is Jesus. "Wherever" can be a strange and fearsome place, because it can include places like Uganda.

To say that we are willing to go wherever Jesus goes is not saying something in addition to saying that we are willing to follow Jesus. It's saying the same thing. Saying that we are willing to go "wherever" with Jesus is merely spelling out what it means to follow Jesus. We either sign up to go wherever with him, or we cannot go with him at all. This does not mean that we must all become foreign missionaries, though for some it can mean that. But saying that we are willing to go wherever with Jesus does mean that we are willing to be sent forth as apostles beyond our home, our church, and the circles in which we usually travel and are comfortable.

We often hear the reminder that "charity begins at home," and there is an element of truth in that admonition. We would not want to be so farsighted that we could only recognize need in faraway places, remaining blind to the faces of need in our own family and community. There would be something wrong with stepping coldly over a person sleeping in our own doorways on our way to some mission on another continent. We would certainly be distressed if the Good Samaritan of Jesus's parable were deserting his ailing wife and hungry children to set out on his famous trip from Jerusalem to Jericho, even if he did help a stranger in need along the way. There would be something awfully strange—and strangely awful—if that were the case.

When people use the expression "charity begins at home," or some more sophisticated equivalent, it is most often to set limits on the scope of our concern. Because most of us do not get much past the beginnings of charity, charity can begin and end in the same place—at home, or very close to home. The more telling question is "Where does charity end?" Does it end with our family, our community? Or does it end only when it reaches the person in need, no matter who that person is or where that person lives? Most people will probably recognize that a family member in need has a claim on them. But those who follow Jesus must go on to affirm that a person in need anywhere has a claim on Christians everywhere.

That is why it is significant that, in Jesus's parable, it is a Samaritan, of all people, who is commended to us. Samaritans and Jews did not have any dealings with each other. They lived separately and believed different things. They were bitter enemies. Ordinarily, if a Samaritan saw a Jew beaten and bleeding by the side of the road, it would be an occasion for some satisfaction. Among all those who saw the injured Jew, the Samaritan had the best reason to ask, "What has he to do with me?" But this Samaritan did not see a foreigner or a stranger or an enemy. This Samaritan saw a person in need. It is important to remember that the parable was offered in answer to the question "Who is my neighbor?" In other words: Who am I obliged to love? My family members? Those who live next door or in my country? Those who believe the same things I do? Jesus makes clear through the parable that our neighbor, the one who has a claim on us, is anyone in need. If our actions are to reflect God's care for God's children, then our precious earthly distinctions of tribe, creed, and nationality simply fade into irrelevance.

Beyond Charity to Advocacy

In our efforts to minister to individuals, we inevitably encounter larger societal issues. William Lee Miller asks us to imagine:

> Suppose the good Samaritan came upon the wounded man and took him to the inn and cared for him, and then came the next day and found another man in the same condition, and dealt again with

his wounds in the same way. Then suppose that on the next day and the next he met wounded travelers at the same place beside the same road, that he helped and cared for each of them. Suppose this went on for weeks.

Would we not think that there was something deficient in his faith if he never thought to ask who was patrolling that road against bandits?

Suppose he were a person of power in the community. Would there not be something deficient in the faith that never thought to use that power to try to prevent the attacks on travelers?

What if the servant of God would give his last bread to a starving stranger in a bread line, yet never think to ask questions about economic conditions that cause the bread line to exist?[5]

We have already considered the ways in which worship itself is a kind of political activity. As Miller's example demonstrates, however, there are times when our encounter with God in worship and our encounter with human need in the world will lead us to involvement in more conventional political activities. That is, there are times when the church will approach the seats of power to plead the cause of those in particular need on behalf of the God who demonstrates special care for the least, the last, and the lost. This advocacy can take many familiar forms—lobbying Congress, organizing boycotts, joining in protest marches, even civil disobedience—that are commonly engaged in by those who want to have an effect on the political process.

As important and appropriate as the church's involvement in public advocacy can be, a danger can accompany it. As we have seen, Christians do not care for the world because of some universal impulse to do the right thing, but rather in response to the unique story of God's care for the world in the life, death, and resurrection of Jesus. But the meaning and authority of this story is not recognized in the public sphere, filled as it is with people who do not see this story as theirs. So when Christians enter the public sphere, our concerns are often translated into terms that might make more sense to the world at large. For example, some Christians may oppose capital punishment because they believe that the God who gives life is the only one with the authority to end life. But such an argument holds no weight for those who do not believe in God; so Christians who oppose capital punishment need to interpret their opposition in ways that have more general appeal. We will argue against capital punishment because it is an ineffective deterrent to crime, or because it is costly, or simply because it seems wrong.

There is nothing wrong with translating the peculiarly Christian perspective into terms that can be more generally understood in the culture at large. After all, politics is a matter of finding common ground and building coalitions. The danger is that, in the search for common ground, the uniqueness of the Christian perspective can be lost entirely. The church can come to represent just another lobbying group making the same arguments that could be heard elsewhere. Denominational gatherings can begin to resemble political conventions, the more liberal denominations talking like Democrats with a slight religious accent, the more conservative denominations saying little that could not be heard at a Republican Party convention.

There is a further danger that, in attempting to speak the language of the surrounding culture, in addressing a culture that does not share the Christian story, we can neglect or even forget the unique dimensions of that story. The Christian story, rightly told, reflects different concerns. It seems strange to the world, and because we are in part people of the world ourselves, there are times when it seems strange to us. It is a story filled with heroes and martyrs, foremost among them the one who died on Golgotha, for whom survival was definitely not the issue. In this story, it was the Romans who were willing to put Jesus to death out of a concern for national survival. By contrast, our forebears in the faith were not ultimately concerned with the rise and fall of nations because they also saw themselves as citizens of another realm. They were willing to die rather than to kill because they viewed their own survival as being less important than following the one who was willing to die rather than take up the instruments of violence. Needless to say, this is not a commonsense approach. But then, the world does not need the church to supply common sense; there are plenty of other sources. The church serves the world when it offers a decidedly uncommon perspective that is not otherwise available to the culture at large.

The abortion debate provides a telling example. Liberal churches, citing a right to choose, square off against conservative churches, proclaiming a right to life. In so doing, neither side adds anything to the public debate because both positions are already amply represented in the political arena. Furthermore, when we speak of rights, we are speaking in a language that derives not from the Bible but from Enlightenment philosophers, which has become the language of the modern democratic state. By contrast, the Bible speaks not of rights but of duties, which we owe to God and to our neighbor. Dale Rosenberger reminds us: "For us, life is not a right, but a gift. Life is a gift of God and belongs wholly to God, despite any appearances to the contrary. And when we receive gifts, obligations spread out in every direction."[6] Notice that, if Christians were to bring this perspective to the issue of abortion, there might still be differences of opinion, but the entire debate would be recast. Instead of echoing positions that are already well-worn in public debate, Christians would bring different and fresh questions to bear, questions such as: What are our obligations to the unborn? What are our obligations to fathers- and mothers-to-be who do not want or cannot care for children?

There will be times when we Christians can appropriately speak in ways that are commonly understood, such as when we can appeal to commonly held standards of right and wrong. We may also join with non-Christians if, in a particular instance, they are fighting the same evil we would fight or pursuing the same good we would pursue. Even so, such alliances with fellow travelers will always be on an ad hoc basis. Inevitably, a time will come when we will have to travel our own way because our destination is ultimately on the road less traveled, the one that leads to the cross and the empty tomb.

Big Things from Small Beginnings

Jesus proclaimed that nothing less than the realm of God was near, and he invited his followers to work toward the fulfillment of God's reign in tangible ways. But when we consider all that this entails—feeding the poor, sheltering the homeless, comforting the sick, clothing those who have inadequate clothing, receiving the stranger, working for peace, appealing for justice—our quite natural reaction can be to shrink from the enormity of the task. After all, the mandate is momentous. Our own efforts can seem puny by comparison. Where to begin? Why even try? But Jesus made it clear that the realm of God does not start out on a grand scale. It starts out small. It all begins with something no larger than a mustard seed, the tiniest of all seeds, which grows into a tree large enough for a bird to nest in its branches (Luke 13:18-19).

In his memoirs, Oscar Wilde told of being brought from prison, where he was held after being found "guilty" of homosexuality, to face the additional indignities of the Court of Bankruptcy:

> When I was brought down from my prison between two policemen, [a man I know] waited in the long dreary corridor so that, before the whole crowd, whom an action so sweet and simple hushed into silence, he might gravely raise his hat to me, as, handcuffed and with bowed head, I passed him by. . . . I do not know to the present moment whether he is aware that I was even conscious of his action. I store it in the treasure-house of my heart. I keep it there as a secret debt that I am glad to think I can never possibly repay. . . . When wisdom has been profitless to me and philosophy barren, and the proverbs and phrases of those who have sought to give me consolation as dust and ashes in my mouth, the memory of that little lovely silent act of love has unleashed for me all the wells of pity, and brought me out of the bitterness of lonely exile into harmony with the wounded, broken, and great heart of the world.[7]

Desmond Tutu, the black Episcopal Archbishop of South Africa who won the Nobel Peace Prize for his ongoing nonviolent struggle against apartheid, was once asked to recall the formative experiences of his life. He replied: "One incident comes to mind immediately. When I was a young child I saw a white man tip his hat to a black woman. Please understand that such a gesture is completely unheard of in my country. The white man was an Episcopal bishop and the black woman was my mother."

These two stories remind us that God's realm can start in just that way, with something as small as a mustard seed. Even a gesture as small and fragile as a mere tip of the hat can communicate the largest and most powerful of all realities—the love of God. Perhaps the realm of God starts out small so that we will not shrink from the enormity of the reality in which we are invited to share, so that we can all take our part. Yet a mustard seed can be overlooked or dismissed as too small to be of consequence. We assume that it takes something large and impressive to grow a tree: surely it takes more than we have to make big things grow—more faith, more courage, more skill, more time. We turn our pockets inside out and say, "See, nothing here." To which God replies, "Look again. There in the fold of your pocket, nestled in the dust, is a mustard seed. Plant that. I will supply the rest." God does not ask more from us than we have, and sometimes what we have is not any larger than a mustard seed. Sure enough, if we do not plant the seed, it will remain small and of little consequence. But if we plant it, God can use it (oh, how God can use it!) and it will grow beyond anything we can envision.

We can no more bring about the dominion of God than we can make a tree grow. The parable of the mustard seed is not a kind of credo for the positive thinker. Jesus does not say that we can do some big things, or big things with God's help, but that God can do big things, even establish a dominion on earth, if we but dare to plant the tiny seed that has been entrusted to us.

CHAPTER 13

Sharing the News

According to Luke's Gospel, when the resurrected Jesus gathered with his followers one final time, he gave them a brief summary of his ministry and reminded them that he was raised from the dead to fulfill the ancient scriptural promises (Luke 24:44–49). Then, immediately before being lifted up into heaven, Jesus said, "You are witnesses of these things." As if they needed to be told! Of course they were witnesses. They could not have denied it even if they had wanted to. They were witnesses who did not fully know what they were witnessing, during those days when Jesus seemed like nothing more than a wise teacher with uncommon insight into the ways of God. They were witnesses when they saw something that only the eye of faith could see, that this Jesus was God's chosen one, the Messiah. They were witnesses when they would rather not have been, when Jesus died on a cross. And they were witnesses when they might have concluded that their eyes had deceived them—when they saw Jesus alive again.

The word "witness" has two meanings, both in our language and in Greek. First, a witness is someone who has seen something, as in "eyewitness"; second, a witness is someone who gives testimony to what he or she has seen, as in a witness who appears in a court of law. Thus, by calling his followers "witnesses," Jesus was not only saying that they had seen these things, but also that, as witnesses, they were now to declare what they had seen—that is, what God had done through Jesus. It is necessary to tell the story because the Christian faith is not something that you can "get" from a hike in the mountains or by contemplating eternal truths. There is no other way to become a Christian except by hearing the story.

Yet, even here Jesus seems to be telling his followers to do something that they would do anyway, for seeing what they had seen and telling others about it would seem to be inextricably connected. To instruct them to tell what they had seen seems about as necessary as telling a mother who has just given birth to a child that she must go and tell others about it. To witness such an event is to declare it. We would think it strange if it were otherwise. We cannot imagine the father of a slave family mentioning casually after dinner, "Oh, I almost forgot, we were set free today. We're not slaves anymore." There is something about news like this that does not wait until after dinner. It has a sense of urgency that makes it demand to be told.

So the followers of Jesus went into the public arenas and private corners of their world and told what they had seen to anyone who would listen, and even to those who would not. They told the story of Jesus as if they could not keep from telling it. They told it with the urgency and conviction of people who knew that there was nothing that the world needed more than to hear what they had to share, as if they knew the way out of a burning building or were bringing bread to the starving. It was urgent news, important news, and—above all—it was good news. There is another word to describe this form of witness: evangelism.

Recoiling from the Call to Evangelism

Many of us recoil from the call to evangelism because of what we associate with the word, which may conjure up images of a rigid biblical literalism. We may associate "evangelism" with manipulative tent-meeting revivalists or their modern equivalents, television preachers. We may think of a time when someone thrust a religious tract into our hands, perhaps accompanied by intrusive professions of concern for our eternal destiny. We may assume that being an evangelist means accosting others with questions such as "Are you saved?" We may have concluded that evangelism is just another name for religious imperialism, the arrogant attempt to bring others, at all costs, into our particular religious fold. When we encounter these forms of evangelism, we might very well respond with the poet William Wordsworth, "Great God! I'd rather be a pagan suckled in a creed outworn...."

David H. C. Read reminds us that, despite these associations with the word "evangelism," the literal meaning reflects positive connotations:

> The first discovery to be made as we track down the etymology of "evangelism" is that it is a beautiful word. If it has become, as I have suggested, an ugly word for some today, this is simply because of unfortunate associations that have been attached to it. The word is, in itself, exquisite since it has the prefix *eu*, meaning "good," which we find attached to happy words like euphoria, euphonious, eutopia, and eupepsia. The opposite prefix, *dys*, meaning bad, gives us words like dyspepsia and dysentery. Perhaps we need the word "dysangelism" to describe some of the worst methods of spreading the Christian gospel. Then it also—perhaps you have never noticed—contains the lovely word "angel." An angel is a messenger, one who brings news. So evangelism is nothing other than the bringing of good news.[1]

Read reminds us that it is important to make a distinction between the methods of evangelism we sometimes see in use and the call to evangelism. We may reject certain methods that are used by those who call themselves evangelists, but the call to evangelism, to share the good news, remains.

Beyond the odious associations with the word "evangelism," even beyond our objection to methods of evangelism we sometimes see being used, there is another reason why we may shrink from the call to evangelism: we are uncertain witnesses. We are all too aware that, compared to our oceans of doubt, our faith would scarcely fill a cup. Our experiences of God are most often fleeting and tenuous.

In response, there may be times when we feel able to whisper an affirmation of faith, but we don't want to declare aloud what we don't know with something like certainty. We tell ourselves that when God is revealed more clearly in our lives, then we might respond with commensurate clarity. But when God is present in our lives only as a still, small voice, we prefer to use a still smaller voice in response. Is it any wonder, then, that we often act less like we are spreading the good news than like we are spreading the good secret?

Just What We Have Seen and Heard

A couple of years ago I attended a denominational gathering for clergy and lay leaders on the subject of evangelism. After worship and a few lectures, we divided into various workshops. One workshop seemed to start later than the others because the people who had been assigned to it were lingering around the coffeepot. That workshop was entitled "Learning How to Talk about Your Faith." After three cups of coffee, I joined that group. When I entered the conference room, I noticed that people had notebooks out, pencils poised, probably hoping that they would be given a comprehensive lecture on how to talk about our faith—and probably also hoping that they would not have to do any of the talking themselves.

The leader of the group, a local church pastor, began by passing out some printed material, including an outline of his presentation and a bibliography. That was certainly a good sign. But never once did he refer to the printed material. Instead, he began by telling stories. The first was about a man in his parish, a prominent business leader, who once made a lunch date with the pastor to discuss what the man described as "something very important." Over the course of the lunch, after they had bobbed on the surface of pleasantries for some time, the businessman finally got around to the reason he had asked his pastor to lunch. Several years earlier, he confided, he had had an intense religious experience. He told his pastor that, as strange as it might sound, he was convinced that he had actually heard the voice of God. He still did not know what to make of the experience, but he knew that he would never be the same again. In response, the pastor said, "Well, that's wonderful. Would you be willing to share that experience with the members of our congregation?" The man replied, "Are you kidding? I haven't even told my wife!"

After telling that story, the workshop leader talked a bit about his cancer surgery and described the ways in which, at certain points, he felt an almost palpable sense of the presence of God. He went on to tell a few other stories about other experiences that were less dramatic perhaps, but no less real to him. When he finished, he invited those present to share some stories of their own. There was a long silence. People began to open their notebooks and shuffle through their handouts. But then, perhaps to save us all from this awkward silence, someone finally said, "I have a story to share." She told about reconciling with her father after years of being unable even to look at him without anger.

Then the stories began to flow. There is, after all, no better response to a good story than to tell another. Someone else told about the birth of his child. After that, someone told about how she was able to stop drinking. I told about some remarkable events surrounding the death of my father. We told one story after another, some of which seemed like dramatic revelations of God, and some of which were about more everyday happenings. In each instance, however, the stories we told were about some moment when we had at least an intimation of the presence of God. Many of these stories had never been told before. That gathering reminded me of a story told by Fred Craddock:

> As a boy I spent pleasant summer evenings gathering fallen stars. As I think back on it, the spent stars were worthless, but it was something to do. My brothers and I would go to a field near the house, climb up on tree stumps and wait for stars to fall. From these perches we could see exactly where the stars fell, and it was not uncommon to have the pockets filled within an hour. Sometimes, whether in greed or out of compassion for fallen stars that might otherwise go unnoticed, I do not know, we would sneak from the back porch with Grandma's clothes basket and harvest

the remaining stars still flickering on the ground. And sometimes, dragging the heavy basket home left us too tired to empty it. "We will do it in the morning," but in the morning Grandma was already fussing about a residue of gray ashes in her clothes basket. (Everyone knows that you cannot save stars over until the next night.) We denied charges of having kindled a fire in her basket and snickered off to play, protected from punishment by the mystery. But during her last illness, Grandma called me to her bed and told me, almost secretively, that she knew what we had been doing with her basket. My guilty silence was broken by her instruction for me to bring to her from the bottom of an old chest a package wrapped in newspaper. I obeyed and then waited the eternity it took for her arthritic fingers to open the bundle. "Oh, it's gone," she said, showing me where it had been. In the bottom of the package was a little residue of gray ashes. We stared at each other.

"You, too, Grandma? Why didn't you tell me?"

"I was afraid you would laugh at me. And why didn't you tell me?"

"I was afraid you would scold me."[2]

Over the years, I have often reflected on Craddock's story, and I believe that I have seen it reenacted many times. Someone will tell me—quietly, reluctantly—about a moment when he or she caught a glimpse of the mystery that crackles just below the surface of life, a moment of uncommon beauty, or insight, or what might be called revelation. Groping for ways to describe such an experience, he or she will sometimes use religious words, although seldom without apology: "I know this may sound crazy to you, but ..." Or "I have never really thought of myself as a religious person, but ..." The moment may have taken place at a singular event, such as the birth of a child, or it may have been during the most commonplace of Tuesdays. It might have happened during a worship service, or while talking with a friend. The settings vary, but the settings don't really matter because they are but a backdrop for the experience.

We all gather such moments in our own lives, but for the most part we hide them from one another as if they were dark secrets, rather than the deep and shining experiences they are, brighter than any falling star. The author of the first letter of John wrote: "What was from the beginning, what we have heard, what we have seen with our eyes, what we have looked at and touched with our hands, concerning the word of life ... what we have seen and heard we proclaim to you" (1 John 1:1, 3).

Evangelism, then, does not begin with a recitation of doctrine, but with what we have seen and heard, with our own experiences of the word of life, no matter how halting or momentary or ambiguous those experiences may have been. Evangelism begins with talk about our lives and the times when we may have sensed our lives intersecting with the life of God. It's true that even putting it this way does not make evangelism easy. God revealed in our lives? If we start talking like that, what will people think? Yes, we have heard that God is supposed to be revealed in ordinary lives—but surely not in lives like ours.

But then, even in lives like ours, something can happen. It may be a moment of awe when we suddenly recognize that there is more to life than is dreamed of in the world's philosophies. It may be at the moment of birth, when we are overtaken by the sacredness of life, or at the moment of death, when we know beyond doubt that death does not write the final chapter. It may be in a word that unexpectedly finds a home in our hearts, and we know that we have been waiting our whole lives to hear that word of peace or challenge. It may be a silent prayer that is shared with hundreds of others, a silence that is deeper and richer than the silence of the stars. Just what we have seen and heard. No more than that.

When we begin our evangelism here, with what we have seen and heard, some remarkable things happen. We discover that this form of religious talk is less threatening than others. If we only tell what we have seen and heard, that leaves room for others to tell what they have seen and heard. Told in this way, stories of faith can stand alongside stories of doubt. They are both valuable. They need not be reconciled into some kind of neat doctrine. The Bible is a collection of stories, the stories of people's encounters with God and the absence of God. These stories are not brought into some kind of system, because life is not a system, but they're simply stories brought between two covers because in the end they are all part of the same story. Beyond this, if we begin to talk with one another about what we have seen and heard, we will be more attuned to the often subtle, partially hidden movement of God in the world. That is, we will begin to see more and hear more. If the moments when we sense the presence of God seem rare in our lives, that is all the more reason to be part of a community of people who tell what they have seen and heard because, in those times when we have no story to tell, we can be sustained by the stories of others.

Our Stories and the Story

Although evangelism may begin with what we have seen and heard in our own lives, it does not end there. We also place our own individual stories alongside other stories of God's interaction with the world that are found in the Bible and in other historic witnesses, showing that our own stories are caught up in the sweep of a larger story. Set in this context, our own stories gain clarity and depth. We can begin to recognize that the God who seems to steal in and out of our lives on occasion is the same God who is bound in covenant with us and has promised never to abandon us. The God who remains largely hidden beneath the clutter of our days is the same God who is revealed in Jesus Christ. Ultimately, we are sustained, not by our own stories but by this larger story of which our stories are a part. And because we are sustained by this story, we endeavor to share it with others.

Martin Luther once defined evangelism as one beggar telling another beggar where to find bread. (Perhaps it is no coincidence that Luther's dying words were: "We are all beggars, every one.") It is our obligation to share the knowledge of where to find sustenance. If we derive strength from God, it is our obligation to share that with those who seek strength. If we receive peace from the continuing presence of Christ, it is our obligation to share that with those who yearn for peace. If our lives find meaning in the Christian story, it is our obligation to share that story with those who long for their lives to have meaning. We have been called to share what has been given to us with all beggars—that is, with everyone—as surely as if we had a surplus of bread in a hungry world. As we have been invited to feast on the presence of God, we are also called on to extend that invitation to others. Evangelism, then, is an invitation to personal faith, an invitation to a community of faith, and an invitation to be a disciple in the world. (This threefold invitation of evangelism has been spelled out most helpfully by Allan Johnson, particularly in his pamphlet "Evangelism for Today."[3])

Invitation to Personal Faith

John records that Philip, soon after he had accepted Jesus's call to follow him, sought out his friend Nathanael and made this remarkable statement of faith: "We have found him of whom Moses in the law and also the prophets wrote, Jesus of Nazareth, the son of Joseph" (John 1:45). Nathanael, who had never met Jesus, did not need to hear any more to dismiss the claim out of hand. "Can anything good come out of Nazareth?" he asked. His rhetorical question, of course, was drenched in sarcasm. Is there any other way to react to the preposterous claim that the savior of the world comes from such a Godforsaken backwater little town? Philip could have responded by repeating his claim with greater verve or by carefully marshaling all of the reasons he believed the claim to be true, or he could have simply walked away. Instead, he offered a simple invitation: "Come and see." That invitation is the essence of evangelism: "Come and see for yourself. I can tell you what I have seen, but I cannot give you faith. I cannot even adequately describe what I see in this person. I can only invite you to come and see for yourself so that you can make your own decision." It was not after Nathanael heard Philip's credo, but only after Nathanael accepted Philip's invitation and went to see and hear Jesus for himself, that his skepticism became affirmation, that his question marks became exclamation points.

Evangelism is, in part, an invitation to personal faith. It is personal, first, because we are not invited to respond to a set of beliefs; rather, we are invited to encounter a person, Jesus of Nazareth. Second, it is personal because it takes root in our own personal experiences and involves a personal commitment. No one can make that commitment for us; there are no secondhand Christians. Uruguayan biblical scholar Mortimer Arias encompasses both dimensions when he reminds us: "Discipleship is not only obeying a commandment or following the teaching of Jesus, but a personal commitment to one person. 'If you want to be *my* disciple ... take up your cross and follow *me*.'"[4]

Faith is personal, but it is not private—an important distinction that is often lost. Faith is personal in that it involves an individual commitment of one person to another. If faith were private, however, we would not share it. The invitation "Come and see" reflects the understanding that a personal faith is meant to be shared. We have all, on occasion, received invitations that deteriorated into coaxing or even came to resemble threats. Many people associate so-called evangelism campaigns with this kind of coercive invitation. Needless to say, however, when we are inviting others to encounter our gracious God, our invitations must be gracious invitations. That is, they must be invitations that are freely offered and to which a person may respond—or not respond—freely.

Invitation to a Community of Faith

If the Christian faith were only a matter of personal commitment and devotion, then no other invitation would be necessary. But because Christianity is a religion of community first and last, a further invitation is extended to join the community of faith. In our time, we invite others to "come and see" Jesus in the ongoing life of the church. The church, which Paul called "the body of Christ," attempts to embody the love of Christ in tangible ways. As Christ's body, the church is charged with being Christ's heart and hands and with carrying on the ministry of Christ in the world. In fact, receiving and showing hospitality toward the stranger is itself one of the ways in which the church carries out the ministry of the one who received strangers and called them brothers and sisters.

When we invite others to a church, we are not only inviting them to witness the continued presence of Jesus as manifest in the church; we are also inviting them to help show this continued presence as they themselves become part of the church. Beyond inviting others to witness the mystery of how the work of Christ can continue through frail and flawed humanity, we also invite them to become part of the mystery themselves.

Some people may be discouraged from extending an invitation to their church because they do not see anything in their church that they would want to invite others to "come and see." We may not see the ways the work of Christ continues in the life of our church, so how can we invite others to see it? There are, of course, two possible reasons for our discouragement. One possibility is that the shortcomings of our church may be so glaring that we have become blind to the ways in which Christ's work continues in the life of our church. Another possibility is that there may not be much to see after all. In this latter instance, the call to evangelism becomes a challenge to the church to exhibit greater faithfulness. Before we invite someone into our home we often consider how we might make our home a more inviting place. For example, we may clean up the clutter that otherwise might have gone unnoticed. Similarly, it may be as we consider inviting someone to "come and see" Jesus in our church that we will pay attention to our life together with renewed dedication and will consider the ways in which our church might exhibit more fully the love of Christ, both within the community of faith and in the world. The South African scholar David J. Bosch reminds us:

> Evangelism is possible only when the community that evangelizes—the church—is a radiant manifestation of the Christian faith and has a winsome lifestyle. Marshall McLuhan has taught us that the medium is the message. This is eminently true of the church-in-evangelism. If the church is to impart to the world a message of hope and love, of faith and justice, something of this should become visible, audible, and tangible in the church itself. According to the book of Acts the early Christian community was characterized by compassion, fellowship, sharing, worship, service

and teaching (Acts 2:42–47; 4:32–35). Its conspicuously different lifestyle became itself a witness to Christ.[5]

It is chastening, but inescapably true nonetheless, that we invite others to faith not only by what we say, but also by who we are as the faith community.

Evangelism is sometimes confused with the concern for church growth. Church growth may be desirable, but it is not synonymous with evangelism: it is an institutional concern originating in a need or desire for more members. The goal of church growth is to have more people join our particular church. Evangelism, sharing the good news, has different goals: it is not concerned with the growth or survival of any one particular church. Evangelism certainly does include the invitation to share in the life of a church; but a person may respond to such an invitation by joining a church other than the one we are members of. If, for example, the members of a Lutheran church were to share the evangel, the good news, in such a way that a majority were to respond by joining Baptist and Episcopal churches, they could be perceived as failing to foster the growth of their particular church, but they would have been successful evangelists.

Authentic evangelism may also, in fact, cause people not to join any church at all because of the cost involved.[6] There are those who will respond to the evangel, the good news, the way the one rich young man responded to Jesus's invitation to follow. He seemed eager—that is, until he learned what such a commitment entailed (Luke 18:18–23). We have to be prepared to let others respond to our invitation in just that way. In fact, we have no other choice. We can extend the invitation to others, but we cannot respond for them. Confusion on this point can cause our attempts to share the good news to degenerate into an assaultive proselyting that distorts the true nature of invitational evangelism. The invitation we have to offer is an open invitation; it is open to both the workings of the Spirit and a variety of responses.

Invitation to Discipleship in the World

Even as we invite others to join us in the church, we also invite them to join us in leaving the church to take up our ministries in the world. We can share the word of life, the good news, not only by what we say but also by what we do. The letter of James charges us to be "doers of the word" (James 1:22). This command can be fulfilled when we refuse to imitate the violent ways of the world or when we show the special care Jesus demonstrated toward those who had been cast off by life. It can be fulfilled when we give shelter to the homeless in the name of the one who said, "Foxes have holes, and birds of the air have nests; but the Son of Man has nowhere to lay his head" (Matt. 8:20). This mandate can be fulfilled when we invite the poor to life's table, as Jesus did—not to eat the leftovers, but as the guests of honor. We can make an eloquent, even though silent, witness to the love of God in many and varied ways, as many and as varied as the ways of Jesus.

There can be something powerful in an unspoken witness. Our ministries in the world can themselves be a form of invitation. In fact, we may even be inclined to think that no other form of invitation is necessary. In one church discussion group I was leading, a man said, "I never say anything about my faith. If you want to know what I believe, watch what I do." At that point, a good friend of his interjected, "You may have to watch very closely...." The two friends laughed together, and then the rest of us joined in. For all of us, it was the humbling laughter of recognition. The witness of our lives is seldom clear without the aid of words. The problem with saying that we would rather act out our faith than talk about it is that it sets up a false choice. Bosch observes: Evangelism "consists in word *and* deed, proclamation *and* presence, explanation *and* example. The verbal witness remains indispensable, not least because our deeds and our conduct are ambiguous; they need elucidation."[7]

Although invitational evangelism involves both word and deed, that does not mean that each is found in equal measure. Sometimes our verbal witness will be no more imposing or obvious than a footnote. In the college I attended, there was a "plagiarism code" that enumerated the rules of scholarly citation and the punishments for their infraction. One of my professors liked to give what he called a "positive interpretation" of the code. Instead of focusing on the imperatives and punishments, he said this: "You must footnote. In a scholarly community, we owe it to one another to point to our source so that, if readers have interest, they can look to the source for themselves." We could say something similar about our verbal witness: it can be a footnote to our actions. If our care for those in need derives from our faith in God, we are obliged to footnote our actions so that others can turn there as well. If we work for peace because we have been claimed by the Prince of Peace, that needs to be footnoted so that others can turn to the source of our actions. Our actions may be a most powerful expression of our witness, but a word—sometimes no more than a word—is necessary for our witness in the world to take the form of an invitation.

Inviting and Invited

In the book of Acts we read about a Roman centurion named Cornelius who had a vision in which an angel (a messenger) told him to send for a man named Simon Peter. Even though the message came without any further explanation, Cornelius did as he was told. When Simon Peter entered Cornelius's home, he announced that he did not usually do such things, that as a Jew he was forbidden from entering the home of a Gentile, and he demanded to know what this was all about. At that, Cornelius told Peter about his vision, and he asked to hear about Peter's god. That was all Peter needed to hear. And he declared: "I truly understand that God shows no partiality, but in every nation anyone who fears him and does what is right is acceptable to him" (Acts 10:34-35). This story is sometimes referred to as the "conversion of Cornelius," but it might more appropriately be called the "conversion of Peter." It was Peter who showed a complete turnaround (*conversion* can best be translated "turnaround"). Peter had thought that the good news was only for Jews; but after visiting Cornelius, he saw that it was for all people. Perhaps he entered Cornelius's house with a willingness to share his understanding of who

Christ is; but he certainly left it with a whole new understanding of who Christ is.

Those who set out to share the good news often discover that they are changed in the process. Good news does not always travel a one-way street. Those doing the inviting need to remember that they, too, are continually being invited to new understandings of God and a renewed relationship with God. We may hear the good news in the things we ourselves do or the words we ourselves say, when our own actions or words echo back to us with the word of life. And we need to continually receive the silent and spoken witness of others—of those inside and those outside the church. We not only invite others to join us, but we also respond to the invitation to join others, to learn what they have seen and heard of God's ways and God's word. We join together in an unfolding journey of discovery and discipleship.

PART FOUR

Conclusion

CHAPTER 14

The Invitation

Let's be frank. We may be wary of the notion that we are invited to be Christ's disciples. We may not know all that is implied by such a commitment, but we do know that we are not qualified for it. We are all too aware of our shortcomings. Our beliefs seem small and frail because they have grown in the shadow of great doubt. It is important for us, in response to these feelings, to remember that the invitation to discipleship may be an awesome privilege, but it is no great honor. Here's an example of how Jesus went about choosing the twelve original disciples: He was walking along the shore of the Sea of Galilee when he saw two brothers, Simon and Andrew, fishing. He said to them, "Follow me, and I will make you fish for people" (Matt. 4:19).

Allow that scene to surprise you. We have no indication that Jesus knew these two fishermen. No interviews were held, no letters of reference submitted. Jesus chose these disciples, not because they exhibited the proper qualifications, but almost at random. Jesus did what he invited Peter and Andrew to do. Like one fishing for followers, Jesus simply cast out his net and hauled in whoever happened to be there. That day Jesus brought in a motley catch: a few uneducated fishermen, a tax collector, and a hotheaded zealot.

We don't particularly like to think about that. We'd like to think that Jesus chose extraordinary people for this extraordinary task of discipleship. We might even imagine that Jesus could intuit something about the people he called, look into their hearts from fifty paces and see some glimmer of a diamond when all that was visible to the human eye was rough coal. That might explain why the twelve disciples seemed to be such simple, unqualified people to begin with; but it would not explain why the disciples *remained* so simple and grossly unqualified for their task throughout Jesus's ministry. Their faith didn't commend them. More often than not, they misunderstood Jesus's teachings. They couldn't perform miracles or work wonders. When Jesus was arrested and the going got tough, they got going all right—as far away as they could get. And if Jesus chose his disciples on the basis of what he perceived as some latent virtue in them, that would not explain why someone like Judas was called. Yet these twelve, including Judas, were Jesus's chosen.

If these characterizations of the disciples sound harsh, perhaps that's because we have done, in retrospect, what we wish Jesus had done to begin with. We assume that any great leader would surround herself or himself with the best people available, so we make the disciples the kind of people we would have chosen—people of faith, great loyalty, and understanding. But there is another, more compelling, reason for us to believe that the disciples were called because Jesus perceived some hidden qualities in them. Quite simply, we can, with that understanding, escape the call. When Jesus goes fishing for disciples, we are off the hook. If Jesus were looking only for people of certain qualifications of faith and understanding to be his disciples, then we need not answer the call—because we know we don't have the necessary qualifications. By contrast, if Jesus called his disciples without regard to qualifications—if he called just anybody—that would mean that he could call you or me.

Indeed, God's ways are not our ways, and if we are honest, we have to admit that we often prefer our ways. After all, if we take seriously the way Jesus recruited his disciples, then we might be asked to drop what we are doing to follow him. Our incompetence, our doubts, and our obvious unsuitability for the job are no refuge. We, too, can be caught in Jesus's sweeping net. And that is frightening. We would rather idolize the disciples than see that they are not different from us. We would rather sit back and admire them than realize that we might be called to stand up and join them.

Who, Me?

There is a kind of "Who, me?" quality in every call to discipleship. We don't believe that Jesus could want us and, what's more, we are not sure that we trust a savior who would want us, for we are acutely aware of our own flaws and frailties. Groucho Marx once said, "I would not belong to any club that would have me as a member." Who would want to be a part of a savior's circle of trusted disciples that was composed of people like us? But that is precisely the mystery that the gospel proclaims, and that may be why Jesus chose his first disciples without regard to their qualifications—so that those who follow will not believe that discipleship is a special honor bestowed on people who have proven themselves qualified. We know that we were not specially chosen because of our virtue, faith, or understanding. The apostle Paul is blunt about it: "Consider your own call, brothers and sisters: not many of you were wise by human standards, not many were powerful, not many were of noble birth. But God chose what is foolish in the world to shame the wise; God chose what is weak in the world to shame the strong" (1 Cor. 1:26-27).

Paul speaks of us as he would speak of himself. He calls us fools—and we are. We are more given to doubt than to faith, more to selfishness than to virtue, and we are usually far from understanding. If God chose what is foolish to shame the wise, then God must have stacked the deck by choosing the most foolish of all. This only underscores the mystery of what the gospel proclaims. After all, it would not be anything special if God did super things with super people—no miracle in that. But it takes the mysterious power of God to do super things with very ordinary people, with disciples chosen from humanity at its most common and flawed.

The invitation to discipleship is not an invitation to live up to our human potential, for there may be less of that potential in us than we like to imagine. Rather, the invitation to discipleship is an invitation to live up to our divine potential, to realize the potential God has to work through us and the potential we have to make us channels of the power of God and the love of Christ. Those who have heard Jesus's invitation to follow may still be uncertain about how to respond; after all, it is such an unlikely invitation to come to unlikely people like us. But, as I hope this book has made clear at every turn, it is the kind of surprisingly wonderful thing that God has always done and is still doing.

The Question Jesus Asks

Simple questions are often the most difficult to answer, and so it is with the question that Jesus asks. Jesus's question reaches across history and into our very lives. It is at the heart of the invitation to discipleship. It is a question that sooner or later demands an answer from each of us, for though we can avoid making up our minds, we cannot avoid making up our lives. It is one of those questions that we may choose to ignore, but can never fully escape.

The question is raised while the disciples are with Jesus in Caesarea Philippi (Matt. 16:13-23). They have just left Galilee, where they endured the constant presence of eager crowds and the press of human need. Now they are in a place that is far from the swelling crowds, and they have a chance to reflect and talk within the inner circle. The disciples are aware that there is a lot of speculation going around about who Jesus is and who he isn't, and Jesus himself seems content to steer clear of the subject. Then, in Caesarea Philippi, Jesus asks the question himself: "Who do people say that the Son of Man is?" The disciples are able to answer that question with ease: "Some say John the Baptist, but others say Elijah, and still others Jeremiah or one of the prophets"—all of them leaders, Jewish tradition holds, who will prepare the way for the coming Messiah.

Jesus then follows up that question with another: "But who do you say that I am?" This question drops like a silver dollar on a slate floor—followed by a deafening silence. No one wants to answer it. I imagine that some of the disciples must have cast down their eyes like students who are hoping and praying that they will not be called on by the teacher. I also imagine that other disciples looked at each other the way my parents looked at each other when I asked if there

really is a Santa Claus. It was a desperate look that says, "Are you going to take this one, or must I?"

Why was that question so difficult to answer? By this time, the
disciples had already traveled many long miles with Jesus; they had
heard him preach; they had seen the lame walk and the blind blink
their eyes with new sight after encountering Jesus. Indeed, the disciples had already risked their lives for Jesus. Certainly, they must have
already answered this question in the privacy of their own hearts.
Why was it so difficult to give voice to their answer?

We all know, for instance, how difficult it is to be the first to say "I
love you" to another. It is difficult to be the first to break the silence
with such a large truth. One does not say anything like that for the
first time without sweaty palms and a dry mouth. We may hesitate,
not because we doubt that the words are true, but because we know
how powerfully true they are, and because, having spoken the truth,
we can no longer ignore its implications for our lives.

Peter, never one to be shy, broke the silence: "You are the Christ,
the Son of the living God." That took a lot of courage to say: if it was
true, it would be enough to turn the world upside down; if it was not
true, saying it would be dangerous blasphemy for which one would
have to suffer the consequences. Anyone saying such a thing might
not be around long enough to say anything else.

But Peter said it anyway, and in response, Jesus gave him the only
beatitude he ever pronounced on a single individual in his lifetime:
"Blessed are you, Simon Bar-Jona" (i.e., "Simon, son of John"), Peter's
formal name, which would be used only on special occasions. Then
Jesus called him Peter (i.e., "the rock"), telling him that he was the
rock on which he wanted to build his church. If there was a higher
honor, Peter couldn't imagine it. And what qualified Peter for that
honor was simply a blessed glimpse of the truth and his willingness
to be the first disciple finally to give it expression.

The other disciples were probably more than a little relieved to
have someone say it at last, and perhaps a bit grateful that they themselves did not have to answer Jesus's question. They could raise their
eyes again because Peter had answered the question for them. Or so
they thought. Because, of course, no one can answer such a question

for us. Anyone who wants to be a disciple must eventually answer it—and that includes every one of us.

The Inescapable Question

The first question—"Who do people say that I am?"—is as easy for us as it was for the original twelve disciples. To find out what answer people give, we could conduct on-the-street interviews, or go to books for the answers provided by the keenest historical and contemporary minds. Or we could simply Google it! We will find no shortage of answers.

Bruce Barton, an American businessman, said that Jesus was the greatest salesman who ever lived. The poet Algernon Swinburne's bitter line refers to Jesus as "the pale Galilean who has caused the world to grow grey from his breath." Karl Rahner depicted Jesus as "a perfected human person." Latin American theologians view Jesus as the great liberator. John A. T. Robinson claims that he was "the human face of God." Edward Schillebeeckx uses the image of Jesus as "the sacrament we encounter." Dietrich Bonhoeffer sees him as "the man for others." Jürgen Moltmann declares that he was "the crucified God." When our daughter was four years old, she called Jesus "God's best friend."

"Who do people say that I am?" Just listen or read, and you will find more answers than anyone could possibly need. And you can answer a question like that without offending anyone. We can answer that question in the public schools and not jeopardize the separation of church and state. A student can safely answer that question historically or sociologically; it asks for no commitment of any kind. A person can answer that question and still follow the cynic's creed: "Consider everything, commit to little, keep moving."

But then comes the second question: "Who do *you* say that I am?" Although only a single word in this question is different, that one word makes all the difference. The answer to this question is not found in the words of others or in the thousands of books about Jesus. Paul wrote to the Corinthians that our faith cannot rest on the wisdom of others, but on the power of God. This question is so difficult because the answer is found so terribly close, as close as one's own heart. There is no escape into comfortable objectivity. One cannot merely sit on the fence and describe what one sees on both sides. One must jump to one side or the other. This question demands not so much the insight of our minds as the allegiance of our lives. And though it has been answered in countless ways in countless lives, the possible answers are more limited than we might like to think. C. S. Lewis says that we have but two options:

> [My aim is] to prevent anyone from saying the really foolish thing people say about Him, such as "I'm ready to accept Jesus as a great moral teacher, but I don't accept His claim to be God." That is the sort of thing that we must not say. A man who was merely a man and said the sort of things Jesus said would not be a great moral teacher. He would either be a lunatic—on a level with the man who says he is a poached egg—or else he would be the Devil of Hell. You must make your choice. Either this man was, and is, the Son of God; or else a madman or something worse. You can shut Him up for a fool, you can spit on Him and kill Him as a demon; or you can fall at His feet and call Him Lord and God. But let us not come with any patronizing nonsense about his being a great human teacher. He has not left that open to us. He did not intend to.[1]

Many students prefer true-or-false questions on a test because, even if they have absolutely no idea which answer is correct, they still have an even chance of guessing correctly. But with a question like "Who do you say that I am?" such an absolute either/or is uncomfortable. The options are too starkly presented, the choices too few. When faced with the need for decision, we are tempted to ask, "Don't you have any essay questions?" We want to be able to qualify our answers. We want to be able to say, "Yes, but on the other hand ..."

Jesus himself seemed to recognize how difficult the question was. Notice that he did not ask it of the disciples until after they had traveled many miles together, not until after they had already seen lives changed with a mere word from his lips or a touch of his hand.

And even after that, the disciples did not feel fully prepared to answer such a question. One never does.

A Truth with Power

"Who do you say that I am?" No one can answer that question for us or fully prepare us to answer it for ourselves. We may hear others say, "Jesus is the Christ, the Son of the living God," but, no matter how eloquent or impassioned the testimony, it is not enough to help us see the truth of it. Rather, in a very real sense, it may be only after we hear ourselves say it that we will see all the dimensions of that truth, for it is then that we can see that it is a truth with great power.

Having spoken the truth, we can see that it has power to give meaning to our lives. We can then let go of the fear that our lives are merely restless wanderings—going to work in the morning and coming home again, eating, sleeping, talking to friends, loving a few people, going on a few trips, having a couple of children—for once we have affirmed that Jesus is the Christ, we can see that our lives are caught up in the great drama of God's redemptive plan for the world.

Having affirmed such a truth, we are prepared to understand the powerful force of love and hope that we can see let loose in the world. We can then understand why those who have been claimed by this Jesus seem to exhibit such strange behavior, why the poor in spirit are so rich in hope, why the ones once counted as outcasts are now guests of honor, why those once paralyzed with fear have hearts that dance, why those left for dead by the world are singing like children, why the jagged pieces of broken lives are put back together.

Answering with Our Very Lives

I wish I could say that the story ends there. But it does not. After receiving the blessing of Jesus, Peter was feeling pretty good. He tried on the mantle of authority, and he liked how it felt. It gave his gait a certain swagger. But before Peter had much time to relish his new status as the foundation of the church, Jesus announced that he had to go to Jerusalem to suffer many things. Peter didn't want to hear it. After all, he pictured entering Jerusalem at Jesus's right hand in a triumphant parade; now Jesus's description was beginning to make it sound like a funeral procession. Peter was sure that it didn't have to be that way. He knew better, and he responded as Adlai Stevenson did when he confessed that he often prayed, "Use me, God, oh use me ... but of course in an advisory capacity." Peter said to Jesus: "God forbid, Lord! This shall never happen to you." Jesus pivoted and fired back: "Get behind me, Satan! You are a stumbling block to me [literally, 'the rock on which I crack my shins']; for you are setting your mind not on divine things, but on human things."

Why was Jesus so upset? Why did he curse the one he had just blessed? In part, Jesus responded so strongly because he heard in Peter's plea the voice of the Tempter. At the beginning of his ministry, in the wilderness, Jesus had heard such a voice offering him all manner of glory and reward. There he was given an opportunity to do the spectacular, to claim privilege and adoration, to avoid suffering and alleviate hardship. It was a temptation because it was attractive. Who would not be drawn to such a path when the only other alternative was going to end up on a cross? Jesus could either accept the world's definition of success or he could follow God's plan, which would end in triumph, to be sure, but only after first passing through the regions of suffering and death.

Jesus was able to turn aside this temptation at the beginning of his ministry. Nevertheless, like all real temptations, it was not something that could be defeated for good. It was always there lurking nearby, waiting for another opportunity to strike. And here it came again, this time striking from very close, from the very one he had just blessed, from his most trusted disciple. I know that it is always a temptation for me as a preacher and teacher to want to present Christian discipleship as something appealing and easy, as something so obviously attractive that any fool would want to sign on: "Come and board the glory train!" Who doesn't want to deliver or receive a message like that? It is tempting to always say pleasant things to pleasant people, to emphasize what is promised and touch lightly on what is required, to promise that Christian discipleship will confer immediate rewards. Most of us would be tempted to give up Easter if we could do without Good Friday in the bargain. But God's ways are not our ways. We are tempted because we often prefer our ways.

Let's be reminded, as Peter was, that before the glory train reaches its final destination, it will make a few stops along the way at places we would rather avoid but cannot, places like the upper room, the Garden of Gethsemane, and Golgotha. The journey of discipleship is not so immediately attractive that any fool would want to sign on. In many ways, it is so awesome that you have to be a special kind of fool—what Paul calls "a fool for Christ"—to get on board.

Jesus responds to Peter so emphatically because Peter is in danger of negating his answer to the question "Who do you say that I am?" After all, it is a question that must be answered—not once, but many times. We might answer such a question first with our lips, but then we have to answer it many times with every step we take. If Jesus is the Christ, as Peter affirmed, then we must be willing to follow him wherever he goes, and that includes a lot of places that we would not otherwise choose to go. To claim new life with Christ, we must be willing to go to Jerusalem and to all the valleys of the shadow in our own world.

"Who do you say that I am?" Every step we take is answer to that question.

"Who do you say that I am?" Martin Luther King Jr. answered that question by marching on Washington.

"Who do you say that I am?" Mother Teresa answered that question by going to the ghettos of Calcutta to dispense medical care and hope.

"Who do you say that I am?" Some people answer that question by serving meals at a local shelter.

"Who do you say that I am?" Others answer that question by sharing a prayer with someone who is confined to a bed of pain.

"Who do you say that I am?" Still others answer that question by approaching the seats of power to plead the cause of the least, the last, and the lost.

"Who do you say that I am?" Still others answer that question by seeking out the very one whom everyone else makes a point to avoid.

Jesus asks every one of us: "Who do you say that I am?"

If you have already traveled for some time with Jesus, the time for answering that question may have arrived. And if you have not, travel with him for a time. The question awaits you down the road. However, even after we have given voice to the answer we have found in our hearts, and after we have received the blessing reserved for those who are able to say, "You are the Christ, the Son of the living God"—something remains. It remains for us to express our answer with our feet, for us to be willing to go to Jerusalem and beyond with the one who makes each of our journeys a holy pilgrimage.

Notes

Chapter 1

1. Lawrence Boadt, *Reading the Old Testament* (New York: Paulist, 1984), 110.

Chapter 3

1. William Muehl, *Why Preach? Why Listen?* (Philadelphia: Fortress, 1986), 69–70.

Chapter 4

1. In Leonard I. Sweet, *New Life in the Spirit* (Philadelphia: Westminster, 1982), 31.
2. In Sweet, *New Life in the Spirit*, 32.
3. Sweet, *New Life in the Spirit*, 36.

Chapter 6

1. Raymond E. Brown, *Responses to 101 Questions on the Bible* (New York: Paulist, 1990), 29.
2. Brown, *Responses to 101 Questions on the Bible*, 37.
3. Martin Copenhaver, *Living Faith while Holding Doubts* (Cleveland: Pilgrim, 1989), 78.
4. William Shakespeare, *Hamlet*, Act 1, Scene 5.

Notes

Chapter 7

1. Frederick Buechner, *Wishful Thinking: A Theological ABC* (San Francisco: Harper and Row, 1973), 97–98.
2. In William H. Willimon, *With Glad and Generous Hearts* (Nashville: Upper Room, 1986), 83–84.
3. Willimon, *With Glad and Generous Hearts*, 83–84.
4. In Willimon, *With Glad and Generous Hearts*, 84.

Chapter 8

1. William H. Willimon, *Remember Who You Are* (Nashville: Upper Room, 1980), 21–22.
2. In James White, *Introduction to Christian Worship*, rev. ed. (Nashville: Upper Room, 1990), 21–22.
3. *Book of Worship: United Church of Christ* (New York: UCC Office of Church Life and Leadership, 1986), 139.
4. White, *Introduction to Worship*, 218.
5. White, *Introduction to Worship*, 204.

Chapter 9

1. Halford Luccock, *Halford Luccock Treasury* (Nashville: Abingdon, 1963), 301.
2. Frederick Buechner, *Wishful Thinking* (San Francisco: Harper and Row, 1973), 12.
3. *Book of Worship: United Church of Christ* (New York: UCC Office of Church Life and Leadership, 1986), 32.
4. William H. Willimon, *Sunday Dinner* (Nashville: Upper Room, 1981), 240.

Chapter 10

1. Benjamin Spock, *Baby and Child Care* (New York: Pocket Books, 1991), 1.
2. George Buttrick, *Prayer* (Nashville: Abingdon-Cokesbury, 1942), 42.
3. François Fénelon, *The Spiritual Letters of Archbishop Fénelon* (London: Rivington, 1877), 205–6.
4. C. S. Lewis, *Letters to Malcolm: Chiefly on Prayer* (New York: Harcourt, Brace and World, 1964), 90.

5. C. S. Lewis, *Reflections on the Psalms* (New York: Harcourt, Brace and Co., 1958), 90.

6. Lewis, *Reflections on the Psalms*, 95.

7. Buttrick, *Prayer*, 72.

8. C. S. Lewis, *The Joyful Christian* (New York: Macmillan, 1977), 99–100.

9. Buttrick, *Prayer*, 112.

10. Anthony Bloom, *Beginning to Pray* (New York: Paulist, 1970), 26.

Chapter 11

1. Walt Whitman, *Leaves of Grass* (New York: Crown, 1961), 14.

2. Raymond Moody, *Life after Life* (St. Simons Island, GA: Mockingbird Books, 1975), 22.

3. William Shakespeare, *King Lear*, Act 4, Scene 1.

4. John Bunyan, *The Pilgrim's Progress* (New York: Penguin, 1964), 147.

5. Hans Küng, *Eternal Life?* (Garden City, NY: Doubleday, 1984), 112.

6. Clarence Jordan, *Cotton Patch Parables of Liberation* (Scottsdale, PA: Herald, 1976), 27.

7. Küng, *Eternal Life?* 136.

8. Clarence Jordan, *Power from Parables* (Americus, GA: Koinonia Partners, 1968).

9. Frederick Buechner, *Wishful Thinking* (San Francisco: Harper and Row, 1973), 22.

Chapter 12

1. Jim Wallis, *The Call to Conversion* (San Francisco: Harper and Row, 1981), 142.

2. William Willimon, "Beyond the Mixing of Politics and Religion," *New Oxford Review*, April 1986.

3. Malcolm Muggeridge, *Something Beautiful for God* (San Francisco: Harper and Row, 1971), 130.

4. David J. Garrow, *Bearing the Cross* (New York: William Morrow, 1986), 58.

5. William Lee Miller, *The Protestant and Politics* (Philadelphia: Westminster, 1965), 24.

6. Dale Rosenberger, "In Collision with Divine Truth" (unpublished paper).

7. Oscar Wilde, *De Profundis* (New York: Modern Library, 1926), 29.

Notes

Chapter 13

1. David H. C. Read, *Go and Make Disciples* (Nashville: Abingdon, 1978), 30–31.

2. Fred Craddock, *Overhearing the Gospel* (Nashville: Abingdon, 1978), 21.

3. Allan Johnson, "Evangelism for Today" (pamphlet) (Cleveland: UCBHM).

4. Mortimer Arias, "The Great Commission: Mission as Discipleship," *Journal of the Academy for Evangelism in Theological Education* 4 (1988–89): 22.

5. David J. Bosch, "Evangelism: Theological Currents and Crosscurrents Today," *International Bulletin of Missionary Research* (July 1987): 101.

6. Bosch, "Evangelism," 101.

7. Bosch, "Evangelism," 101.

8. Bosch, "Evangelism," 101.

Chapter 14

1. C. S. Lewis, *Mere Christianity* (New York: Macmillan, 1960), 55–56.

Selected Bibliography

Bloom, Anthony. *Beginning to Pray*. New York: Paulist, 1970.

Boadt, Lawrence. *Reading the Old Testament*. New York: Paulist, 1984.

Book of Worship: United Church of Christ. New York: UCC Office of Church Life and Leadership, 1986.

Brown, Raymond E. *Responses to 101 Questions on the Bible*. New York: Paulist, 1990.

Buechner, Frederick. *Wishful Thinking: A Theological ABC*. San Francisco: Harper and Row, 1973.

Buttrick, George. *Prayer*. Nashville: Abingdon-Cokesbury, 1942.

Copenhaver, Martin. *Living Faith while Holding Doubts*. New York: Pilgrim, 1989.

Craddock, Fred. *Overhearing the Gospel*. Nashville: Abingdon, 1978.

Garrow, David. *Bearing the Cross*. New York: William Morrow, 1986.

Jordan, Clarence. *Cotton Patch Parables of Liberation*. Scottsdale, PA: Herald, 1976.

Küng, Hans. *Eternal Life?* Garden City, NY: Doubleday, 1984.

Lewis, C. S. *The Joyful Christian*. New York: Macmillan, 1977.

———. *Letters to Malcolm: Chiefly on Prayer*. New York: Harcourt, Brace and World, 1964.

———. *Mere Christianity*. New York: Macmillan, 1960.

———. *Reflections on the Psalms*. New York: Harcourt, Brace and Co., 1958.

Miller, William Lee. *The Protestant and Politics*. Philadelphia: Westminster, 1965.

Moody, Raymond. *Life after Life*. St. Simons Island, GA: Mockingbird Books, 1975.

Muehl, William. *Why Preach? Why Listen?* Philadelphia: Fortress, 1986.

Muggeridge, Malcolm. *Something Beautiful for God.* San Francisco: Harper and Row, 1971.

Read, David H. C. *Go and Make Disciples.* Nashville: Abingdon, 1978.

Sweet, Leonard I. *New Life in the Spirit.* Philadelphia: Westminster, 1982.

Wallis, Jim. *The Call to Conversion.* San Francisco: Harper and Row, 1981.

White, James F. *Introduction to Christian Worship.* Rev. ed. Nashville: Upper Room, 1990.

Willimon, William. *Remember Who You Are: Baptism, a Model for Christian Life.* Nashville: Upper Room, 1980.

————. *Sunday Dinner.* Nashville: Upper Room, 1981.

————. *With Glad and Generous Hearts.* Nashville: Upper Room, 1986.

For Further Reading

Chapter 1

Anderson, Bernhard W. *Understanding the Old Testament.* Englewood Cliffs, NJ: Prentice Hall, 1966.

Brueggemann, Walter. *The Bible Makes Sense.* Atlanta: John Knox, 1977.

Napier, Davie. *Song of the Vineyard: A Guide through the Old Testament.* Philadelphia: Fortress, 1981.

Chapter 2

Buechner, Frederick. *The Faces of Jesus.* San Francisco: Harper and Row, 1989.

Johnson, Robert Clyde. *The Meaning of Christ.* Philadelphia: Westminster, 1968.

Kee, Howard Clark. *What Can We Know about Jesus?* Cambridge, UK: Cambridge University Press, 1990.

Muggeridge, Malcolm. *Jesus: The Man Who Lives.* San Francisco: Harper and Row, 1975.

Nouwen, Henri J. M. *Letters to Marc about Jesus.* San Francisco: Harper and Row, 1988.

For Further Reading

Chapter 3

Borg, Marcus. *Meeting Jesus Again for the First Time: The Historical Jesus and the Heart of Contemporary Faith.* San Francisco: HarperSanFrancisco, 1994.

Johnson, Luke Timothy. *Living Jesus: Learning the Heart of the Gospel.* San Francisco: HarperSanFrancisco, 2000.

Spong, John Shelby. *The Easter Moment.* New York: Seabury Press, 1980.

Chapter 4

Berkhof, Hendrikus. *The Doctrine of the Holy Spirit.* Atlanta: John Knox, 1964.

Sheed, F. J. *The Holy Spirit in Action: Why Christians Call Him "The Lord and Giver of Life."* Ann Arbor: Servant, 1981.

Sweet, Leonard I. *New Life in the Spirit.* Philadelphia: Westminster, 1982.

Chapter 5

Brown, Robert McAfee. *The Significance of the Church.* Philadelphia: Westminster, 1966.

Guthrie, Shirley C., Jr. *Christian Doctrine: Teachings of the Christian Church.* Atlanta: John Knox Press, 1968. Chapter 18.

Küng, Hans. *The Church.* New York: Sheed and Ward, 1967.

Chapter 6

Barr, Robert R. *What Is the Bible?* Minneapolis: Winston, 1984.

Brown, Raymond E. *Responses to 101 Questions on the Bible.* New York: Paulist, 1990.

Charpentier, Etienne. *How to Read the Bible: Two Volumes in One.* New York: Gramercy, 1991.

Gomes, Peter J. *The Good Book: Reading the Bible with Mind and Heart.* New York: Morrow, 1996.

Willimon, William H. *Shaped by the Bible.* Nashville: Abingdon, 1990.

Chapter 7

Copenhaver, Martin B., Anthony B. Robinson, and William H. Willimon. *Good News in Exile: Three Pastors Offer a Hopeful Vision for the Church*. Grand Rapids: Eerdmans, 1999.

Hickman, Hoyt L. *A Primer for Church Worship*. Nashville: Abingdon, 1984.

White, James F. *Introduction to Christian Worship*. Rev. ed. Nashville: Abingdon, 1990.

Willimon, William H. *With Glad and Generous Hearts: A Personal Look at Sunday Worship*. Nashville: Upper Room, 1986.

Chapter 8

Marty, Martin E. *Baptism*. Philadelphia: Fortress, 1977.

White, James F. *Introduction to Christian Worship*. Rev. ed. Nashville: Abingdon, 1990. Chapter 7.

Willimon, William H. *Remember Who You Are: Baptism, a Model for Christian Life*. Nashville: Upper Room, 1980.

Chapter 9

Marty, Martin E. *The Lord's Supper*. Philadelphia: Fortress, 1980.

White, James F. *Introduction to Christian Worship*. Rev. ed. Nashville: Abingdon, 1990. Chapter 8.

Willimon, William H. *Sunday Dinner: The Lord's Supper and the Christian Life*. Nashville: Upper Room, 1981.

Chapter 10

Bloom, Anthony. *Beginning to Pray*. New York: Paulist, 1970.

Buttrick, George A. *Prayer*. New York; Nashville: Abingdon-Cokesbury, 1942.

Jones, Timothy. *The Art of Prayer: A Simple Guide*. New York: Ballantine, 1997.

For Further Reading

Lewis, C. S. *Letters to Malcolm: Chiefly on Prayer.* New York: Harcourt, Brace and World, 1964.

Nouwen, Henri J. M. *With Open Hands.* Notre Dame, IN: Ave Maria Press, 1972.

Chapter 11

Küng, Hans. *Eternal Life?* Garden City, NY: Doubleday, 1984.

Nouwen, Henri J. M. *Beyond the Mirror: Reflections on Death and Life.* New York: Crossroad, 1990.

Shinn, Roger Lincoln. *Life, Death, and Destiny.* Philadelphia: Westminster, 1957.

Chapter 12

Copenhaver, Martin B., Anthony B. Robinson, and William H. Willimon. *Good News in Exile: Three Pastors Offer a Hopeful Vision for the Church.* Grand Rapids: Eerdmans, 1999. Pages 91–106.

Hauerwas, Stanley, and William Willimon. *Resident Aliens: Life in the Christian Colony.* Nashville: Abingdon, 1989.

Wallis, Jim. *The Call to Conversion.* San Francisco: Harper & Row, 1981.

———. *The Soul of Politics: A Practical and Prophetic Vision for Change.* New York: New Press, 1994.

Chapter 13

Arias, Mortimer. *Announcing the Reign of God: Evangelization and the Subversive Memory of Jesus.* Philadelphia: Fortress, 1984.

Armstrong, Richard Stoll. *Service Evangelism.* Philadelphia: Westminster, 1979.

Read, David H. C. *Go and Make Disciples.* Nashville: Abingdon, 1978.